MYANMAR'S LONG ROAD to NATIONAL RECONCILIATION

The **Institute of Southeast Asian Studies (ISEAS)** was established as an autonomous organization in 1968. It is a regional centre dedicated to the study of socio-political, security and economic trends and developments in Southeast Asia and its wider geostrategic and economic environment.

The Institute's research programmes are the Regional Economic Studies (RES, including ASEAN and APEC), Regional Strategic and Political Studies (RSPS), and Regional Social and Cultural Studies (RSCS).

ISEAS Publications, an established academic press, has issued more than 1,000 books and journals. It is the largest scholarly publisher of research about Southeast Asia from within the region. ISEAS Publications works with many other academic and trade publishers and distributors to disseminate important research and analyses from and about Southeast Asia to the rest of the world.

Asia Pacific Press, based at the Australian National University, is a specialist publisher on economics, development, governance and management in the Asia Pacific region.

As well as book publishing, Asia Pacific Press has developed electronic publishing of research through the outline journal Labour and Management in Development, Pacific resources online, Pacific Economic Outlook and Studies Online. APSEG Online Papers are searchable by title and author and are available to download free of charge.

Asia Pacific Press also houses the influential journals *Asian-Pacific Economic Literature* and *Pacific Economic Bulletin*.

MYANMAR'S LONG ROAD to NATIONAL RECONCILIATION

edited by
Trevor Wilson

ISEAS

INSTITUTE OF SOUTHEAST ASIAN STUDIES
Singapore

ASIA PACIFIC PRESS
The Australian National University
Australia

First published in Singapore in 2006 by ISEAS Publications
Institute of Southeast Asian Studies
30 Heng Mui Keng Terrace
Pasir Panjang
Singapore 119614
E-mail: publish@iseas.edu.sg
Website: http://bookshop.iseas.edu.sg

First published in Australia and New Zealand by
Asia Pacific Press
Asia Pacific School of Economics and Management
The Australian National University
Canberra ACT 0200
Australia

*The responsibility for facts and opinions in this publication rests exclusively with the
authors and their interpretations do not necessarily reflect the views or the policy of the
publishers or their supporters.*

ISEAS Library Cataloguing-in-Publication Data

Myanmar's long road to national reconciliation / edited by Trevor Wilson.
  A collection of papers originally presented at the 2004 Myanmar/Burma
  Update Conference organized by the Dept. of Political & Social Change, The
  Australian National University Research School of Pacific and Asian Studies,
  Canberra, on 18–19 November 2004.
  1.   Burma—Politics and government—1988- —Congresses.
  2.   Burma—Economic conditions—1948- Congresses.
  3.   Agriculture—Economic aspects—Burma—Congresses.
  4.   Civil society—Burma—Congresses.
  I.   Wilson, Trevor.
  II. Australian National University. Dept. of Political and Social Change
  III. Myanmar/Burma Update Conference (2004 : Canberra, Australia)
DS530.4 B972 2004   2006

ISBN 981-230-362-6 (soft cover)
ISBN 981-230-363-4 (hard cover)

For Australia and New Zealand, this soft cover edition is co-published by Asia
Pacific Press, The Australian National University, Australia.

Front cover: Painting by Shwe Maung Thar, an artist from Rhakhine State in
Myanmar.

Typeset by Superskill Graphics Pte Ltd
Printed in Singapore by Utopia Press Pte Ltd

Contents

Acknowledgements

As co-convenor of the 2004 Myanmar/Burma Update Conference and editor of this volume, I am indebted to Professor Jim Fox, Director of the Research School of Pacific and Asian Studies at The Australian National University for giving me this opportunity to bring together a wide range of viewpoints on Myanmar/Burma at this defining moment, and for his strong personal commitment to the Conference. I am grateful to my co-convenor, Dr Ron May, for his assistance, as well as for his patience and for passing on the benefits of his experience in organizing previous update conferences at the ANU. Similarly, I thank my ANU colleague Morten Pedersen for his strong support and wise advice, as well as for his invaluable assistance on the ground in Yangon. My warm thanks go above all to those who have contributed to this volume, for their confidence in me and their unflagging support, both for the Conference and for this publication. I also appreciate the firm backing of the Institute of Southeast Asian Studies for the ANU Conference and for the publication of this volume. Last but not least, I wish to thank my wife, Christine, who, in her usual meticulous fashion, undertook the copy editing at my request, despite her many other commitments.

EDITOR'S NOTE

This book generally follows UN practice in using the name Myanmar when referring to the country. However, it also follows the growing practice of respecting the personal preference of the authors of individual chapters in how they wish to refer to the country. The conference title uses "Myanmar/Burma" to reinforce the continuity with previous ANU Update Conferences, which used the name "Burma" in their title.

The Contributors

Graeme Batten
Dr Graeme Batten, Professor of Irrigation in the School of Agricultural and Veterinary Sciences at the Wagga Wagga campus of Charles Sturt University, gained Bachelor's and Master's Degrees in Rural Science from the University of New England in 1969 and 1977 respectively, and a PhD from the Australian National University, Canberra, in 1985. During his career, he has specialized in the links between fertilizers, soils, plant nutrients, food quality, and the sustainability of agro-ecosystems. Dr Batten teaches soil science, irrigation, water management, and rice production, and supervises postgraduate students, while maintaining strong links with farmers, agri-business, and research and extension staff in regional Australia and in other countries. In recent years, he has concentrated on establishing links with producers and researchers in developing countries, and on identifying ways to encourage technology transfer to enhance the amount and quality of food produced.

John Copland
Dr John Copland is Research Program Manager (Livestock/Animal Science Program Manager for Myanmar, India, Thailand, Indonesia, Laos and Cambodia) at the Australian Centre for International Agricultural Research (ACIAR), Canberra. He has been working in Asia and the South Pacific for almost two decades, developing livestock research projects and programmes. He was the foundation Research Program Manager for two Animal Science programmes and for the Fisheries programme in ACIAR in collaborative research and development projects that involve a partner country and Australian institutions. He visited Myanmar several times prior to the commencement of the two small ACIAR projects in 2003. Prior to 1975, Dr Copland spent seven years working in the livestock sector,

National Veterinary Laboratory, Port Moresby. Subsequently, he was based in Jakarta and for two years served as team leader of a review of the Indonesian agricultural sector.

Karl Dorning

Mr Karl Dorning joined the Burnet Institute, Centre for International Health, Melbourne in 2003, after spending nearly eight years in Burma with World Vision Myanmar. During this time, he was responsible for the oversight and management of government and multilateral-funded programmes in a broad range of areas including HIV/AIDS, children in difficult circumstances and child rights, trafficking, and community development programmes more broadly. He maintains a particular interest in the impact of HIV/AIDS on youth and children and has published work on HIV and mobility and the impact of HIV on street children. He coordinated a five-country study into child abuse and neglect for World Vision International and was a senior child rights advocate for some years, representing World Vision at international forums such as the UN Special Session on Children in May 2002.

Larry Jagan

Mr Larry Jagan works as a freelance journalist in Bangkok. He is a specialist on Southeast Asia, especially Myanmar. He has been reporting from Bangkok for four years, during which time he has been one the few journalists allowed to visit Burma regularly. He reports predominantly for the BBC and the *Bangkok Post*, but also contributes regularly for Radio Australia, the *South China Morning Post* and Deutsche Welle. Previously, he was the BBC World Service's Regional News and Current Affairs Editor for Asia Pacific for more than ten years. He has been a prolific writer on Burma for more than twenty years.

Richard Jones

Mr Richard Jones was a Director of First&42nd where he lead the Corporate Social Responsibility (CSR) team. He has worked extensively with multinational companies in planning and delivering on CSR strategies. Companies he has advised operate in many areas, including in oil and gas (Premier Oil, Norsk Hydro), in chemicals (BASF), in tobacco (British American Tobacco), and in mobile telecommunications (Orange). He was closely involved in Premier Oil's CSR initiatives in Myanmar from 1999 to 2003. After leaving First&42nd, he started CSR Africa, a management consultancy with a focus on sustainable business strategies for companies with corporate responsibilities at their core. He is currently working with Total, Premier Oil, Marathon Oil, and Philosophy Design.

U Myint

U Myint has a PhD in economics from the University of California, Berkeley. In Yangon he has held the posts of Head, Economics Department, Institute of Education, and Chief, Economic Division, Ministry of Foreign Affairs. Subsequently, he served for a number of years as Senior Economic Affairs Officer, United Nations Economic and Social Commission for Asia and the Pacific in Bangkok. He is now retired and lives in Yangon.

Zaw Oo

Zaw Oo is a Myanmar national with graduate degrees in international affairs and international development from Columbia University and American University. He is the Director of the Burma Fund, a Washington-based think-tank working on the issues of democratization in Burma and on overseas policy research projects on democratization, civil-military relations, economic transition, transitional justice, reconciliation and migration. Zaw Oo has over fifteen years of experience in working with marginal communities in Myanmar and has served as a consultant for the International Institute of Democracy and Electoral Assistance (IDEA), the Center for International Private Enterprise, and Radio Free Asia. He has attended the annual sessions of the United Nations Human Rights Commission in Geneva between 1989 and 1991 to testify on human rights violations and the issue of protection of Myanmar refugees in Thailand.

Morten B. Pedersen

Mr Morten B. Pedersen is a research scholar in the Department of Political and Social Change, Australian National University. Since 2001, he has worked as a senior analyst for the International Crisis Group in Brussels, and as a consultant for various governments and international organizations on Burma. He is the co-editor and co-contributor to the book *Burma/Myanmar: Strong Regime, Weak State* (Crawford House, 2000) and the author of a number of reports on international policy on Burma and on political, social, and economic developments within the country.

Martin Smith
Mr Martin Smith is a writer and analyst who has reported about Burma/Myanmar for a variety of media, non-governmental, and academic organizations during the past two decades. He is author of *Burma: Insurgency and the Politics of Ethnicity* (Zed Books, 1991 and 1999) and *Fatal Silence? Freedom of Expression and the Right to Health in Burma* (Article 19, 1996). His most recent publications include *Burma (Myanmar): The Time for Change* (Minority Rights Group International, 2002) and "Burma: The Karen Conflict", in *Encyclopedia of Modern Ethnic Conflicts*, edited by J. Rudolph (Greenwood Press, 2003).

David I. Steinberg
Dr David I. Steinberg is Distinguished Professor and Director, Asian Studies, School of Foreign Service, Georgetown University. He is the author of four books and monographs on Burma/Myanmar, the latest being *Burma: The State of Myanmar* (Georgetown University Press, 2001,) and of some forty-five articles and book chapters about that country. As Director of Philippines, Thailand and Burma Affairs in the United States Agency for International Development, Department of State, he negotiated the re-entry of United States' foreign assistance to Burma in 1979. From 1958 to 1962 he was Assistant Representative of The Asia Foundation in Burma. He was educated at Dartmouth College, Lingnan University (China), Harvard University, and the School of Oriental and African Studies, University of London. He also writes extensively on Korean affairs.

Robert H. Taylor
Dr Taylor is Senior Visiting Research Fellow, Institute of Southeast Asian Studies, Singapore. He was formerly Professor of Politics at the University of London, Pro-Director of the School of Oriental and African Studies, and Vice-Chancellor of the University of Buckingham. He studied at Yangon University in 1978 and 1982 and has been a frequent visitor to Myanmar since 1975. The author and editor of a number of volumes including *The State in Burma* (1987) and *The Politics of Elections in Southeast Asia* (1995), he is a contributor to a new history entitled *The Emergence of Modern Southeast Asia* (2005), edited by Norman Owen. He is joint editor of *Myanmar:*

Beyond Politics to Societal Imperatives (2005). He lives in London, from where he provides consultancy services on Southeast Asian affairs, especially Myanmar.

David Tegenfeldt

Mr David Tegenfeldt is currently based in Yangon as Senior Advisor, Hope International Development Agency, working on issues of conflict, peace-building, reconciliation, social development, and social change. From 1993 to 2001, he worked as Country Director for World Concern, working at first in Chiang Mai, Thailand, with responsibility for Thailand and Myanmar (1993–1995), then moved to Yangon and was responsible for Myanmar. For the past ten years he has been a regular speaker at conferences on Burma/Myanmar. He has a BA in Sociology from Westmont College, Santa Barbara; a Master's degree in Health Policy and Management from the University of Michigan; and a Master's degree in Conflict Transformation from the Eastern Mennonite University in Virginia. He was born in Burma and has spent twenty years living in Burma.

Kyaw Than

Dr Kyaw Than obtained his Bachelor of Agriculture degree from the Institute of Agriculture of Myanmar in 1966. He continued his studies at the Imperial College of Science and Technology, London, in 1974 and received his doctorate in 1978, his studies specializing on Insect Systematics. He joined the Institute of Agriculture (now Yezin Agricultural University or YAU) in Pyinmawa, Myanmar, as a member of the teaching staff in 1966. He was promoted to Professor of Entomology in 1992. In the last twenty-six years he has been heavily involved with teaching and research at YAU. He has published extensively on the prospects for agricultural development and agricultural education in Myanmar. He is presently Rector of YAU and is a member of the Academy of Myanmar Agriculture, Forestry, Livestock and Fishery Sciences.

Sean Turnell

Dr Sean Turnell is an economist and former central banker with a long-time interest in Burma's financial system. Based at Macquarie University in Sydney, he teaches and undertakes research in the Economics Department. He is currently completing a book on the political economy of money and banking in Burma for the Nordic Institute of Asian Studies.

Since 2003 he has edited *Burma Economic Watch,* an on-line newsletter on the Burmese economy.

Trevor Wilson

Mr Trevor Wilson is a Visiting Fellow at the Department of Political and Social Change, Australian National University, Canberra. He retired in August 2003 after working for more than thirty-six years for the Australian Government, thirty years of which was spent with the Department of Foreign Affairs and Trade. He served as Australia's Ambassador to Myanmar for three years from mid-2000 to mid-2003. He was assigned to Australia's Embassy in Tokyo three times, first in the late sixties, then in the early eighties, and finally as Deputy Head of Mission in the second half of the nineties. He also had tours of duty in Washington and Laos. In Canberra he also worked in the Defence Department, the Prime Minister's Department, and in the office of the Minister for Foreign Affairs, Gareth Evans.

Myo Win

Mr Myo Win is Lecturer in Agricultural Engineering, Charles Sturt University, Wagga Wagga. Born and educated in Myanmar, with a degree in Agricultural Engineering from Rangoon Institute of Technology, he also has a post-graduate degree from the University of Melbourne. His father, U Ba Tin, was a pioneer in Myanmar agricultural development and served as an agricultural advisor for over sixty years, finishing as a CEO with the Agricultural and Rural Development Corporation (ARDC). During U Ba Tin's service, he was posted in major agricultural regions, and Myo Win had many opportunities to see Myanmar agriculture in action. Since 1982, Myo Win has been lecturing in agricultural engineering, specializing in irrigation and soil conservation, at Charles Sturt University in the NSW rural city of Wagga Wagga.

Glossary

ACIAR	Australian Centre for International Agricultural Research
ADB	Asian Development Bank
ADP	Area Development Program
AFPFL	Anti-Fascist People's Freedom League
ASEAN	Association of South East Asian Nations
AusAID	Australian Agency for International Development
BSI	Bureau of Special Investigation
BSPP	Burma Socialist Programme Party
CBO	community-based organization
CEC	Central Executive Committee (of the National League for Democracy)
CFN	Child Focussed Network
CGIAR	Consultative Group for International Agricultural Research
CIAT	Centre for International Tropical Agriculture
CIFOR	Centre for International Forestry Research
CNF	Chin National Front
CPB	Communist Party of Burma
CRPP	Committee Representing the People's Parliament
CSO	Central Statistical Office
CSU	Charles Sturt University (Australia)
DKBA	Democratic Karen Buddhist Army
EIU	Economist Intelligence Unit
FAO	Food and Agriculture Program
FHAM	Fund for HIV/AIDS in Myanmar

HIV/AIDS	Human Immuno-deficiency Virus/Acquired Immuno-deficiency Syndrome
ICRISAT	International Crops Research Institute for Semi-Arid Tropics
IFPRI	International Food and Policy Research Institute
IMF	International Monetary Fund
INGO	International Non-governmental Organization
IRRI	International Rice Research Institute
IWMI	International Water Management Institute
KIO	Kachin Independence Organization
KNU	Karen National Union
LNGO	Local Non-governmental Organization
MAS	Myanmar Agricultural Service
MMA	Myanmar Medical Association
MMCWA	Myanmar Maternal and Child Welfare Association
NDF	National Democratic Front
NGO	Non-governmental Organization
NIB	National Intelligence Bureau
NLD	National League for Democracy
NMSP	New Mon State Party
ODA	official development assistance
OIE	International Office for Epizootics
PDC	Peace and Development Committee
SEAFDEC	South East Asian Fisheries Development Centre
SLORC	State Law and Order Restoration Council
SNLD	Shan Nationalities League for Democracy
SPDC	State Peace and Development Council
SSA	Shan State Army
SSA-N	Shan State Army-North
SSA-S	Shan State Army-South
UN	United Nations
UNA	United Nationalities Alliance
UNDP	United Nations Development Programme
UNHCR	United Nations High Commissioner for Refugees
UNICEF	United Nations Children's Fund
UNLD	United Nationalities League for Democracy
USAID	United States Agency for International Development

UWSP	United Wa State Party
WFC	World Fish Centre
WFP	World Food Programme
YAU	Yezin Agricultural University
YMCA	Young Men's Christian Association
YWCA	Young Women's Christian Association

Overview

Trevor Wilson

The 2004 Myanmar/Burma Update Conference, the sixth in a series, took place in the context of an overall political situation little changed from that of five years ago. The same military regime remains in control of the country, functioning in much the same repressive way as before, and there is still no clear prospect of substantial change or of the genuine political and economic reforms that would allow the people of Myanmar the hope of enjoying the prosperity and freedom being enjoyed by their neighbours in Southeast Asia. Yet the particular dynamics of Myanmar's political, social, and economic circumstances had gone through quite significant changes in the previous eighteen months, leaving the country facing more uncertainty than for many years.

October 2004 witnessed the most dramatic, and probably the most far-reaching, changes in the leadership of the State Peace and Development Council (SPDC)[1] since the forced retirement of General Saw Maung in 1992. All the more surprising because they were almost unforeseen, these changes ended the previous strong sense of collegiality and cohesion amongst the top SPDC leadership. There had long been speculation about differences among the top three leaders — the SPDC Chairman, Senior General Than Shwe; the Vice Chairman, Deputy Senior General Maung Aye; and the Prime Minister, General Khin Nyunt — but hitherto the leadership had clearly attached highest priority to regime stability and cohesion, and had handled occasional internal problems, such as accusations of corruption, with the minimum of outward fuss. In this instance, however, the top leaders went so far as to abolish one of the military institutions — Military Intelligence — that was critical to the regime's maintenance of tight controls over the country and its people, on the presumption that it was a tool of the fallen Prime Minister. They also instigated a wholesale purge of military intelligence officers and their close associates, on a scale unprecedented under the current government.[2] Parallel with this, they initiated a wide-ranging Cabinet reshuffle in which a number of relatively inexperienced generals with no obvious qualifications for ministerial jobs replaced long-serving, experienced (and, in some cases, relatively capable) Ministers.

Two aspects of the changes had the immediate effect of increasing the constraints on any international organization or foreign individual who needed to work with the government. First, there were various indications that the regime seemed to be turning the clock back on more than a decade of gradual change, and was much less receptive to new ideas and any relaxation of tight state controls. This was shown in harsher official propaganda, in overt knee-jerk negativism towards dealing with foreigners, and in a reversion to earlier inward-looking military-style attitudes. Second, while the international community lacked direct knowledge of the new decision-makers, conversely, the incoming generals who had been appointed to senior SPDC or government positions displayed a striking lack of international exposure or experience. This does not bode well for the immediate future of Myanmar's international relations, nor does it suggest any great sensitivity on the part of the regime to international opinion — at least in the absence of some new, explicit decisions being taken in favour of international cooperation, something that seemed rather unlikely for the moment.

The 2004 Myanmar/Burma Update Conference also took place against the backdrop of the National Convention that the SPDC re-convened in May 2004 after an eight-year hiatus. The National Convention was a key part of the "road map" launched by the SPDC in August 2003 as an obvious (but doomed) attempt to neutralize international opprobrium after being generally held responsible for the attack on Aung San Suu Kyi and her National League for Democracy (NLD) followers at Depayin in May 2003.

The National Convention eventually resumed in February 2005, operating in much the same way as it had functioned the previous year, but with some personnel changes among the delegates. By re-affirming its intention to re-convene the National Convention, the SPDC acknowledged that political transition has to be accomplished in one way or another. This would in normal circumstances have been taken as a welcome step, seen as indicating that the new SPDC leadership maintained its commitment to a quasi-consultative political process.

However, in terms of both its composition and its operations in 2004, this "home-grown" National Convention would not pass any normal tests of representative-ness, transparency, credibility, and, therefore, legitimacy.[3] Moreover, the SPDC proceeded with the second phase of the current Convention apparently unconcerned about the exclusion of so many of the opposition political parties that had won the majority of the seats in the 1990 elections.

The SPDC leadership made no serious attempt to create the conditions for the NLD to reconsider its decision not to participate, despite some reports of wavering by the NLD leaders who had attended the earlier National Convention up until 1995.[4] To compound matters, the SPDC forced the Shan Nationalities League for Democracy, the party that won the second largest number of seats in the 1990 elections, out of the convention permanently by arresting its leaders on the very eve of the Convention's resumption. It is difficult to draw any conclusion other than that the SPDC's military leadership is even more reluctant than before to allow "normal", uncontrolled, law-abiding activities by political parties. At the very least, this would make highly suspect any form of "multi-party democracy" that might be eventually installed as a product of this process.

The SPDC continued to determine arbitrarily which delegates would participate in the National Convention, but in fact nominated a wide range of representatives. Included among the delegates were some quite prominent figures, many of whom (not surprisingly) had a record of cooperating with the regime, but not all of whom could be termed "supporters" of the regime by any means. One of the unusual features of the Convention was the extraordinary measures the SPDC adopted to maintain the isolation of the delegates from interaction with the community while the sessions were in progress. But although delegates were kept at the venue for lengthy periods in specially-prepared accommodation, they were allowed to return to their families from time to time, and some inkling of what had gone on behind the scenes leaked out. This was probably encouraged by the authorities to some extent, or at least was not actively discouraged.

Despite its obvious shortcomings, the National Convention process was a very substantial exercise. Built-to-purpose facilities were constructed in a green-fields site, a remarkable logistic and administrative support operation was maintained during sessions, and superficially impressive reporting arrangements were also put in place. Although the sessions took place behind closed doors, the SPDC took the unusual (for the SPDC) step of maintaining a website, as well as a stream of reports in the official media giving selective accounts of the content of speeches and topics considered.

The initial sessions of the resumed National Convention — in May–July 2004 and then from February 2005 — left as many questions unanswered as they answered. For example, the focus of the Convention proceedings was on formulating "principles" for the Constitution; no announcement was made about how, when, and by whom the Constitution would actually be drafted. While this essentially confirmed (as was widely suspected) that the SPDC was determined to move ahead with the draft constitution (that had been produced by the government in the first phase of the National Convention in the early nineties but not been formally accepted), it transpired that a number of groups were able to force the SPDC to allow discussion of highly sensitive, but important, issues such as power-sharing. Some participants report that the Convention sessions seem not to have been entirely the sterile set-piece statements that the Government prefers.

The 2004 sessions of the resumed National Convention dealt with the various constitutional issues selectively, but by no means avoided all sensitive issues. While the Convention considered the all-important matter of power-sharing, how — and indeed whether — larger constitutional goals such as the independence of the judiciary, freedom of the press, and freedom of association and assembly, which have not existed in Myanmar for generations, are likely to be achieved remains doubtful. At the end of the day, it still remains to be seen whether any discussion inside the National Convention that falls outside the SPDC's preferred outcomes will lead either to any substantive changes to the draft Constitution or to any meaningful concessions from the SPDC. But just as importantly, it is still unclear what time-frame is envisaged for elections that would lead to a transition to an elected government. This contrasts with the recent example of Pakistan, where the military regime has laid down a timetable for a political transition.

During 2004, one major development was the promise of a ceasefire between the SPDC and the Karen National Union. While this has yet to materialize, and the KNU still remains outside the current National Convention process (as it has from all domestic political negotiations since before independence), the KNU will find it difficult to revert to armed resistance in the face of the increasing determination of the Burmese army to defeat them militarily, and their capitulation is probably a matter of time. Should they waver on their course towards negotiation of a ceasefire with the SPDC, they can probably expect sharp military reprisals to force them back into line. Equally, however, their agreement to a ceasefire (if it were finalized) would be a big prize for the SPDC, and would enormously strengthen the SPDC's ability to claim to speak for the whole country. It would effectively mean an end to more than fifty years of insurgency against the government in Yangon.

More than ever since President Ne Win was forced to hand over power in 1988, future political developments in Myanmar depend almost entirely on the capacity of one man, SPDC Chairman Senior General Than Shwe. Gone is the earlier sense of SPDC collegiate government. This may prove a major challenge, both for Than Shwe, who is ageing and whose continued health cannot be assured, as well as for the loyalty of those closest to him. But if this loyalty holds, and if his own men remain in the ascendancy, the way might be open for Than Shwe to stand aside, to move to the background. It now seems increasingly clear that the younger group of generals promoted into positions of higher authority since 2002 will eventually take over the reins of government fully. They will have done so after what might prove to have been a surprisingly smooth — but certainly not uneventful — "transfer of power", and after as much preparation or "on the job training" as could probably be expected in Myanmar. But the key question remains unanswered — does the military regime really propose to hand over power to an elected government, notwithstanding their own claim to be a "temporary" government?

Observers are increasingly concluding that the NLD now faces even greater marginalization than ever before. This is clear from the continued detention of Aung San Suu Kyi, from the NLD's complete exclusion from the National Convention, and from the continued harsh clamp-down on all kinds of political activity. Aung San Suu Kyi's own dominance over the opposition could also be called into question as her isolation from the political process becomes ever more profound.[5] This coincides with new, and surprisingly unheralded, signs that some leading figures in the expatriate struggle against the SPDC, as well as some "neutral" Burmese living overseas, are rethinking their outright opposition to the SPDC, and are beginning to open lines of communication with the SPDC.[6]

Current trends, if they continue, will undoubtedly further weaken the struggle for democracy being waged by overseas Burmese communities, who have little to show for more than fifteen years of struggle. Hitherto, despite their high international profile, such groups have been essentially marginal to the central political struggle; they have been weakened by their own divisions and remoteness from the situation on the ground, and by their inability to present themselves an alternative source of legitimacy. Despite continuing efforts to make headway in building coalitions, in order to overcome their intractable factionalism, cohesion is lacking. These groups cannot boast a great record of achievement so far, other than pressuring a small number of Western investors to close down their operations in Myanmar, as part of their informal sanctions campaign. Although their campaign against tourism has intensified in the past three years, tourist numbers reported by the government have increased, albeit from a very low level.

Yet, the overwhelming flow of international funds to opposition or "democratic" groups continues little changed, while the volume of international funds going to the people living in Myanmar remains miniscule. Apart from broadening the scope of unofficial sanctions, with decidedly mixed social and economic impact, funds directed to the overseas Burmese movements have resulted in little more than a highly unbalanced and essentially self-serving flow of public information, media coverage, and political advocacy in relation to Burma, especially in the United States and the United Kingdom. Not only does this seem quite remote from the actual needs of the Burmese people, it reflects a rigid tactical approach that appears incapable of brokering any compromise or opening the way to negotiations that might end the long-lasting political deadlock.

Despite the persistently poor performance of the Myanmar economy, the consequent socio-economic decline has been neither a catalyst for economic collapse nor for political or economic reform. In a situation probably not seen anywhere else in the world in such a sizeable country, SPDC management of the economy occurs almost entirely without input from the world's international financial institutions or from influential investors. In recent years, foreign direct investment into Myanmar has dwindled to insignificant levels, as much because of the unfavourable economic conditions arising from the nature of economic policy-making as because of any campaigns against investment in, and tourism to, Myanmar. The informal sanctions campaign by Burmese opposition groups has claimed some high-profile successes, with companies such as Triumph and British American Tobacco withdrawing their investments in 2002 and 2003 respectively. The closure of such factories and the consequent loss of jobs, particularly evident in the textiles sector, has been acknowledged as having a detrimental impact on ordinary wage earners,[7] but there is no evidence of any impact on the military regime's hold on power.

During the last few years the number of international and national non-government organizations (NGOs) operating in Myanmar has grown considerably. While their ultimate influence is limited, international non-government organizations will continue to have an important role to play, if for no other reason than that they provide services and capacities that the Myanmar Government will still be unable to provide. The imperatives for provision of humanitarian assistance will remain as great as ever, and will continue to be independently attested to by objective and well-informed assessments by United Nations (UN) agencies, who have a wealth of experience operating on the ground in Myanmar. International NGOs are uniquely placed to implement projects at the community level, dealing directly with real problems faced by the people, and working in conjunction with local people to help produce practical responses to basic problems.

Whatever the arguments about engagement or pressure, when it comes to international NGOs, opinion in Myanmar seems overwhelmingly to favour their direct and full-blooded involvement. From humanitarian groups to intellectuals, from farmers to professional associations, Myanmar people recognize and welcome the positive encouragement and substantive gains that they obtain from the involvement of international NGOs. People who argue against this are in a minority in Myanmar. Of course, everything depends on the nature of the international NGOs' engagement, but as is evident in the contributions in this book, international NGOs are well aware of the need to manage their engagement carefully.

KEY THEMES

One of the underlying objectives of the 2004 Update Conference was to sharpen perceptions of the situation in Myanmar, in the hope that this might illuminate a better understanding of underlying conditions.

With the new National Convention process under way, whatever credibility problems it might face, it is clearly more important than ever to know what drives all the key players in the process, including the military. This may be even more important than before, since the views of the National League for Democracy seem increasingly likely to have little direct influence over the final outcome. Given a new line-up of little-known military leaders, who have much less exposure to international issues than their predecessors, it is vital for the international community to penetrate the thinking of this leadership group and identify whether or not it might be possible to encourage change to occur more rapidly, and the extent to which, and the ways in which, this might happen.

The most useful perceptions will always be based on a rigorous analysis of the situation, and not on biased or preconceived views. They will be based on direct contact and experience of the circumstances and the participants in those circumstances, and an objective but well-informed understanding of prevailing conditions and the personalities. They must also be founded on a sound strategic approach, rather than being driven by short-term opportunistic tactics. It is surprising how much of the Burma debate is not based on these essential criteria.

Most conferences dealing with Myanmar rely heavily on the expertise of the expatriate and (mostly Western) academic communities on Myanmar, but do not always have the benefit from much first-hand, recent or direct experience of Myanmar. This conference was consciously different. Accordingly, several chapters in this book are by knowledgeable practitioners who are working, or have worked, in Myanmar, who bring realism and credibility to their contributions. Others are by world-renowned experts who visit the country frequently and maintain extensive contacts there, and whose invaluable insights have over the years proven remarkably accurate. So whatever interpretations the different contributors might offer, and whatever ideas they might espouse, the aim was to present assessments that could claim great immediacy and practicality by virtue of being formulated in the current operational environment of Myanmar, unlike the positions that many Burma activists overseas advocate.

Political Dynamics Inside Burma/Myanmar

The chapters by **Robert Taylor** and **Larry Jagan** examine broad political developments, issues thrown up by recent political changes, and the current thinking of the military leadership and their objectives for the future. They do so from different perspectives, namely that of an academic and that of a journalist, but fundamentally agree on the prognosis for continued assertion of military control.

Against the background of debate about forms of power-sharing amongst the many communities in Myanmar, **Martin Smith** argues that the dynamics surrounding ethnic involvement in political process have shifted significantly since the National Convention last took place in the mid-nineties, only a short time after some of the ceasefire agreements had been signed. Ceasefire groups have developed increasing confidence in articulating their demands for political as well as economic and territorial rights, and will try to benefit more directly from their compliance with SPDC policies than they have to date by securing some gains in the process. They see the National Convention as an important, albeit rare, opportunity to lay out their claims and to push for them as hard as circumstances permit. There is no doubt, for example, that while groups such as the Kachin have benefited greatly from the ending of hostilities with the army — and while their compliance with the terms of the ceasefire has been valuable for the SPDC — they have not been able to secure the social and economic benefits that they expected would follow, and which they now value even more highly. Yet there is no immediate prospect of a more equitable, mutually satisfactory arrangement being offered by the SPDC.

The Weaker Position of the International Community

Together, ASEAN and Myanmar's Asian neighbours enjoy more influence in Yangon than Western countries do, but precisely how they will use this influence remains to be seen. India, China, and Japan seem likely to continue to compete for strategic influence in a rather empty contest, and each will be less than satisfied with the highly nationalistic and non-rational policy responses of the SPDC. But whether India, China or Japan would ever be prepared to play a more direct role to encourage political change remains to be seen. So far each of these countries has been at pains to avoid taking on such a thankless role. Whether anything might come out of any Indonesian messages that convey quietly but directly to the regime their concerns about its lack of forward movement is also still unclear.

A stronger anti-UN sentiment seems to be emerging amongst the new SPDC leadership, and this could lead to even greater difficulties for UN Special Envoy Razali, for the ILO presence in Yangon, and perhaps even for other more established UN activities in Myanmar. Whether any hiccups are just short-term, and can be overcome with patience and persistence, or whether they will translate into longer-term problems, remains to be seen. If such setbacks to the broader role played by the United Nations were to eventuate, it could take some time for this ground to be recovered.

At the same time, while the intensity of the limited Western sanctions against the regime has increased over the past three years, the political impact of sanctions is negligible, and will remain so as long as Myanmar's powerful neighbours, China and India, continue to underpin the country, as seems most likely. Indeed, the use of non-UN sanctions has probably, if anything, hardened regime attitudes on whether or not to concede to demands for change from the international community. The judgments on this question by Robert Taylor and by **Morten Pedersen** in their chapters are difficult to gainsay. They reinforce the carefully-balanced assessment made two years earlier in the conference on "Reconciliation in Myanmar and the Crises of Change" at Johns Hopkins University that "there is little evidence to support the idea that sanctions alone have played a significant role in causing the changes in Burma/Myanmar since 2000".[8] Morten Pedersen makes the case for a more intelligent, comprehensive approach to providing assistance that does not exclude working with decision-makers but rather seeks to influence them.

Whereas in some other conflict-torn states, returning expatriates have made a significant contribution both to national reconstruction and national reconciliation, there is little sign yet of this occurring in any significant way in Myanmar. **Zaw Oo** presents a comprehensive description of the successful move to internet campaigning by the Burma opposition groups overseas. Yet he, too, acknowledges their difficulties in achieving the primary goal of regime change.

In the context of the debate in recent years over sanctions versus "engagement", several speakers were asked to focus on the nature of international assistance inside Myanmar, and to provide real life "case studies" in various sectors. Little coverage of such experiences can be found in conferences on Burma or in published literature until now, because such activities are clearly not regarded as "politically correct" by the most vocal activists and by some foreign governments. The relatively positive outcomes from much of this sort of assistance also remain less well known, and it is not sufficiently recognized for its contributions, but equally have yet to demonstrate that its undoubted improvements can be sustained.

Viewing the situation from a Myanmar perspective, **U Myint** demonstrates that there is considerable scope for international assistance to influence policy development and implementation in a much more "hands on" way.

Reinforcing Civil Society as an Alternative?

One of the underlying reasons why change in Myanmar has not been propelled by pressures from within the country is the extremely debilitated state of civil society structures. Anyone visiting or working in the country, even briefly, cannot but be surprised by the present sorry state of affairs. So it was reasonable for the 2004 Update Conference to examine once again the role, if any, of civil society in promoting change.

As **David Steinberg** reports in his chapter, domestic civil society has been so comprehensively suppressed, not only under the SLORC/SPDC regime but also during the Ne Win period, that it will remain weak and in an embryonic state for the foreseeable future. In most countries civil society forms the strong and essential underpinning for the creation of democratic forces, but in Myanmar it has been drastically weakened by decades of active official restriction and is unlikely to play a determining role in achieving national reconciliation at this stage. But the momentum towards adopting the new Constitution has increased, however slightly, and it will be hard for the SPDC to turn back increasing grass-roots interest in greater community participation in development and empowerment. As Steinberg cogently demonstrates, the military regime's lack of legitimacy and the absence of broad-based civil society structures are closely linked.

David Tegenfeldt and **Karl Dorning** provide unique first-hand insights in asking how international non-government organizations can contribute through strengthening civil society structures and encouraging positive change. Taking examples of how civil society roles in some other key internal conflicts were an essential ingredient in the major transformations that occurred, and with the insights that come from their many years of immersion in Myanmar society and culture, both are optimistic about the capacity of Myanmar people to respond although they recognize the enormity of the residual problems.

David Tegenfeldt calls for more strategic and more conscious efforts to promote change in Myanmar than have been applied in the past. His suggestion of drawing lessons from other historically significant internal conflicts is neither far-fetched nor theoretical. Karl Dorning details how international NGOs are already playing a significant role in re-building civil society, but also argues that this is nowhere near enough, given the manifest needs in Myanmar.

Far-Reaching Economic Reforms Needed

So far there has been little spill-over from the very limited presence of foreign investors in Myanmar. The main reason for this, apart from the general imperviousness of the country to outside influences under the military regime, is the reality that most foreign investors are obliged to operate through joint ventures with government-run or government-directed organizations.

Richard Jones explains how foreign investors inevitably encounter certain compromising situations in their relationship with the authorities, but outlines how these can be dealt with effectively by suitable preparations and sensitivity. In carrying out its social programmes in Myanmar, Premier Oil systematically sought input from a range of experts in order to ensure — to the extent this was possible — that its commercial activities and related social programmes were carried out in a way that was sensitive to community concerns. These experts — mainly from universities — advised Premier Oil on social and humanitarian aspects of their operations (Warwick, Essex Universities in the UK, Monash and Western Sydney Universities in Australia) as well as on the particular cultural and political contexts in which Premier Oil was functioning in Myanmar. Given that interaction between foreign investors and the government authorities is a fact of life in a country like Myanmar, it behoves foreign investors to be extremely sensitive to local conditions and to assume a measure of ethical responsibility for their activities in a systematic way. There is no evidence to date of foreign investors being punished by the authorities for taking principled positions on workplace issues and on the social and economic context in which they are operating. But there is also not much evidence yet of improved working conditions and labour practices arising from the presence of foreign investors. This could easily change if foreign direct investment were to grow more rapidly in the future, but this seems unlikely for the moment, given the recent extension of sanctions by certain Western countries.

Sean Turnell's incisive snapshot of the SPDC's mismanagement of the financial and banking problems during 2003–04 demonstrate both the compound impact of inept military controls of the economy and the resilience of the subsistence economy. One key point in his analysis is the absence so far of any measurable macro-economic impact from sanctions.

As Turnell notes at the end of his assessment of the economy, while the broad economic impact of sanctions is still difficult to measure, there have been undeniable short-term adverse effects on employment, business activity and (indirectly) on overall living standards. But this does not foreshadow the economic collapse of the regime. In all probability, any impacts from sanctions will continue to be mitigated in various ways, with flows of assistance from China, India, and Japan picking up in recent years. Without a move to more universal sanctions, a collapse arising from sanctions can be ruled out. Any move to wider, UN-based sanctions clearly remains out of the question, however.

Agriculture was given considerable attention at this 2004 conference, as health had been on previous occasions. Arguably, agriculture can also be the source of powerful humanitarian welfare improvements, and certainly in Myanmar it occupies a leading place in economic development. Interestingly, when in 2002 the SPDC sought to show Aung San Suu Kyi examples of progress under their administration, it was agricultural infrastructure and power generation projects that they took her to see. From her point of view, Aung San Suu Kyi did not dispute this choice, and subsequently told observers in Yangon that she was impressed by some of the government projects and respected the dedication and skills of government technicians.

Clearly, the main requirement for greater progress in agricultural development is to allow market forces to function without intervention from the government, while ensuring that the government provides an overall strategic policy that takes account of food security needs, and of Myanmar's domestic diversity of climates and natural endowments, at the same time as ensuring consistency and predictability of policy.

Graeme Batten and **Myo Win** argue that improvements in infrastructure are an essential pre-requisite for achieving progress in efficient and sustainable agricultural development. They provide a wealth of information about the agricultural sector, while identifying shortcomings and areas for future international assistance aimed at improving food security and thereby alleviating poverty, which they argue should be accorded the same priority as health by the international community. Theirs is a more optimistic perspective than that of Ardeth Maung Thawnghmung in the 2002 Myanmar Update.[9] They also acknowledge the underlying constraints arising from the absence of a fully-developed, market-driven macro-agricultural policy. But modest changes have been occurring in agricultural policy, and the Rector of the Yezin Agriculture University, **Dr Kyaw Than**, in his introductory commentary openly recognizes many shortcomings and the need for international assistance to help overcome various obstacles.

John Copland provides an experienced and balanced view of Myanmar's agricultural needs, based on his extensive experience of working in the developing agricultural economies of Southeast Asia. He also offers publicly, for the first time, case studies of two projects currently under way in Myanmar with financial support from the Australian Centre for International Agricultural Research (ACIAR). Aung San Suu Kyi, who was consulted about these projects before they began, was impressed by the way in which they were designed to ensure that direct benefits would go to the people.

* * *

Despite Western and Asian expressions of concern about the excessively "leisurely" pace of change, realistically the maximum one might expect might be the completion of a referendum and establishment of a transitional government under the military by mid-2006. National reconciliation is likely to be a drawn-out gradual process, rather than a single event or agreement.

The new leadership will probably remain highly risk-averse for the immediate future, and there is little sign so far of the major change in attitude necessary if they are to accomplish their own agenda in any reasonable time-frame. A move into a period of isolationism cannot be ruled out, but this is likely to be short-term, because Myanmar's integration with the region is too great to be ignored or reversed, and because the SPDC depends on assistance from China and India in particular.

Severe cleavages in society need to be mediated. While it is not clear how this might be achieved, given the lack of organizations with a track record of success in dealing with the military authorities, perseverance with any practical form of engagement helps. In the meantime, the SPDC's essential lack of legitimacy — and their basic inability to overcome this through their current approaches — will remain a major obstacle to a long-term political solution. While it is increasingly hard to identify what might prove to be the catalyst for change, it is nevertheless important to keep trying to find solutions that can break the deadlock between the two opposing sides. A more pro-active — but mutually acceptable — political role by the United Nations could still be a long way off, but this would only be possible if key UN member states such as China, the United States, and Myanmar itself, could agree on it.

Notes

1   Formerly known as the State Law and Order Restoration Council (SLORC).
2   A similar investigation into associates of former President Ne Win and his family occurred after the arrest of Ne Win's family in early 2002, but that was on a much smaller scale.
3   It was criticized for these shortcomings by the United Nations Secretary General, Kofi Annan. "Secretary-General Reiterates that Myanmar's National Convention Must Be All-Inclusive To Be Credible", Statement, SG/SM/9309, 17 May 2004. Available at: http://www.un.org/News/Press/docs/2004/sgsm9309.doc.htm. Accessed 6 July 2005.
4   Invitations to NLD Chairman, U Aung Shwe, and some other NLD delegates were issued by the Government, but it was clear that any NLD participation would be decided by a party executive decision. NLD Central Executive Committee members were allowed to meet Secretary-General Aung San Suu Kyi and Vice Chairman Tin Oo while they were in detention to deliberate on this matter.
5   Nandar Chann offers an unusually gloomy analysis in "Opposition Blues", *Irrawaddy Online Edition*, February 2005. Available at: http://www.irrawaddy. org/aviewer.asp?a=4426&z=104. Accessed 10 July 2005.
6   In particular, the case of Zarni, the young leader of the US-based Free Burma

Coalition who controversially returned to Yangon for secret talks with the SPDC leadership in May 2004, as part of a wider ongoing SPDC campaign to cultivate selected influential members of the Burmese diaspora. Zarni has set out publicly the reasons for the shift in his thinking in the May Kha List at Listserv.Indiana.edu/archives/maykha-l.html of 6 September 2004, in the form of a letter to one of his questioners, "My One Day Trip to Rangoon and Our Track II Initiative". (Accessed 12 July 2005)

[7]   US Department of State, "Conditions in Burma and U.S. Policy Toward Burma for the Period September 28, 2003–March 27, 2004", Press release by the Bureau of East Asian and Pacific Affairs, U.S. Department of State, 13 April 2004.

[8]   See, School of Advanced International Studies, Johns Hopkins University, "Conference Report: Burma: Reconciliation in Myanmar and the Crises of Change", Report of conference held 21–23 November 2002, Washington DC, p. 6. Available at:http://www.sais-jhu.edu/programs/asia/SEA/SEA_Publications/Southeast%20Asia/Burma%20Conference%20Report_Final.pdf (Accessed 8 July 2005).

[9]   Ardeth Maung Thawnghmung, "Agricultural Implementation Processes in Burma/Myanmar: Problems and Limitations", in *The Illusion of Progress: The Political Economy of Reform in Burma/Myanmar*, edited by David S. Mathieson and R.J. May (Crawford Press, Adelaide, 2004).

I

Perspectives on Recent Political Developments

1

"One Day, One Fathom, Bagan Won't Move": On the Myanmar Road to a Constitution

Robert H. Taylor

Introduction: Background to Possible Futures

The Myanmar proverb quoted in the title of this paper was first told to me by a friend when, more than twenty years ago, I lamented the slow pace at which we were then travelling in a frequently malfunctioning Volkswagen bus up the old winding road from Mandalay to Maymyo. When, in the reign of King Mindon, a young man was, in his turn, lamenting the slow pace at which they were travelling by ox cart on a pilgrimage to Bagan, his wise father assured him that "if we travel merely a furlong a day, where can Bagan go?"

The road to Myanmar's third constitution has now been travelled for more than sixteen years, but only in August 2003 were we shown a skeletal "road map" to the eventual destination. The reputed cartographer has now left the stage, but the map remains intact. How closely it will be followed remains to be seen, though the government was quick to emphasize that Prime Minister General Khin Nyunt's departure would have no effect on policy. An estimated twenty per cent or more of the population of the country has been born since, in September 1988, the military abrogated the old one-party constitution of the Burma Socialist Programme Party (BSPP) and announced vague plans for elections to choose an assembly to draft a new constitution. But still we have no idea when the journey might end. Readers who have followed Myanmar affairs during the past decade and more will doubtless suffer a sense of *déjà vu* if they read further. But travel on we must, because it is the only political destination we know of, even though we have little inkling of what the weather will be like when we get there or whether the journey will provide the boon so fervently sought.

What passes for analysis and comment on contemporary Myanmar's politics might be better done by a librettist with Wagnerian tastes than by conventionally-trained political scientists and historians.[1] We know that events occur, we observe the occasional changes in the leading personnel of the government,[2] we see the results of decisions made somewhere by someone or some collective, but we have little or no idea why events occur when they do, what the leading players think or know, or how decisions are made. While this is true of our efforts to understand the current military government of Myanmar, the State Peace and Development Council (SPDC),[3] so also does this predicament apply to our understanding of the behaviour of the civilian and para-military opposition to the military, the National League for Democracy (NLD) and other political parties, and the various ceasefire or peace groups such as the Kachin Independence Organization (KIO), the United Wa State Party, or the Pao National Organization.

The topic of the holding of a reconstituted national constitutional convention[4] has dominated Myanmar politics for the past several years. Since August 2003, when the then Prime Minister, General Khin Nyunt, seized the initiative and redefined the immediate major political issues of the country by announcing a seven-step road map to constitutional government, questions have been posed about the nature of that convention. Would it be inclusive of all the groups which claim a right to speak on behalf of some or all of the population of the country? Would the proceedings of the convention be open and fair? Would the army compromise with their political critics and opponents, or, even less likely, abandon their grip on political power? Would the decisions reached at the first session of the convention be open to revision or interpretation? Would subsequent amendment of the eventual constitution be permissible?

Whereas the events of 2003 provided high drama and large surprises, plunging the emotions of the participants in, and observers of, Myanmar's political life from highs of anticipation to depths of gloom and back again,[5] 2004 demonstrated the apparent unchanging certainties of the country's politics since the time of independence. Ultimately, the Myanmar armed forces and their rigidly hierarchical chain of command determine what is politically possible. The ouster of Prime Minister General Khin Nyunt on 18 October, after sixteen years as the leading public figure in the regime, confirmed that not only do the defence services dominate the polity, but that infantry (*tatmadaw kyi*) dominate the defence services. General Khin Nyunt's attempt to maintain his authority as Prime Minister based on his role as head of Military Intelligence[6] and the larger National Intelligence Bureau (the latter abolished in the wake of his departure) demonstrated once more Chairman Mao's adage that political power grows out of the barrel of a gun, not the "ball pen".

It would require massive changes in attitude and approach to the issues of governing a highly fissiparous society to produce eventually, following the conclusion of the constitutional convention, a regime in which the military shares power with civilian politicians from the majority and minority ethnic communities of Myanmar. There has appeared little evidence that this will be possible, though the convention process itself suggests that some limited progress in the direction of the beginning of a new order may be possible. As one sagacious commentator remarked earlier this year, Myanmar needs less a road map to democracy than a *dah*[7] to cut a path through the jungle to make a path to constitutionalism.

From the time of the release from house arrest of Daw Aung San Suu Kyi in May 2002 until the attack on her convoy at Depayin at the end of May 2003, many observers held to the hope that the army leadership and the General Secretary of the NLD would be able to cooperate in some manner in order to end the political stalemate that has gripped the country since the elections of May 1990. Even as late as May 2004, after Daw Aung San Suu Kyi and the Vice-Chairman of the NLD, former General Tin Oo, had been held in prison or under house arrest for another year, some observers, and even one or two participants in the Myanmar political drama, still held fast to the hope that the two sides might compromise.

The demands of the NLD, reiterated in January 2004, that the results of the 1990 election, as the party understands them, be implemented and that all NLD members jailed for political activities be immediately released, indicated that their side of Myanmar's multifaceted political equation had not adjusted its opening bargaining position, if indeed it was willing to compromise at all. The army government, with no need, in its view, to concede publicly or privately the moral equivalency, let alone assumed legitimacy, of its most formally organized, but now badly depleted, civilian opponents, merely ignored the party's demands and proceeded on a path of its own choosing.

The advent of the constitutional convention was accompanied by a great deal of international attention as Asian and European governments sought some way in which to assist the process of political reconciliation in Myanmar. The high point of that effort was a meeting held in Bangkok in December 2003 and hosted by the Thai government, to allow the Myanmar government to explain its plans for the future and gain international support and understanding for them. The meeting was remarkable for the governments that were *not* invited as for those that were invited and attended. Neither the United States nor its closest ally, the United Kingdom, the former colonial power — the two most judgemental critics of the SPDC and its predecessor regime — were included on the invitation list. The ten invited nations[8] represented those states more willing to concede the necessity for external engagement with the political process within Myanmar. These governments tend to see the continual ritual condemnation of the SPDC and all its works, backed with economic sanctions and a restating of unquestioned support for Daw Aung San Suu Kyi, as ineffectual, if not counterproductive. What became known as the Bangkok process was, however, short-lived, and what had seemed to some to be an international opening in Myanmar politics once more proved illusory.[9]

Thus, looked at from outside or from the perspective of those who insist that Daw Aung San Suu Kyi and the NLD must have a role in the current constitutional convention, the political situation in Myanmar looked as bleak at the start of 2005 as it did in May 2003.[10] However, when examined from the perspective of the need to resolve the deepest fissure in Myanmar politics since independence was regained, perhaps the situation is not so disheartening. The virtual civil war between the government of Myanmar (whether under former Prime Minister U Nu's civilian governments or General Ne Win's military Revolutionary Council and subsequent BSPP regime) and the ethnic insurgents was marked by various attempts to negotiate a political solution to the issues raised by demands for local autonomy and economic and political rights in the name of ethnicity within an essentially unitary state. Each of these attempts failed because of the unrealistic demands of the ethnic leaders or the unbending insistence by the government that the insurgents abandon their arms in order to complete an agreement. The remarkable achievement of the SLORC/SPDC regime has been to enter into tacit or real ceasefire agreements with all of the major insurgent groups and many of the minor ones. While this has allowed an end to the endless cycle of killing that marked the civil war period, the political issues which fuelled the conflict have yet to be resolved. The inclusion of twenty-eight former insurgent groups in the constitutional convention[11] suggests, however, that not only have conditions on the ground in the minority areas begun to change, but that the means for enabling a political solution to Myanmar's ethnic conflicts may also be found.

The Convention: Who is In and Who is Out?

The prospects for political reconciliation and social consolidation, in the context of a political opening in Myanmar, momentarily looked promising at the beginning of 2004. Not only were twenty-nine members of the NLD released from detention, following the ending of the house arrest of five leading members of the party in November 2003, but a termination of the country's oldest insurgency appeared to be in prospect. The key leader of the Karen National Union (KNU) during its more than half a century of armed struggle, General Bo Mya, met with Senior General Than Shwe, the Chairman of the SPDC, in Yangon in January 2004, raising expectations that a formal ceasefire agreement between the two sides, to replace the verbal "stand down" understanding which had been reached previously, would be concluded. Talks between the SPDC and KNU, Myanmar's oldest and most entrenched ethnic insurgent army, had commenced in November 2003 and had progressed through a second phase in December. The arrival of a twenty-man KNU group led by Bo Mya (coinciding with his 77th birthday which was celebrated at a dinner hosted by Prime Minister General Khin Nyunt) was made possible as a result of the KNU accepting the government's terms for ceasefire talks.[12]

The talks between the KNU and the government in January 2004 did not prove to be conclusive, however, and efforts to reach a final agreement continued during the year. Reports emerged of occasional armed clashes between government troops and KNU forces or splinter groups in both November 2004 and January 2005. It would appear that a conflict erupted amongst the KNU leadership as to the desirability or necessity of a ceasefire deal with Yangon. Factions emerged, and some foreign groups involved in supporting the KNU clearly hold out the prospect that the insurgency can carry on as before.[13] More importantly, there are apparently debates amongst the KNU and other non-ceasefire groups as to whether to maintain alliances with the NLD and other predominantly *Bamar* (Burman) organizations. However, after so many years of fighting by both government troops and rival ethnically-labelled insurgent groups over the right to tax local populations and to control regional smuggling routes, one might surmise that unless the isolated insurgent bands that still exist can enter the political process in some way, they may operate more like dacoits than guerrillas fighting for a political cause.

The KNU returned to Yangon on 18 October 2004 for five days of further talks, but left to return to their camps on the Thai border two days later when, following the ouster of Prime Minister General Khin Nyunt, their interlocutors in Military Intelligence became embroiled in the issues arising from the departure of their superior officer, the reputed architect of the ceasefire agreements. Once more factional conflict played a hand, potentially perpetuating a major issue in the search for a permanent peace in Myanmar. While the details are not yet fully clear, it would appear that the KNU's government interlocutors were drafted into the process of reassuring the ceasefire groups in the Shan and Kachin states that the deals previously reached by them with the government under General Khin Nyunt's auspices remained intact. This apparently entailed trips to Myitkyina and Lashio by the new Prime Minister, Lt. General Soe Win, and his successor as the new Secretary 1 of the SPDC, Lt. General Thein Sein. The latter, who also has chaired the revised constitutional convention, assured the public soon after General Khin Nyunt's removal, which some described as a "palace coup", that the road map process would continue to be implemented because it was not merely General Khin Nyunt's policy, but that of the SPDC as a whole.

The prospects for the sustainability of the KNU insurgency, and that of the remaining armed groups along the Thai border amongst the Kayah and Shan, look particularly bleak, since the government has clearly increased its capacity to penetrate and dominate border areas. Unlike conditions in the 1980s when travel was considered safe only in the central regions, today virtually the entire country is open to frequent and unimpeded journeys.[14] This has, allegedly, led some of the members of the ceasefire groups to query whether their leaders have not conceded too much in exchange for the benefits they received by abandoning armed conflict. As some of their former military strongholds were occupied by government troops, and their leaders grew prosperous as a result of the businesses they were allowed to conduct, sometimes in conjunction with the army or Military Intelligence, the basis for new factionalism amongst the ethnic groups became apparent. In earlier years, such a situation might have led to the renewal of armed conflict.

Furthermore, even if factionalism does ensure the continuation of low-level insurgency, the Thai government is no longer willing to tolerate, let alone assist, anti-Yangon insurgent groups, and the presence of more than 100,000 Kayin (Karen) and other refugees in Thailand has become a major social and political problem for the local Thai authorities. The continuation of insurgent activities in the border area is also seen as a hindrance to the economic development of these regions. As the government of Thaksin Shinawatra has begun to achieve the reality of former Prime Minister Chatichai Choonhaven's 1990 dream of turning the battlefields of Thailand's neighbours into market places, the capacity of the Myanmar state to tax, police, and develop the border regions has increased. Moreover, the increased mobility of the Myanmar armed forces and the atrophying of what had been the "rear base areas" of the insurgents in neighbouring states has meant that a renewal of armed conflict has become an increasingly dangerous, and therefore unlikely, course for any ceasefire group.[15] Indeed, finding a constitutional way to protect the economic and administrative rights that they have gained through the ceasefires has become ever more necessary.

Since 1989, the army government appears to have achieved by compromise, patience, negotiation, and material and psychological persuasion what its predecessors failed to do through armed confrontation. Though the peace achieved has not been cost-free to the regime, it has resulted in the government now having a greater say in the future of the border areas than at any time in the past, including during the British period, when these areas were known for their "light" administration or indirect rule. Thus, when it came to forming the constitutional convention, the government, while it went through the ritual of consulting with the leaders of the ethnic communities before inviting them to the participate, had at its disposal the capacity to foreclose any options they might have considered if uncooperative.[16] Speculation to the effect that some of the ceasefire groups would walk out of the convention, or not return to it when it resumes, has remained simply that — speculation. Indeed, government spokespersons claimed that they were assured by the leaders of the ceasefire groups after General Khin Nyunt's departure that they would attend the next session of the convention, which, it was announced, would resume on 17 February 2005. This was confirmed by the publication, unusually, of statements by the leaders of several of the groups in the official Yangon press.

Do the NLD and its Supporters Have a Future?

Though the convening of the constitutional convention provided an opportunity for the ethnic ceasefire groups to join a process which might eventually ensure a degree of autonomy and legality for their *de facto* semi-autonomous zones and businesses, the National League for Democracy is not taking part in the convention. Whether the NLD's exclusion from the convention is the result of a decision willingly made by them, or the result of allegedly unreasonable conditions placed by the SPDC on their participation, is a matter of interpretation. In the weeks leading up to the opening of the convention, the Central Executive Committee (CEC) of the party was permitted to meet on several occasions with Daw Aung San Suu Kyi and Vice-Chairman Tin Oo; both of them remained, nonetheless, under house arrest. The CEC proceeded to negotiate the terms of their participation in the convention. These included the possibility that the "six objectives" and "104 principles" agreed at the previous sessions be considered as merely suggestions, and that the NLD would be allowed to choose its own delegates to the convention as the ceasefire groups had been allowed to do. While the government remained studiously ambiguous on the first of these points, according to a statement released by the party on 14 May, the right to choose their delegates was conceded, even though individual invitations to NLD members who had attended the earlier sessions had already been issued.

However, on two other points no compromise was possible. The party would not be permitted to re-open its branch offices, closed following the Depayin incident, though its central headquarters had been re-opened; nor would Daw Aung San Suu Kyi or former General Tin Oo be released. While some contend agreement was nearly reached on all these points, only to be withheld at the last minute by the highest authority in the SPDC, others argue that the conferring of moral equivalency between the government and the NLD implicit in such a compromise ruled it out from serious consideration from the time the demands were made. In any event, the NLD chairman, former General Aung Shwe, announced on 14 May that "The NLD ha[d] come to the conclusion that it will not benefit the nation by participating in the national convention. Therefore it has been decided that the NLD will not attend the convention."[17] The Shan Nationalities League for Democracy (SNLD), the party that won the second largest number of assembly members-elect in 1990, following the NLD's lead, also decided not to attend according to its leader, Hkun Htun Oo.

Although the NLD had participated in the first sessions of the constitutional convention in 1993, 1994 and 1995, during which time Daw Aung San Suu Kyi was under house arrest, soon after her release the party made a decision to withdraw from the assembly on the grounds that its procedures were undemocratic and its decisions, especially the guarantee of a leading role for the military in any future constitutional regime, were unacceptable.[18] The non-participation of the NLD in the convention because of its unswerving reliance on demands that the political process be more fully open on its terms, and that the eventual decisions reached be acceptable to it, points to a fundamental dilemma for the party. Should it stick to its high democratic principles in the hope of eventually turning Myanmar into a fully-fledged constitutional democracy of some as-yet-undefined form, or should it be willing to broker deals with the generals in order to begin to share power with the military, as the ceasefire groups are hoping to achieve? The NLD's all-or-nothing strategy wins it strong praise from powerful quarters in the West, but over a period of fourteen years has not been successful in opening any political space in which the party can operate. Some amongst the exile community who previously campaigned in support of Western sanctions in support of Daw Aung San Suu Kyi have finally begun to argue for a more gradualist, process-oriented, approach.[19]

The NLD, an organization as old as Myanmar's current military regime, was born as a loose coalition of anti-BSPP, anti-army, pro-change students, veteran politicians, and former army officers who had served in, and fallen out with, the governments of General Ne Win over the previous quarter-century and more. It rose like a phoenix from the ashes of the old socialist order around its charismatic Delhi and Oxford-educated General Secretary, Daw Aung San Suu Kyi. As the daughter of Myanmar's national independence hero, General Aung San, a man whose brief political career can be interpreted to justify almost any form of politics, Daw Aung San Suu Kyi became a magnet for those opposed to the army, thus contributing significantly to the success of the NLD in the polls in 1990. Without her, and the national and international acclaim she has achieved since 1988, the NLD might merely be one of a number of political parties that arose between 1988 and 1990 in the hope that their leaders might have a role in the future government of Myanmar.

Daw Aung San Suu Kyi's iconic status is thus the main strength of the party, but also arguably its greatest weakness, for without her the party's future is in doubt, and not merely because as it has excluded itself from the only political process in the country which is possible under the current military regime. Time is not on the NLD's side. The average age of eight of the nine CEC members, excluding the General Secretary, is nearly eighty-one.[20] It would appear that the NLD CEC is unable to reach a policy determination without the presence of Daw Aung San Suu Kyi. According to a number of separate reports, following the party's May 2004 meetings a number of local-level party activists requested a briefing from the members of the CEC. When they received no satisfaction, individuals elected in 1990 met with the senior leadership for clarification of the party's future plans. They replied that they were making no decisions in regard to the future until Daw Aung San Suu Kyi was released. Asked if that date was not until after the convention had concluded, they had no answer but sat "like tombstones".[21]

The air of unreality which seems to surround the NLD CEC was then compounded when about forty of the NLD members-elect wrote to the Committee Representing the People's Parliament (CRPP), composed of the eight NLD CEC members and some senior ethnic minority party leaders and independents. Having previously told the elected members that they could not have a meeting with the CRPP, the CEC members took offence and attempted to summon such impudent "young" men to the

NLD headquarters for disciplinary action. While similarly unrealistic activities have been proposed by other aging politicos living in the leftist politics of the past, such as the formation of an AFPFL-type "united force" led by the NLD, the younger activists of the party have been constrained on one pretext or another. As a result of the party being unable to act as long as Daw Aung San Suu Kyi remains in detention, rank and file members are said to be drifting away from it, with some apparently joining the government-sponsored Union Solidarity and Development Association (USDA) in order to gain the patronage which derives from that body.[22]

The strategy of many who oppose the army government, both within Myanmar and among the exile community, appears to depend largely on the support that their cause generates in the United States and other Western countries. As the seventy-one-year-old U Than, who was elected in 1990 under the Rakhine League for Democracy banner and now resides in India, said on 25 October 2004, "… we are struggling for democracy in Burma, [but] there's so much international pressure that's building up — so we are going to have democracy soon."[23] This hope, fervently held by opponents of the military in Myanmar since the first days of demonstrations against the governments of Brigadier General Sein Lwin and Dr Maung Maung in front of the United States Embassy in Yangon in August and September 1988, appears after sixteen years to be increasingly pious.

The Future of the SPDC

While the travails of the NLD and its supporters receive little media attention, signs of discord and disagreement within the SPDC are seized upon as harbingers of the possible collapse of the military order in Myanmar. The dramatic removal of the Prime Minister in October 2004, only hinted at prior to the event itself, was one of the few instances of public discord amongst the top leadership of the regime. The resulting situation created conditions for the government of Myanmar unprecedented in the SLORC/SPDC period and provides the possibility of a new beginning, though when and how significant political change might occur remains in the realm of speculation. Moreover, none of the imagined scenarios for the future I can see suggest that the road to constitutional government, or even democracy, will be travelled any faster than before as a result of the changes in the SPDC.

The SLORC/SPDC has undergone various mutations since it took power on 19 September 1988. Initially, the senior members of the regime were more or less peers in terms of their experiences and seniority. None had served in the old BSPP government, other than the first chairman of the State Law and Order Restoration Council, General Saw Maung.[24] Indeed, a new rank, Senior General, had to be invented for the chairman in order to differentiate him from his peers. None of the members of the SLORC held the old order in high regard, perhaps as a result of their having served as BSPP regional party committee chairmen and central committee members, and they plunged into government with a verve unknown in recent Myanmar experience. No clear hierarchy had yet emerged among them, each was able to manage his sphere of responsibility relatively independently, and entrepreneurship and initiative became possible even for members of the once-moribund civil service. Brigadier General Khin Nyunt, who had been known for his service to General Ne Win, the senior figure in Myanmar government for the previous twenty-six years, became Secretary 1 of the SLORC, and although junior in the hierarchy, became the most publicly active member of the regime. With his picture often in the press and on television, and his frequent visits to all parts of the country, Secretary 1, who also held the post of head of Military Intelligence, became a crucial member of the regime. Military Intelligence, through organizations such as the now-defunct Office of Strategic Services (OSS), was seen as serving as a think-tank for the regime. The learning curve of the government after 1988 was quite steep as the military sought to reposition itself and the larger government of Myanmar both domestically and internationally.

The collective nature of the early SLORC was underscored in 1992 by the removal of Senior General Saw Maung following a nervous breakdown. At that time the other members of the organization were either able not to involve themselves in their colleagues' affairs or able to work together relatively harmoniously to resolve a problem. A solution for one difficult issue that faces all military regimes, the need to provide reasonably steady and predictable promotion possibilities, was also available to the early SLORC because, relatively speaking, the upper levels of the Myanmar armed forces were not bloated with numerous senior-ranking officers. The army under General Ne Win had been noted for its relatively anaemic organizational structure. Also, the SLORC period was one of rapid expansion of the armed forces, which created many promotion opportunities.

However, time, the enemy of all politicians in power, was not standing still, and by 1997 the free-wheeling days of the SLORC were numbered. In that year, the members of the SLORC still in command of troops or intelligence units moved against those who had taken on increasingly governmental responsibility.[25] The result was the beginning of the creation of a greater sense of hierarchy within the regime. With the removal of former regional commanders-turned-ministers and other members of the SLORC in mid-November 1997, simultaneously with the renaming of the ruling council as the SPDC, the structure at the top came to reflect an evolved ethos and *modus operandi*. Senior General Than Shwe had only two senior members of the SPDC with whom to cope, the ever-resourceful Lt. General Khin Nyunt, and the commander-in-chief of the army, General Maung Aye. The new members of the SPDC, largely former regional commanders, were in no position to argue with their seniors on the council, but merely waited in the hope of their demise.

For the six years between the formation of the SPDC and the removal of General Khin Nyunt, the Senior General has had the responsibility of balancing the plans, ambitions, and views of General Maung Aye and General Khin Nyunt. Most recently promoted Vice-Senior General, Maung Aye formally stood as the Senior General's deputy as well as commander of *tatmadaw kyi* (or the operational commands of the army). During most of the time since the formation of the SPDC, any potential clashes between the Senior General's two most senior colleagues were kept in check not only by his ability to arbitrate between them, but also by their mutual attention concerning their shared political problems, especially the delicate matter of how to deal with Daw Aung San Suu Kyi while coping with the international pressures that have faced the government. With both of these issues in stasis in October 2004, even if only temporarily, steps were taken which eventuated in the removal of General Khin Nyunt.

After regular troops were ordered to raid Military Intelligence and related units along the Shan State border with Yunnan Province, evidence of corruption and malfeasance was allegedly discovered. The raid, which took place while General Khin Nyunt was on an official visit to Singapore, prolonged briefly for minor medical treatment, produced allegations that the head of Military Intelligence, either knowingly, or unknowingly and therefore also in dereliction of duty, had allowed his subordinates to become involved in corrupt transactions. This provoked a crisis perceived as insubordination, which required resolution.[26] General Khin Nyunt's departure from the government had obvious repercussions throughout the governmental structure of the country. His long and active career had made a number of individuals hostages to his fortune, many of whom would be now called to account as part of moves to "clean up" the situation he had allowed to be created. This situation suggests that in the future the government of the SPDC may be more risk-averse and cautious than it has been for the past sixteen years.[27]

Some Historical Parallels

Why might this be the case? Two periods in Myanmar's relatively recent history give some clues. In 1984, the year after the bomb attack by North Korean agents that nearly ended the life of the then South Korean prime minister who was visiting Yangon, Military Intelligence was re-organized. It was brought together with the Home Minister's Bureau of Special Investigation (BSI) and the regular police Special Branch under the umbrella of a newly-created National Intelligence Bureau (NIB) composed of the Home, Finance and Planning, and Defence Ministers and chaired by the Prime Minister . The intention was to ensure that the intelligence failure that had followed from the sacking of General Ne Win's assumed heir apparent, General Tin Oo,[28] on corruption charges, and that allowed the North Koreans to enter the country and plant the deadly bomb, would not be repeated because of lack of coordination amongst the government's various intelligence units. The NIB, which was abolished after the removal of General Khin Nyunt as being "no longer suited",[29] was possibly a solution to a problem that was only partially responsible for the intelligence failure that permitted the bombing incident to occur.

An equal, if not greater, cause for the inadequacy of the security services in 1983 was the chaos which resulted from the removal of General Tin Oo and his entourage, reportedly down to the level of captain. When such events occur, those who remain in the system spend more time looking over their shoulders in order to ensure that their positions are secure than in undertaking their security duties. Changes in Military Intelligence at that time had further long-term consequences for the regime. The new head of Military Intelligence after 1984 was the relatively junior

Colonel Khin Nyunt.[30] Even more than his much more senior and experienced predecessors, Colonel Khin Nyunt was unlikely to have had the courage to bring unwelcome news to the attention of the one man who could make things happen in Myanmar at that time, BSPP Chairman Ne Win.[31] As U Ne Win became increasingly isolated and cut off from realistic information about the condition of the country, the government of socialist Burma effectively ground to a halt other than for the performance of ritualistic activities. The result was the moral and financial bankruptcy which led to the popular upheaval of 1988.

Similarly, during the crucial months of July, August, and September 1988, between the announcement of the resignation of U Ne Win as Chairman of the Burma Socialist Programme Party and the military *putsch* that installed the SLORC, it can be argued that Military Intelligence and the other security services of the state stopped operating effectively, thus limiting the regime's capacity to cope with the political demands that faced it at that time. Only after the military reasserted its authority and provided the necessary security to allow Military Intelligence to re-establish its various monitoring mechanisms were public political activities controlled, if not eliminated. It may be that the present period is again a time in which the remaining Military Intelligence organization spends more time worrying about its own future than checking up on the political activities of the citizenry.[32]

Even if history does not repeat itself in the manner suggested above, the SPDC is clearly in a new situation in terms of its own internal *modus operandi*. Senior General Than Shwe will no longer have his previous role as arbiter determining the balance between his two most senior colleagues; nor is it likely that he will be the recipient of unwelcome news, even in the unlikely event that the new head of Military Intelligence were to report directly to him as General Khin Nyunt had done. This raises the prospect that the government of Myanmar could be about to repeat the experience of the 1980s. There are, however, some factors that work against this scenario, two that are internal to the structure of the regime and two that are external.

One internal factor is the inexorable passage of time and the necessity for the army to provide satisfactory career paths for officers as they seek advancement. This places inevitable pressure on the top-most people to give way to those rising from below. For example, the regional commanders, who have been in place since the last reshuffle of SPDC members in 2001, will before long be expecting their turn to sit in the offices of power in Yangon, while the incumbents will be thinking about when their chance for the top jobs will come. Most military regimes, lacking mechanisms for orderly succession, fail to manage this dilemma satisfactorily. Unlike in the days of the BSPP, when the army had the ability to resolve this problem by moving ambitious but less competent officers into the party or finding them posts in the bureaucracy, the present-day army will need to find room for them within its own increasingly bloated structures. The Senior General may also find that without a parallel and independent head of Military Intelligence reporting to him, his knowledge of potential plots against him within the armed forces is limited.

A second internal factor which may ensure that the entropy that allowed the events of 1988 to occur is not repeated, is the necessity for economic development. This may drive the army not only to insist on more rational and business-sensitive economic policies, but also to provide an opportunity for civilians to begin to share power with the military. Alfred Stephan, in his book *Rethinking Military Politics: Brazil and the Southern Cone*,[33] described how, because of the desire by politicized conventional armies to have new and expensive equipment, such groups seek overall economic growth in order to increase government revenues. This tends to turn the infantry against the intelligence corps, which, with its much-less-mechanized operations, is primarily concerned with political control rather than with economic growth. Aware as it is of its own strategic vulnerability, and more aware of the advanced economies and weapons systems of the country's neighbours than it was in the days when General Ne Win determined security policy, the army may insist on putting economic growth higher up the policy agenda than has previously been the case.

It may not be insignificant that the first public meeting at which the new Prime Minister spoke included not only senior government officials but also what were described as indigenous entrepreneurs from the Chamber of Commerce and other business organizations. By including what the *New Light of Myanmar* quoted him as describing as "the very well to do" in the meeting, he implied that they too had a role in the future of the country as seen from the perspective of the new order.[34] It is, perhaps, not insignificant that also present on this occasion and speaking about the business climate was General Thura Shwe Mann, third in the new hierarchy of the regime and Joint Chief of Staff of the Army, Navy and Air Force.[35]

This meeting stands in contrast to the last large address to senior members of the government given by General Khin Nyunt in August 2003, when he announced the constitutional roadmap. Apparently no members of the private sector were invited to attend.

Myanmar More Engaged with the World

The major external factor which makes a repeat of the scenario of 1983–88 unlikely is the marked change in Myanmar's international position. This has come about as a result of the end of the Cold War, the increasing economic integration among the economies of Asia, and the SPDC's own more vigorous diplomacy as it has sought to defend itself from the effects of criticisms and economic and political sanctions applied by the United States and the European Union. Myanmar's membership of the Association of South East Asian Nations (ASEAN) is one element of this diplomatic effort. Only minor aspects of the changed situation in which Myanmar found itself in 2004 are reversible. Moreover, although there are, no doubt, members of the top levels of the army and government who hold what the rest of the world has to offer in the kind of disdain which demonstrates that they are the true sons of General Ne Win, even the most die-hard among the military know that the technology and economic modernization they seek in order to enhance the national defence capabilities (let alone their own personal interests) is only available through the ever-increasing integration of Myanmar into the larger Eurasian economy.

This realisation came simultaneously with the creation of the SLORC. Ministers at that time proudly announced how many international organizations their respective ministries had joined or rejoined. Invitations for foreign capital to invest in Myanmar were issued almost immediately after the military resumed sole control of the regime. "Socialism is dead; long live the Myanmar road to capitalism, with the help of our foreign friends" might well have been the slogan of the early SLORC. Changes in China were fundamental to this, not least the withdrawal of support by the Chinese Communist Party for the Burmese Communist Party nearly a decade earlier and China's turn to the capitalist road. Not only did this pave the way for the ceasefire agreements with the Kachin, Wa, and Kokang on the Chinese border, but it also meant that China came to be seen both as a market for Myanmar and as a source of capital and technology as well as military equipment. The arms embargoes that most

North American and Western European countries applied following the army's suppression of the "pro-democracy" demonstrators in 1988 were, consequently, little noticed except by Western arms exporters.

The economic sanctions that have been applied increasingly stringently by the United States and the European Union since the United States Congress in 1996 passed legislation banning all new investments by American companies have politically had an equally negligible effect on the regime. The ever-tightening sanctions policy has limited the overall degree of economic growth in Myanmar, but has also had the effect of making the regime both more self-reliant and more indebted to its Asian neighbours, while increasing its defensiveness in dealing with Western governments. Sanctions have merely confirmed in the minds of the generals the soundness of their policies and the traitorous behaviour of those Myanmar citizens inside and outside the country who advocate the maintenance of existing sanctions and organize boycotts of Myanmar goods and the Myanmar tourist industry.[36]

While the sanctions that the United States has applied have received most international attention because of their implications for foreign investment and, since mid-2003, for US-dollar-denominated transactions in Myanmar,[37] European Union sanctions have also been in place for some years. Having agreed amongst themselves to withdraw all military attaches from Myanmar and to insist that Myanmar station no official military attaches in European capitals, European governments have thus denied themselves one form of access to the military and, therefore, to the current government. Bans have also been placed on the issuance of visas to senior military figures and their families. Grandchildren as young as toddlers are thus unable to avail themselves of European health and educational services. Assets held by senior Myanmar officials have also been frozen. The elaborate financial trawl necessary for such an asset freeze revealed an extraordinarily small amount of money, almost certainly much less than the cost of the accountants who did the work. In October 2004 the visa ban was extended to include all military officers down to brigadier-general rank and their families unto the third generation.[38]

As American and European interests in human rights in Myanmar are insufficient to threaten, let alone implement, more drastic measures toward the regime, the government has largely dismissed Western pressure from their calculations.[39] In view of the success of the government and some ceasefire groups, with United Nations assistance, in further reducing the production of opium, corroborated independently by joint U.S.-Myanmar survey teams, officials in Yangon must wonder what it takes to get cooperation on specific issues of significance to the international community. The deepening engagement with Asia as both a counter-weight to the minimal consequences of Western sanctions and as a way of gaining access to development resources will ensure that Myanmar remains internationally active. The acceptance of Myanmar at the Asia-Europe summit in Hanoi in October 2004 underscored this reality for the regime.

As a result of the veto which the United States and some other major states have placed on the granting of major structural adjustment and development assistance loans and grants by international financial institutions such as the World Bank, the International Monetary Fund (IMF), and the Asian Development Bank, Myanmar is not integrated into the world financial system. There is no possibility of an IMF president standing over Senior General Than Shwe as he signs a humiliating loan agreement as happened to President Suharto of Indonesia near the end of his reign.

While Western-dominated institutions have no capacity to pressure the regime in Yangon, the same is not true of Myanmar's Asian neighbours. China has extended major loans to Myanmar, including US$400 million in 2004 while writing off US$73 million at the same time. India has also become a major funder of the Myanmar state. Although non-payment of outstanding debt presumably would have little impact on these relationships, if Myanmar seeks additional funding for development assistance or, if the economy does not improve, for recurrent expenditures such as the purchase of petroleum products, good relations with the country's giant neighbours will be essential. Since India and China are likely sources of foreign investment and economic assistance, as are the major ASEAN states and Japan, Asian states will in time develop even more influence in Myanmar.

More immediately, another factor limits the ability of the Myanmar government to ignore its Asian neighbours. This is its membership of ASEAN. Myanmar was scheduled to assume the chairmanship of the association in mid-2006 and host a summit of ASEAN and ASEAN-dialogue partner states in 2007. While it seemed unlikely that the United States and perhaps the European Union would send representatives to such a meeting, it would have been hugely embarrassing to the other members of ASEAN as well as to the government of Myanmar if countries such as Japan and South Korea were to boycott the summit, which seemed highly unlikely. If Japan and South Korea do attend, this would undermine the effect of a Western boycott. The minimum that would be expected before the United States or the Europeans would consider attending a summit hosted by Yangon would be significant progress toward the achievement of a constitutional government in Myanmar.

If measurable progress on the political roadmap laid out by General Khin Nyunt in August 2003 is not achieved by the end of 2005, the competence of the government of Myanmar to fulfil its promises will be sorely undermined. Just as the declaration by the United Nations in 1987 that Myanmar had joined a number of African states as one of the "least developed countries" undermined the tattered legitimacy of the BSPP regime, so a decision by ASEAN to skip the turn of Myanmar to chair the Association would be seen by large parts of the politically-aware public in Myanmar, including within the armed forces, as a demonstration of the incompetence of the SPDC. The possibility of this happening, however, seems extremely unlikely.

Back to the Convention

The resumption of the constitutional convention, previously expected to take place in mid-November but later postponed until 17 February 2005, is the crucial next step in proceeding down the route of constitutional government. After the convention concludes, possibly in April or following a final session in June July 2005, a draft constitution will have to be prepared and readied for a referendum. The organization of the latter, if done in the deliberative manner of the referendum held for the adoption of the 1974 constitution, would take several years. It would seem that to satisfy the concerns of the ASEAN countries (unspoken as yet in public, although they may have been voiced in private), such a leisurely schedule would be unacceptable.[40] While it would probably be impossible by mid-2006 to move further along the path set out by the roadmap than successful completion of the referendum and the establishment of a transitional government under the military, that is the minimum that one might expect.

While this puts pressure on the government to move forward on the constitutional process, this situation does not necessarily bode well for the political future of Daw Aung San Suu Kyi and the National League for Democracy. Asian states have already discounted and grown weary of the double standards that the West applies to Myanmar, in contrast to their relations with, say, some states in the Middle East or elsewhere with even more egregious human rights records. In some ways, the self-isolation of the United States, and possibly of the European Union, from Asian international politics plays to the interests of some major Asian states. So continued exclusion of the NLD from the convention and permanent detention of Daw Aung San Kyi is probably inevitable, without a major change in their political strategy, if not their complete capitulation to the army.

The period between March 2005 and the middle of the year will be crucial for the success of the constitutional process and for the government. The new prime minister probably has significantly less latitude for initiative than his experienced predecessor had (until the final months of his tenure). For the reasons outlined above, the possibility also exists that the entire state machine will become more risk-adverse and conservative than it has been recently. But the government is going to have to deal with issues which are raised by the constitutional convention, not least the desire of the ceasefire groups and other representatives of the ethnic minorities for a viable degree of autonomy as well as a reasonable degree of development assistance. This will not only add to the political pressure on the army but will also highlight the need to develop more rational and consistent market-oriented economic policies.

Given the new political situation that follows from the dismissal of General Khin Nyunt as the third pillar of the SPDC, more now rests on the sagacity and farsightedness of one man than at any time since the fall of Chairman Ne Win. The capacity of Senior General Than Shwe to maintain the support of his military subordinates, to allow rational economic policies to be implemented, to maintain positive relations with China, India, and the major ASEAN member states, particularly Thailand, and to see the successful implementation of the next steps of the roadmap to constitutional government, is a huge challenge. Many variables will be outside his control and events may override intentions. Until now, the Senior General has been remarkable for revealing little of himself and his capacities. That is about to change.

Notes

1   As with *Nixon in China*, the operatic possibilities of the Myanmar situation
     invite a writer with greater creativity than a mere academic such as myself.
     Imagine the possibilities. You have the two queens held in palaces on opposite
     sides of a lake pining through lengthy arias for the lost imaginary worlds of
     their dead fathers. Their palaces are maintained by men in green who provide
     the operatic action as they scurry about on the stage making love and war with
     their colourful neighbours from the hills while trying to guess their master's
     desires. One of them, a senior prince, even finds himself, in the penultimate
     act, detained like the princesses whom he incarcerated before, for his alleged
     dereliction of duty. A chorus of neighbours wishes the men in green well and
     provides friendly encouragement, but off in the distance large drums
     occasionally burst forth. These big noises toll for the inevitable doom and
     gloom they foretell if the men in green do not change their ways and realize
     that their true queen is locked up on the south side of the lake; meanwhile the
     bad queen from the north laments the fate of her sons and husband and the
     good queen waves her highly principled "democracy" wand, casting a spell
     over the big drummers. While the drama unfolds, the master of all meanwhile
     sits in splendid isolation pondering the instability and uncertainty of life.
     Subsequent liberal re-interpreters may even seek to remake the story of the
     detained prince, making him out to be the Prince Charming all had hoped for,
     but who only emerged after his neutering.
2   The Chairman and Deputy Chairman of the ruling State Peace and Development
     Council, Senior General Than Shwe and Vice Senior General Maung Aye, are
     the only remaining members of the cadre of senior military officers that assumed
     power in 1988. All of their former colleagues have been replaced over the
     years, mainly by younger regional commanders.
3   The name "State Peace and Development Council" (SPDC), was adopted by
     the regime in 1997. It had been known formerly as the State Law and Order
     Restoration Council, or SLORC.
4   The Convention initially met sporadically over three years from 1993 and
     drew up "six objectives" and "104 principles" to be followed in the subsequent
     writing of a constitution. The most important of the points agreed at the
     Convention assured a leading role for the army in any future government,
     including in the choice of head of state and the appointment of 25 per cent of
     members in the legislature from the military.
5   For analyses of 2003, see Kyaw Yin Hlaing, "Myanmar in 2003: Frustration and
     Despair", *Asian Survey*, Vol. 44, No. 1 (January–February 2004), pp. 87–92; and
     Robert H. Taylor, "Myanmar: Road Map to Where?", in *Southeast Asian Affairs
     2004* (Singapore: Institute of Southeast Asian Studies, 2004), pp. 171–84.

6   Officially, Military Intelligence, or MI, was known as the Directorate of Defence
     Services Intelligence (DDSI).

7   A *dah* is a knife with a large blade that is used by Myanmar farmers.

8   In addition to Thailand and Myanmar, countries that attended the meeting
     were Australia, Austria, China, France, Germany, India, Indonesia, Italy, Japan,
     and Singapore. Also present was the United Nations Secretary-General's Special
     Envoy to Myanmar, Ambassador Tan Sri Razali Ismail of Malaysia.

9   A second meeting, to have been held in April or May 2004, to which the
     original 13 participants were expected to be joined by Norway and Switzerland,
     lending further credibility to the Bangkok process, was cancelled at the request
     of the Myanmar government. Yangon was said to be too busy planning for the
     constitutional convention to attend. Critics of the regime suggested that the
     cancellation followed on from the fact that a statement by then Foreign Minister,
     U Win Aung, to the effect that Daw Aung San Suu Kyi would be released prior
     to the convention, was unlikely to eventuate. This had created a potentially
     embarrassing international situation best avoided. Senior figures in the SPDC
     may also have seen the "Bangkok process" as an attempt to internationalize
     what they perceive to be an internal matter.

10   This is the view of the United States and United Kingdom governments as well
     as of the United Nations Secretary-General. See, for example, the Secretary-
     General's report to the 59th session of the General Assembly, dated 16 August
     2004, paper A/59/269.

11   See Martin Smith's table in Chapter 3, also reproduced in "Ethnic Politics and
     Regional Development in Myanmar: The Need for New Approaches", in
     Myanmar: Beyond Politics to Societal Imperatives, edited by Kyaw Yin Hlaing, Tin
     Maung Maung Than and Robert H. Taylor, pp. 78–80 (Singapore: Institute of
     Southeast Asian Studies, 2005).

12   Previous KNU requests that third parties be involved in the talks and that they
     be held outside of Myanmar were abandoned. The terms which the SPDC
     offered were apparently similar to those made to other insurgent groups in the
     late 1980s, starting in the Shan and Kachin states. Earlier efforts, such as a
     unilateral ceasefire with the KNU in the early 1990s, failed to draw the
     organization into negotiations with the government.

13   Campaigning groups such as Christian Solidarity Worldwide and the Free
     Burma Rangers.

14   For example, in 1983, at the time of last national census in Myanmar, 830
     village tracts were off-limits to Immigration and Manpower Department officials
     for "security reasons", and another 120 were only partially enumerated in the
     census. It was estimated that nearly 1.2 million people then lived in villages to
     which the government had no access. These villages included 435 in the Shan
     State, 181 in Kachin State, 170 in Karen State, 34 in Sagaing Division, 8 in

Kayah State and 2 in Tanintharyi Division. See Socialist Republic of the Union of Burma, Ministry of Home and Religious Affairs, Immigration and Manpower Department, *Burma 1983 Census* (Yangon, 1986), Table A-1: Area Covered in 1983 Census by State and Division, pp. 1–12. Today there are relatively few places in the country where the writ of the government does not reach, though sometimes it is mediated through the leadership of a ceasefire group.

[15] The withdrawal of Chinese Communist Party support for the Burma Communist Party in 1989 led to the first round of ceasefires with groups in the Kachin and Shan States. Groups operating in Rakhine State are also finding their room for manoeuvre reduced as the governments of India and Bangladesh have increasingly cooperated with the Myanmar armed forces in controlling cross-border insurgent operations and cutting off supply lines to armed groups.

[16] The increased mobility of the armed forces as a consequence of the purchase of new equipment and increased recruitment achieved during the ceasefire period suggests that if one or more ceasefire groups were to return to arms, the capacity of the army to intervene is much greater now than prior to 1988. However, the terrain where these groups operate is very rugged and large areas do remain inaccessible by land for parts of the year.

[17] Both the statement by Chairman Aung Shwe and the NLD CEC statement are available on BurmaNet News, 14 May 2004.

[18] As that decision was made not long after then United States Secretary of State Madeleine Albright visited Daw Aung San Suu Kyi in Yangon, the official media in Myanmar has from time to time contended that the withdrawal was done, if not at the behest of, then with the encouragement of, the United States.

[19] See, for example, Free Burma Coalition, *Common Problems, Shared Responsibilities: Citizens' Quest for National Reconciliation in Burma/Myanmar*, October 2004.

[20] Aung Shwe, 86; Than Tun, 83; Tin Oo, 77; Lwin, 80; Hla Pe, 77; Lun Tin, 83; Nyunt Wai, 78; Soe Myint, 81. Daw Aung San Suu Kyi is now 60.

[21] Personal correspondence and discussions in October and November 2004.

[22] The NLD apparently circulated in July 2004 a country-wide petition to demand the release of Daw Aung San Suu Kyi and Vice Chairman Tin Oo. For this they were accused by the government of "coercing" members of the public. In August 2004 the party also launched a suit in the Myanmar Supreme Court for the release of Daw Aung San Suu Kyi and Vice Chairman Tin Oo and for the re-opening of the party's branch offices. The suit was summarily dismissed as an "irrelevancy".

[23] An Inter Press Service report datelined New Delhi and Bangkok, 25 October 2004, www.rebound88.net/04/oct/25.html. Accessed 8 August 2005.

[24] Though General Than Shwe was appointed Deputy Minister of Defence in the dying days of the regime, in July 1988.

[25] The fact that this event occurred at approximately the same time as the Asian

economic crisis and the beginning of the negative investment consequences of United States economic sanctions tended to obscure the significance of what transpired.

26 There were rumours circulating earlier in the year that Military Intelligence officers were become concerned about their safety. Foreign Minister U Win Aung allegedly said that his Prime Minister "was in a very dangerous situation" and that the lives of both men were at risk. This is according to a report from Bangkok-based journalist Larry Jagan who reports he learned it from two sources who attended a meeting of ASEAN foreign ministers and Ambassador Tan Sri Razali Ismail in June (*Bangkok Post*, 18 September 2004). If indeed the Myanmar Foreign Minister were so indiscreet as to make this claim, even confidentially, another reason for his dismissal was produced. An "end game" situation had been created.

27 An alternative interpretation might lead to the opposite conclusion. That is, relieved of the need to balance the interests and perceptions of his two deputies, the Senior General and those close to him whom he has appointed over the past several years will be able to restore a vigour to the centre of government that has been missing in recent years. Time will tell, but even if this does prove to be the case, lower-level officers are likely to refer decisions that formerly, with General Khin Nyunt's protection, they felt comfortable making, up the line for higher authority to act, thus slowing the decision-making process.

28 This General Tin Oo is not the same person as NLD Vice-Chairman General Tin Oo.

29 According to the Home Minister, Colonel Tin Hlaing, as quoted on 24 October 2004 by Associated Press. Colonel Tin Hlaing and the Minister for Labour and Minister in the Prime Minister's Office, former Ambassador to the United States U Tin Winn, were the other senior members of the government removed following the detention of General Khin Nyunt. They retired on 5 November 2004. Colonel Tin Hlaing had overseen the government's anti-drug programmes and had encouraged human rights training among the civil service and the police, as well as facilitating two visits by Amnesty International to Myanmar. His successor is Major General Maung Oo, a former regional commander. U Tin Winn, who had managed the consequences of the highly politicized campaign to get the International Labour Organization to impose sanctions on Myanmar, was replaced as Minister for Labour by U Thaung, who remained concurrently Minister for Science and Technology. *New Light of Myanmar*, 6 November 2004. Colonel Tin Hlaing and U Tin Winn were Khin Nyunt loyalists and perhaps his closest confidants in the government.

30 A General Tha Kha had been appointed as General Tin Oo's immediate successor but he was replaced by Colonel Khin Nyunt following the bombing episode.

31 Ne Win's mooted abandonment of one party socialism in 1987 reportedly followed threats by Japan to withhold additional economic assistance unless reforms were carried out.

32   Military Intelligence has been reformed as the Office of Military Affairs-Security
     or OMAS. It is under the command of Major General Myint Swe who also
     doubles as Yangon Commander. He is Number 4 in the hierarchy of the
     regime, as published in the official press accounts of events, and is immediately
     above the Prime Minister, Lieutenant General Soe Win. Local intelligence
     officers are presumably now under the command of regional commanders.
     Formerly they had a separate line of command to the Director of Defence
     Services Intelligence, General Khin Nyunt. On a day-to-day basis, DDSI was
     under the command of Major General Kyaw Win who has now retired from
     military service.
33   Alfred Stephan, *Rethinking Military Politics: Brazil and the Southern Cone*
     (Princeton: Princeton University Press, 1988).
34   *New Light of Myanmar*, 25 October 2004.
35   An alternative or additional explanation would be that the regime wanted to
     assure major investors of continuity in government policies and to warn them
     from indulging in corrupt activities with unworthy individuals.
36   Elaboration of these and related arguments may be found in John H. Badgley,
     ed., "Reconciling Burma/Myanmar: Essays on US relations with Burma", *NBR
     Analysis*, Vol. 15, No. 1, March 2004.
37   Largely increasing transaction costs and creating market uncertainties.
38   While one can argue that Western sanctions and consumer boycotts have
     denied Myanmar workers jobs in the textile, tourism, transportation, and
     other industries, the impact of these on the regime has been not only negligible
     but derisory. The European Union member state that has apparently pressed
     most determinedly for sanctions has been the United Kingdom. There has
     been a modest anti-SPDC campaign in Britain for a decade or more, perhaps
     amounting in all to several hundred people spearheaded by an organization
     with a staff of five on a good day. This campaign has, however, been remarkably
     effective in stopping critical thought in the United Kingdom on the subject of
     European policy toward Myanmar. When pressed to provide one example of
     how the European sanctions regime has negatively impacted on the regime in
     Yangon, on behalf of the minister responsible, a senior Foreign Office official
     could only conclude that there is "anecdotal evidence" that the sanctions
     "rankle" the generals. Personal correspondence.
39   It would appear that the efforts by the Secretary-General of the United Nations
     to pressure the regime are placed in the same category as US and EU expressions
     of concern.
40   The sudden departure of General Khin Nyunt has caused concern amongst
     ASEAN governments, although Thai Prime Minister Thaksin, who was
     informed early of the change, appeared sanguine. The unannounced surprise
     visit of the Indonesian Foreign Minister to Yangon on 11 November 2004 to
     discuss developments underscores regional concerns.

2

Burma's Military: Purges and Coups Prevent Progress Towards Democracy

Larry Jagan

Over the last seventeen years, since the army seized power in Burma on 18 September 1988, there has been a series of extended power struggles within the top levels of Burma's ruling military clique that have severely affected the country's move towards democracy. The most crucial of these, perhaps, was the downfall of the prime minister and intelligence chief, General Khin Nyunt, in October 2004.

Khin Nyunt was arrested on 18 October at Mandalay airport, flown back to Rangoon, and placed under house arrest. His supporters in Cabinet and government were subsequently purged in a series of cabinet shake-ups, dealing a severe blow to the pro-democracy movement.

General Khin Nyunt, who was appointed prime minister in August 2003, was a pragmatist, and favoured involving the pro-democracy leader Aung San Suu Kyi in the national reconciliation process — as the military prefers to call plans for political reform. But he was at odds with the country's hard-line leader, General Than Shwe. It is well known that the

Senior General hates even hearing the mention of Aung San Suu Kyi's name.

Within weeks of Khin Nyunt's arrest, hundreds of military intelligence officers were arrested, interrogated, and charged with economic crimes and corruption. Most of them are facing more than thirty years' jail. The military intelligence division was immediately disbanded. More than thirty thousand junior officers and soldiers were summarily dismissed. Some senior officers were allowed to retire and some foot-soldiers were reassigned to infantry divisions and sent to the most isolated and dangerous border regions. Since then, anything to do with Khin Nyunt has been purged. Photographs, posters, and billboards showing him have been taken down. The spire in the famous Shwedagon temple in Rangoon that Khin Nyunt had covered in gold has been boarded up. The authorities have also scoured the civil service and sacked anyone who had got their post as a result of a recommendation from a military intelligence officer. It is reminiscent of the days of the former Burmese monarchs — when the king was overthrown or died, the next king had all the old king's relatives killed.

Before Khin Nyunt's arrest, Burma's top military leadership had been waging a bitter power struggle for some time. At the root of the conflict were major differences between Khin Nyunt and Than Shwe over Burma's political future. On one hand, the prime minister favoured change. He understood that Burma's future depended on political reform and economic development, and that these were linked. On the other, the hardliners around Than Shwe believed the best way to preserve the military's central role was simply to do nothing and maintain the status quo. Despite increased international pressure following the brutal attack on Aung San Suu Kyi and her supporters on 30 May 2003, when she was travelling in the north of the country, Burma's hard-liners clung to their perception that there was no need to compromise with the pro-democracy activists.

Days after Khin Nyunt was made prime minister in August 2003, he announced a seven-stage road-map for movement towards democracy. This involved reconvening the National Convention to draw up a new constitution. (The Convention had originally started its work ten years previously, in January 1993, but went into recess in November 1996 after the National League for Democracy (NLD) walked out.) The draft constitution would then be put to a referendum, followed by fresh elections under the new constitution.

"Although there are seven steps, it won't take seven years to achieve," the Burmese Foreign Minister Win Aung said in the corridors of the Association of South East Asian Nations (ASEAN) summit of leaders in Bali in October 2003.[1] He did, however, concede that the first step was likely to be the most difficult.

Khin Nyunt had frequently told Asian leaders and the UN envoy Razali Ismail that he supported involving Aung San Suu Kyi in the national reconciliation process. He wanted the National League for Democracy to participate in the National Convention. General Than Shwe, on the other hand, has steadfastly refused to allow Aung San Suu Kyi and the NLD to participate in the National Convention. He has always insisted that the political parties would only be given a role in the national reconciliation process after a new constitution was drawn up and new elections called.

After several months of negotiations, the National Convention opened with some ethnic groups involved, but without the major political groups being allowed to participate. Discussions between senior representatives of the State Peace and Development Council (SPDC) and the NLD continued up until the last minute. There was a flurry of meetings between the two sides in the final days before the Convention was due to open. The NLD leaders were allowed to meet Aung San Suu Kyi and Deputy Chairman U Tin Oo, who were still under house arrest, to consult on their position. The NLD insisted on a series of conditions most of which were rejected by Than Shwe, the key one being the release of Aung San Suu Kyi. In the face of the military's unresponsive attitude, the NLD declined to participate in the Convention.

At that point Khin Nyunt's usefulness ran out. Than Shwe was already angry with the prime minister, following UN envoy Razali Ismail's visit to Rangoon in March 2004, when Razali had called for Khin Nyunt to be given a mandate to work with Aung San Suu Kyi on the national reconciliation process. In effect, the UN envoy was calling on the senior general to empower his prime minister. Nothing angers the top leaders more than public suggestions that there are major differences between them — even if there is a bitter power struggle in progress.

From this time, Khin Nyunt and his clique of senior military intelligence officers knew they were on borrowed time. Not long afterwards, Khin Nyunt, who was still nominally head of military intelligence, warned his senior military intelligence officers to be careful as he could no longer protect them. One senior military intelligence officer even told friends in Rangoon that he suspected that his phones, including his cell phone, were being bugged. This kind of paranoia increased amongst the senior ranks of military intelligence in the months before the army moved against Khin Nyunt.

By the end of July 2004, after the National Convention went into recess, things were coming to a head. Relations between Khin Nyunt and Than Shwe worsened dramatically. In mid-June, Than Shwe cancelled Khin Nyunt's scheduled visit to Indochina — his symbolic first visit as prime minister to Cambodia and Laos — and ordered him to go to the National Convention and deal with the ethnic groups who had been resisting the way the Convention was being managed and refusing to back down. The trip was rescheduled, but Khin Nyunt refused to talk directly to the ethnic leaders. This may have sealed his fate.

"My prime minister is in a very dangerous situation," Burma's foreign minister Win Aung told his Asian counterparts and the UN envoy Razali Ismail at the ASEAN foreign ministers meeting in Jakarta from 30 July to 2 August. "And he may have to flee the country," Win Aung said.[2] It is understood that shortly before Khin Nyunt was arrested, one Southeast Asian country informally offered him political asylum. "But he procrastinated until it was too late," a military source said.

Over the past few years there has been growing resentment within the army over the latitude Khin Nyunt had given his military intelligence officers to get involved in business activities. "I can't educate my children," a Burmese army officer once complained to me, "but every MI [military intelligence] sergeant can afford to send their children to school abroad." Tension between the army and military intelligence in the border areas had been growing for months. "It was in part a battle over business interests and resources but it was also a war over status and authority," according to a UN official who works in Burma's border areas. The regional military commander in Lashio in northern Shan State finally moved to end the conflict with military intelligence, at least in Shan State, and called in his boss — army chief General Maung Aye, who took decisive steps to end the dominance of military intelligence. In September 2004, on the orders of General Maung Aye, more than twenty intelligence people were arrested in the border town of Muse on the Chinese border because of their business activities. Over a hundred government employees — customs officials, immigration officers, and border guards were also detained on corruption charges. The military intelligence compound in the northern city of Lashio was surrounded and two officers were arrested for corruption. Both had illegal bank accounts in China.

General Than Shwe was firmly behind the move against Khin Nyunt, and launched the campaign on the pretext of rooting out corruption in the military. Many intelligence officers had indeed been actively involved in business, but now that was used as the excuse to round them up and cashier them. Than Shwe's approach to power is largely drawn from his mentor, Burma's former strong-man General Ne Win, who was a master at eliminating military rivals. Frequent purges were a major characteristic of his rule. In the mid-1970s Ne Win sacked the army commander, Tin Oo, after the soldier's growing popularity within the army and among the people marked him out as a potential rival for power. Ne Win also fired another Tin Oo in the 1980s, and later the military intelligence chief, when his growing power and influence began to rival Ne Win's.

Over the past few years it has been clear that there has been a growing division within Burma's military leadership on how to maintain the army's political role in the future and develop the country. Than Shwe's approach in recent years has been to revitalize the army and strengthen the military. Than Shwe has a clear vision of the future of the military — and it is not one in which the army plays second fiddle to a civilian administration. General Than Shwe has made no secret of the fact that he expects to rule the country for at least another decade, according to a senior military source close to the top general. This has been institutionalized in the draft constitution, in that the president must be a military man, while the defence minister must also be an army commander.

But Than Shwe understands that for the army to remain in a position of control it needs to be strengthened and reformed. With more than 400,000 armed soldiers and officers, it is already the largest standing army in the world apart from that of China. In the two years 2003–04 the army has been making major purchases of hardware, including significant purchases from the Ukraine.

General Than Shwe is renowned for being cautious and xenophobic, as well as authoritarian. He does not trust his subordinates. Several years ago he told a senior army commander that he mistrusted both his immediate subordinates, Maung Aye and Khin Nyunt, because he felt they were "hot-heads" who had a tendency to make snap decisions. In the past few years he has led something of a hermit's life — seeing few people and confiding in even fewer. "He sits in a cocoon — his own padded room — meets few people and listens to none," according to a Western diplomat in Rangoon. But he does spend time surfing the Internet on his computer and understands that this is the future — and one which Burma must encompass, according to a military official in the Senior General's office. (It should be noted that here that many analysts believe Than Shwe does not have a good grasp of English. This is not true. He speaks and understands English extremely well. Both the UN envoy, Razali Ismail, and the former Indonesia foreign minister, Ali Alatas, have told me that they had long conversations with the General in English.)

In 2004 Than Shwe ordered all senior commanders in the army to learn how to use computers and access the Internet. Army officers of the rank of colonel and above were recently told to buy their own personal computers, according to military sources. Several hundred junior military officers have been sent to Russia and India for computer training. Senior officers in the army now have to pass examinations in English to get promotion. This is all part of Than Shwe's vision to revitalize the army and ensuring that it has an enduring role in Burma's political future.

The power-struggle within the military has thrown the future of Burma's national reconciliation process into serious doubt. The National Convention resumed drafting a new constitution in May 2004 and is continuing to prepare for a referendum on the constitution in the future.

The former prime minister Khin Nyunt was often seen as the driving force behind the national reconciliation process, but immediately after his arrest the regime's leaders were at pains to assure the international community that the State Peace and Development Council was committed to the roadmap. Days after Khin Nyunt was ousted, the new Burmese Foreign Minister, Nyan Win, told diplomats in Rangoon that it was "business as usual," according to a Western-based diplomat in Rangoon who attended the Foreign Minister's briefing. Later, the Chairman of the National Convention Convening Commission, Lieutenant-General Thein Sein, said, "[W]ith a view to seeing the emergence of a peaceful, developed and discipline-flourishing democratic state, the State Peace and Development Council will continue to implement the [roadmap] agenda step by step, without changes."[3]

This seems to remain the military rulers' political strategy, the key being the National Convention. Although the main political parties, including opposition leader Aung San Suu Kyi's National League for Democracy, were not able to participate in 2004, the various ethnic rebel groups who have signed ceasefire agreements with Rangoon have been attending. But the continued participation of some of these groups must be in serious doubt. For them, Khin Nyunt's role in the government was crucial, for he was their main point of contact and they believed that he, at least, understood their demands for ethnic rights. Many ethnic leaders were personally loyal to Khin Nyunt and still do not trust Than Shwe or Maung Aye. The Wa and Kachin ethnic leaders remain anxious and uneasy, according to sources close to both groups, despite repeated meetings with the new prime minister, Soe Win, and Secretary One, Thein Sein.

Originally many of the ethnic leaders contemplated withdrawing from the process. "We may now have no alternative but to pull out of the National Convention," said a senior ethnic leader inside Burma, a week after Khin Nyunt's removal. But most of them later believed they had no alternative but to remain at the National Convention. "We need to be there to put our point of view. This may be the last chance we get to influence the content of the constitution," a Kachin leader told this author.[4]

But for the Burmese government and the ethnic groups, the national reconciliation process involves more than simply drawing up a new constitution in which ethnic rights are guaranteed. Although these ethnic groups have ceasefire agreements with the government, most of them have retained their arms. In the months before the National Convention started in May 2004, Khin Nyunt and his intelligence operatives had been telling the ethnic leaders that once the new constitution was drafted, they would have to surrender their weapons. This is something many of them were already reluctant to contemplate; with the purge of Khin Nyunt, they will be even more hesitant to disarm.

Since the fall of Khin Nyunt, Than Shwe and Maung Aye have been taking a very tough line with the ethic groups, according to military sources in Rangoon. This approach has been highlighted by a more combative position towards the main rebel group that has not yet signed a ceasefire agreement, the Karen National Union (KNU), and there were several major skirmishes in December 2004 and January 2005. The KNU and the government had been holding peace talks during the course of 2004.[5] The Karenni, who broke their ceasefire agreement with the SPDC, have also come under intense military fire in the first two months of 2005.

For their part, several ethnic leaders have hinted that returning to armed struggle against the Burmese army is a serious option that will have to be considered. The whole question of demobilizing the ethnic armies remains one of the pivotal issues in the national reconciliation process. It was the key issue that was being discussed between Khin Nyunt and the ethnic leaders in the months after the National Convention went into recess in July 2004. At the time, the two sides seemed to have made significant progress towards a solution that would have seen the ethnic soldiers absorbed into a armed militia, but under the control of the Burmese regional commanders.[6] Disarming the ethnic armies as quickly as possible is now at the top of the military's agenda, while the ethnic leaders' suspicions of the intentions of the top military men means they will resist this move as long as possible.

Although Burma's top leaders continue to insist that nothing has really changed as a result of Khin Nyunt's fall, the reality in Rangoon at the moment is that there is significant sense of uncertainty. There is no doubt that Khin Nyunt is now a totally spent force and has been effectively removed from the scene, but the power struggle at the top has not yet been completely resolved. The struggle now is between Maung Aye and Than Shwe.

At the centre of the continuing tension within the military leadership is the issue of transferring power to the next generation of officers. This is a problem that besets all military dictatorships, and in some countries has led to a period of acute uncertainty that has in turn ended with the eventual transfer of power to a civilian government.[7] When the Foreign Minister, Nyan Win, briefed diplomats on Khin Nyunt's retirement on health grounds, he also pointed out that the regime was beginning to hand over the reins of power to the next generation. There have been clear signs for some time that a new, younger officer class was being groomed to succeed the old men currently in charge.

The transfer of power is far from over. The purge of Khin Nyunt and his supporters is likely to be the start of the process rather than the end General Thura Shwe Mann has been appointed to the important position of Joint Chief of Staff of the Army, Navy, and Air Force, is thus already number three in the SPDC, and is obviously destined for one of the top jobs. But it is unclear at present who else will emerge to replace Than Shwe and Maung Aye in due course. Little is known about the next generation of army officers. Even Shwe Mann is an unknown quantity. He and many others coming through the ranks are believed to favour a more professional and clean army. A few years ago a senior military officer said he believed eighty per cent of colonels in the army believed in the need for political change, and many even privately supported Aung San Suu Kyi, but dared not reveal their feelings to anyone in the army for fear that it would be used against them in the future.

The latest military changes in Burma certainly herald a significant and extensive overhaul of the country's power structure. However, it is by no means clear where that leaves the national reconciliation process. In recent months there have been strong hints that the military government intends to wrap up the National Convention by the end of 2005 to hold a referendum on the constitution before the end of 2006. The regime's leaders are concerned about their ASEAN neighbours who are anxious to see political reform in Burma before Rangoon is considered for the presidency of ASEAN in the next few years.[8]

The ease with which Burma's third-most powerful general was swept from power has revealed how fragile Burma's military control really is. In the midst of this uncertainty and change it is just possible that the emerging generals will opt to try to involve Aung San Suu Kyi and the National League for Democracy in the national reconciliation process.

If so, Khin Nyunt's legacy may still be instrumental in forcing the regime to start a genuine process of handing over power to a civilian government. But Khin Nyunt's vision was always that this would take up to another thirty years. The former prime minister also told the pro-democracy leader that the army never negotiated. If that is the pragmatist's view, political change in Burma is still a very long way off.

Notes

[1] Exclusive interview with the author.
[2] Personal exclusive interviews with several participants in the meetings.
[3] From a statement by Lieutenant-General Thein Sein, "Complete Explanation on the Developments in the Country", *New Light of Myanmar*, 23 October 2004.
[4] Exclusive interview with KIO leader, Dr Tu Ja, in Rangoon.
[5] Talks sponsored by Khin Nyunt and usually conducted by senior military intelligence officers. Ironically, a KNU delegation was in Rangoon at the exact time Khin Nyunt was arrested.
[6] Interview with military spokesman Colonel Hla Min.
[7] In Asia, Bangladesh and the Philippines are cases in point.
[8] Burma unexpectedly stood down as the next president of the ASEAN bloc at the 2005 regional summit of foreign ministers in the Lao capital of Vientiane in July. For further details, see Larry Jagan, "Rangoon lets ASEAN off the hook", *Bangkok Post*, 29 July 2005.

3

Ethnic Participation and National Reconciliation in Myanmar: Challenges in a Transitional Landscape

Martin Smith

Introduction

Since 1988, Burma/Myanmar has remained deadlocked in its third era of political transition following independence from Great Britain in 1948. Military-dominated rule has continued, there has not been a return to elected government, and there have been no substantive benchmarks of political change. And yet Myanmar in the first decade of the twenty-first century is importantly different from General Ne Win's failed experiment with autarchic socialism in the Burma of 1962–1988. Over the years a series of events have refashioned the socio-political landscape. Defining moments include the introduction of a market-oriented economy following the 1988 assumption of power by the State Law and Order Restoration

Council (SLORC, now known as the State Peace and Development Council (SPDC)); the 1990 general election in which the National League for Democracy (NLD) won victory; and Myanmar's membership of the Association of South East Asian Nations (ASEAN) in 1997. Whatever the future holds, in an increasingly globalized world there is little likelihood of Myanmar returning to its hermit-nation status of the Ne Win era.

Myanmar today continues to face a complex diversity of challenges. However, if there is any single issue which is both the key to the political failures of the past and an essential priority for a progressive future, it is the question of national reconciliation and ethnic inclusiveness in the processes of democratic reform. In this respect, the changes in the ethnic landscape have been among the most significant since the SLORC-SPDC assumed power in 1988. Two developments have underpinned such change: first, an ethnic ceasefire movement that was instituted by the military government in 1989 and had spread to over twenty armed opposition groups by the end of the century; and second, the 1990 election in which nineteen ethnic minority[1] parties also won seats, forming the second largest block of pro-democracy parties after the NLD.

At the time of writing, it remains important to stress that there are several ethnic minority areas where conflict has continued, especially in the Thai borderlands. There are also unresolved questions about the involvement of electoral political parties in the SPDC's seven-stage road-map process and the resumed National Convention in 2004 at which the country's third constitution since independence is scheduled to be devised. In late 2004, further uncertainties were raised by the reshuffles in the SPDC government that led to the downfall of General Khin Nyunt, who had been closely identified both with the ethnic ceasefires since their inception and with the road map.

Nevertheless, on the ground the impact of incremental changes in the ways that ethnic issues have been addressed in Myanmar since 1988 remains notable. In particular, the ethnic ceasefires have meant that many long-off-limits regions of the country have become accessible to outside visitors, including international aid agencies and businesses. This has already had marked socio-economic consequences in the field, as well as sharpening international perceptions about what was hitherto one of Asia's least-known frontier regions. For, whether due to the residual ethnic conflicts or the changing landscapes after the ceasefires, Myanmar's ethnic minority borderlands are increasingly regarded as strategic regions of inter-linked human flow and socio-economic contention or opportunity that is only likely to escalate in the twenty-first century.[2] This is a situation that is explicitly recognized by all of Myanmar's neighbours through their post-1988 policies of "constructive engagement" with the country and its peoples.[3] Stated a 2003 report by the Asian Dialogue Society, "The small wars along Myanmar's borders are a form of contained balkanization and it is not in the interest of Myanmar or Asia that a process towards stabilization be derailed. Asia cannot afford to lose Myanmar and Myanmar cannot afford to lose Asia."[4]

As such views highlight, perhaps the most significant change in Myanmar's transitional landscape has been on the ethnic political front. The challenges of democratic reform are yet to be answered, but with the demise of Ne Win's Burma Socialist Programme Party (BSPP), the consequence of both the ethnic ceasefires and the 1990 elections has been to return ethnic politics and nationality parties to the centre of the country's political map. In a country where ethnic minority peoples constitute an estimated one-third of the population of fifty-three million, this was always essential if the country were ever to achieve inclusive peace and reform. But the ethnic parties had been excluded from the public stage for over two decades after Ne Win's 1962 seizure of power, except in the insurgent *maquis* and "liberated zones", through which a diversity of armed opposition groups continued to control most borderland areas during the BSPP era.[5]

Equally importantly, the post-1988 revival of ethnic politics is a reality that, since the early 1990s, has been recognized by the United Nations and other international organizations as an integral element in the "tri-partite" formulation by which dialogue, reconciliation and reform should be achieved — that is, through the military government of the SPDC, the National League for Democracy, and the country's diverse ethnic minority groups.[6] Notably, too, in a marked change from the BSPP precedent, the SPDC chairman Senior General Than Shwe has referred to the ethnic ceasefires as the most defining feature of the SLORC-SPDC era through a policy of what the military government terms "national reconsolidation".[7] Such a claim was reiterated in the state-controlled media on Armed Forces Day in 2004: "Internal insurgency broke out for over 40 years after the independence was regained. Nowadays, national unity has been restored out of goodwill and efforts of the government."[8]

The challenge, however, remains: to move on from a backdrop of such promises and rhetoric, in which many different organizations have been involved, to achieving sustainable peace and reform. Many veteran actors in the country's politics compare the present time of uncertainty and reorientation to the other epoch-shaping moments in post-colonial history, notably during 1947–49 and 1962–64. Indeed, it was recognition of the perceived opportunities provided by Myanmar's transitional landscape that encouraged the country's oldest armed opposition group, the Karen National Union (KNU), to resume formal peace talks with the military government in January 2004. The party's aging leader, General Saw Bo Mya, personally led the delegation to Yangon where he celebrated his 77th birthday. "The present period is like 1947 and 1963; that is why we went to Yangon to meet face to face to see the situation," Bo Mya claimed. "This time there are no preconditions, so we want to solve our problems in political ways."[9]

Somewhat remarkably, the KNU conflict has continued virtually uninterrupted since 1949, in one of Asia's longest-running insurgencies. However, while it is the political crisis that often gains the international headlines, behind the growing desire for peace also lies very real concern on the part of many communities over the desperate humanitarian situation that exists in many areas of the country. As the door to the country increasingly opens, the evidence is inescapable. Once regarded as among the most potentially prosperous countries in Asia, Myanmar today is one of the world's poorest, with an estimated per capita income of just US$300 per annum at the turn of the century.[10] Equally stark, in September 2004 the World Food Programme estimated that a third of all children aged under five in Myanmar are suffering from malnutrition, with many of the worst conditions of poverty in the ethnic minority borderlands.[11] Clearly, the long years of political and ethnic conflict have taken a heavy toll on all aspects of socio-economic life in the country.

In order to comprehend, therefore, how Myanmar became deadlocked in a state of such precipitate decline, it is crucial to understand that the country's political and ethnic challenges are inextricably interlinked. The corollary that must be drawn from these conclusions is that during any process of social and political reform, dealing with ethnic participation and national reconciliation will remain a vital constant. Indeed, this is a reality that has long been recognized in private by many of the key stakeholders and political actors in the country. In contrast with the

Ne Win era, the need for ethnic peace and democratic reform exists today in the vocabulary of all the leading parties and institutions.

Before moving on to examine the present challenges, some initial caveats are required. For the moment, it is still uncertain whether the country is truly on the path towards inclusive reform. As in other pivotal years in Myanmar politics, 2004 was a year of complex change, with both hopes and anxieties raised in uneven balance.

But rather than providing a rationale for further delays or new cautions, this should only serve to elevate the urgency of establishing a durable peace with the ethnic groups and an inclusive process of reform. Many leaders of ethnic nationality groups fear that if inclusive reforms are not achieved now, when so many groups say that they are willing and prepared, then the foundation for yet another generation of division in the country could be laid. Given Myanmar's troubled past, this is not a prospect to be considered lightly. The warnings from history have been repeated and are very clear.

The Legacies of Failure

Myanmar today is a land still suffering the consequences of over five decades of armed conflict. The evidence is manifest as much in the political and humanitarian aspects of life in Myanmar as in the social and economic spheres. Every single part of the country has been affected at one time or another by insurgency and social breakdown. It has not been simply an issue that involved only non-Burmans, nor has it been simply a case of the Burman majority versus the ethnic minorities. There have, for example, been conflicts between armed groups among the Karen and Mon peoples and among the Shan and Wa peoples over the years. Yet it is the ethnic minority communities that have generally been longest in the front lines of conflict, and among those communities the cumulative effect of their sufferings has left a debilitating legacy of under-achievement and loss in a country that, at the time of independence, was still seeking to come to terms with the divisions and destruction of World War II. To the country's long-term cost, these unresolved crises have transcended two constitutions and all three political eras during the post-colonial age.

Following the insurrection of the Communist Party of Burma (CPB) in March 1948, political rebellion rapidly spread to the Karen, Mon, Pao, Karenni, Rakhine and other ethnic groups, who took up arms against the central government in order to gain greater autonomy or, in some cases, to secede. The country's first constitution, drawn up shortly before Burma became independent in 1948, never gained widespread approval during the era of parliamentary democracy (1948–62). The 1947 constitution embodied too many anomalies; for example, it was federal in concept but not in name; and, setting a precedent for the future, too many ethnic parties felt excluded by the political processes of discussion at that time. In particular, the Panglong Conference included leaders of only the Chin, Kachin and Shan peoples from the colonial Frontier Areas, while the KNU boycotted the elections for the 1947 Constituent Assembly, thus excluding itself from future influence or representation in government.[12] Further disruption occurred when remnants of the Kuomintang forces invaded from China and entrenched themselves in the mountains and forests of the northeast borderlands where, with clandestine backing from the United States, they became part of the insurgent mosaic during the 1950s.

Ne Win's monolithic "Burmese Way to Socialism" came no closer to solving the country's many ethnic and political challenges. Instead, the takeover of power by Ne Win in 1962 ushered in a quarter of a century of economic misrule (1962–88). The constitution that was eventually adopted in 1974 introduced, for the first time, the appearance of ethnic symmetry in the country's political map, by the creation of seven divisions, where the Burman majority mostly lived, and seven ethnic minority states: Chin, Kachin, Karen, Kayah, Mon, Rakhine, and Shan. However, the socialist goals of the state, the one-party structure of government (enshrined in Article 11 of the constitution), and the methods of force employed to impose such a system, merely served to increase resistance to the government. Rather than the BSPP crushing opposition, new insurgencies escalated rapidly among the Kachin and Shan peoples, this time spreading to other ethnic groups, including the Palaung, Kayan, and Lahu.

In justifying such tactics, Ne Win expressed implacable opposition to the federal goals of many of the ethnic nationality forces, who subsequently united in the nine-party National Democratic Front (NDF, formed 1976). Indeed, it was to forestall any prospect of federalism, which was then being proposed by the above-ground Federal Movement, that Ne Win claimed to have seized power in 1962. It would, he argued, "destroy the Union".[13]

It is important to stress that during the BSPP era there were numerous insurgent challenges to government, including by the deposed prime minister U Nu, who briefly took up arms in the Thai borderlands with the KNU, New Mon State Party and other erstwhile opponents in the short-lived National United Liberation Front (1970–74). But undoubtedly the most serious military threat came from the revived Communist Party of Burma which, following anti-Chinese riots in Yangon, received full-scale support from China for a decade after 1968. This had a convulsive impact on the direction of armed conflict and ethnic politics in the country. With thousands of freshly-armed recruits among such nationalities as the Wa and Kokang, the CPB was able to seize control of vast new "liberated zones" in ethnic minority lands along the China frontier, from where it attempted to spread insurrection back into urban areas and the central Irrawaddy plains.

This cycle of political paralysis and insurgency was the backdrop to the country's economic collapse during the 1980s. In a country with no real external enemies, an estimated 40 per cent of the national budget was being spent on defence; two insurgent blocks, one headed by the NDF and one by the CPB, controlled most borderland areas as well as much of the thriving black market trades in such lucrative items as jade, opium, cattle and luxury goods; and all the time the social and humanitarian costs were mounting. This decline was graphically exemplified when Burma was accorded Least Developed Country status by the UN, in 1987. There are no reliable statistics for casualty figures, and until the mid-1980s the fighting was little reported in the outside world. But there is little reason to doubt the claim of the first SLORC chairman, General Saw Maung, in a landmark admission about the impact of war, made in 1991, that the true death toll since independence "would reach as high as millions".[14]

It is poignant to note, therefore, how few attempts were made to try and end the fighting by dialogue and political means until the post-1989 ceasefires. Individual talks took place between the government and insurgent groups, but they were few and very far between — notably with the KNU in 1949 and 1960; with Rakhine, Pao and Mon groups during U Nu's "arms for democracy" initiative in 1958; with Muslim Mujahids in 1961; and with the Kachin Independence Organization in 1972 and 1981 (when talks were also held with the CPB). Few talks, however, ended with agreements or lasting ceasefires. Many different counter-insurgency tactics were also attempted by the government over the years, ranging from the political ("people's war") to the repressive (the "Four Cuts").[15] Some of these methods included the recognition of armed opposition groups as local militia, including the Ka Kwe Ye of the 1960s and 1970s (which over the years switched to and from the government side). But the only face-to-face peace talks of any real size or duration was the unsuccessful Peace Parley held during 1963–64, shortly after Ne Win seized power, while the only nationwide amnesty that included armed opposition supporters was as long ago as 1980.

In the meantime, huge rifts in political vision and understanding developed as fighting raged in different parts of the country. Governmental authority, in the main, was confined to the towns and cities, the central lowlands and coastal plains. In many borderland regions, in contrast, there were often a number of parallel organizations of insurgent or quasi-state authority that came to rival a Lebanon or Afghanistan in their complexity.[16]

Against this background, disillusion not only with the failures of central government but also with many insurgent groups was building. In 1988 popular protest was instrumental in the collapse of the BSPP government, as demonstrators took to the streets following General Ne Win's resignation. Within a year the CPB, the country's oldest political party and most long-standing insurgent group, was also swept away. The CPB's demise, however, was triggered by a rather different sequence of events in the aftermath of the events of 1988 — by an upsurge of ethnic nationalism in the northeast of the country, as ethnic minority troops from the CPB's 20,000-strong People's Army along the China border mutinied and deserted.

In the late 1980s, desperation and the mood for change were clearly widespread across the country. This was highlighted in a statement by the fledgling United Wa State Party (UWSP), broadcast by its radio station in May 1989, shortly before the UWSP agreed on a ceasefire with the new SLORC government:

> Every year the burden of the people has become heavier. The streams, creeks and rivers have dried up, while the forests are being depleted. At such a time, what can the people of all nationalities do?[17]

Ethnic Ceasefires and the Changing Landscape

It is a measure of how much the socio-political landscape has changed in Myanmar since 1988 that formerly-insurgent groups among such peoples as the Kachin, Shan, Mon, Pao, and Wa took their places as official delegates in the opening sessions of the resumed National Convention in 2004.

Previously such organizations were referred to in the state-controlled media of the Ne Win era only by such terms as "bandits", "saboteurs", "racists", or as leftist or rightist "extremists" to be "eradicated".[18] At the same time, it is contemporary reflection of the many dilemmas in Myanmar politics that neither the NLD nor representatives of the nine-party United Nationalities Alliance (UNA), which either won or contested seats in the 1990 general election, were there to join the ceasefire groups at the National Convention (see Chart 3.1).

From this paradox, it is apparent that national reconciliation and the SPDC road map have an uncertain way to travel. This concern was publicly reflected by a 17 August 2004 statement from the UN Secretary-General Kofi Annan who, while acknowledging the "potential role" such a body could play in the "transition to democracy" and "national reconciliation", considered that the National Convention did not "currently adhere" to standards laid down by resolutions of the UN General Assembly.[19]

Many questions clearly remain, but for the moment it is important not to lose sight of how much focus was appearing to form in Myanmar politics around the SPDC's seven-stage road map in the months prior to the National Convention's resumption. General Khin Nyunt's announcement of the road map in August 2003 had had immediate and galvanizing effect. In particular, in an otherwise barren landscape, many political strategies and re-appraisals came to be based around it, whether inside or outside the country.[20] Indeed, the possibility of attendance by the NLD and allied ethnic parties at the National Convention appeared to come tantalizingly close in the days immediately prior to the Convention's commencement on 17 May 2004.[21]

Certainly, in terms of ethnic politics the National Convention's resumption was a moment that many nationality parties had long been awaiting, especially the ceasefire groups, who took it seriously as a potential benchmark of change. Not only had armed opposition groups been unable to stand in the 1990 general election (and few were involved in the earlier National Convention between 1993 and 1996), but they regarded the start of face-to-face dialogue in Yangon in 2004 as a culmination of their ceasefire strategies for reconciliation and reform that had begun over a decade earlier. "We want change now — not in another five years," said Dr Tu Ja, who headed the Kachin Independence Organization to the National Convention. "That is our thought and basis."[22]

CHART 3.1
Status of Ethnic Parties, May 2004

1. **Main ceasefire groups at National Convention**

Name in state media	Usual name/other details
Burma Communist Party (Rakhine Group)	Communist Party of Burma (Arakan)*
Kachin State Special Region-1	New Democratic Army (Kachin)*
Kachin State Special Region-2	Kachin Independence Organization**
Kayah State Special Region-1	Kayan National Guard (breakaway group from KNLP)
Kayah State Special Region-2	Karenni Nationalities Peoples Liberation Front*
Kayah State Special Region-3	Kayan New Land Party* **
New Mon State Party	New Mon State Party**
Shan State (North) Special Region-1	Myanmar National Democratic Alliance Army (Kokang)*
Shan State (North) Special Region-2	United Wa State Party*
Shan State (North) Special Region-3	Shan State Army (formerly Shan State Progress Party)**
Shan State (East) Special Region-4	National Democratic Alliance Army (eastern Shan state)*
Shan State (North) Special Region-5	Kachin Defence Army (1991 split from KIO 4th brigade)
Shan State (South) Special Region-6	Pao National Organization**
Shan State (North) Special Region-7	Palaung State Liberation Party**
Shan State National Army	Shan State National Army (1995 split from MTA)
Shan State Nationalities People's Liberation Organization	Shan State Nationalities Liberation Organization*

*Former ally or breakaway group from CPB
**Former National Democratic Front member

continued on next page

CHART 3.1 *(cont'd)*

---

2. Splinter ceasefire groups from larger ethnic forces at National Convention

(a) From the Karen National Union
     (non-ceasefire)

Democratic Kayin Buddhist Association	Democratic Karen Buddhist Army: 1994 split
Haungthayaw Special Region Group	Karen Peace Force (ex-KNU 16th battalion): 1997 split
Phayagon Special Region Group	1998 split: Hpaan district

(b) From the Karenni National
     Progressive Party (non-ceasefire)

Kayinni National Development Party Dragon Group	1999 split
Kayinni National Progressive Party (Splinter, Hoya)	1999 split: Hoya district
Kayinni National Unity and Solidarity Organization	

(c) From the defunct Mong Tai Army
     (1996 "surrender" ceasefire)

Homein Region Welfare and
Development Group
Shwepyi Aye (MTA) Group
Manpan Regional Militia Group

(d) From the National United Party
     of Arakan (non-ceasefire)

Arakanese Army (AA)	Ex-armed wing in NUPA: 2002 split

(e) From the New Mon State Party
     (1995 ceasefire)

Mon Armed Peace Group (Chaungchi Region)	Mon Army Mergui District: 1996 split
Mon Splinter Nai Saik Chan Group	

CHART 3.1 *(cont'd)*

3. **Ethnic parties from 1990 General Election at National Convention**
   Kokang Democracy and Unity Party
   Lahu National Development Party
   Mro-Khami National Solidarity Organization
   Union Kayin League
   Union Pao National Organization
   Wa National Development Party

4. **Ethnic parties from 1990 election in 2002 United Nationalities Alliance (not at National Convention)**
   Arakan League for Democracy
   Chin National League for Democracy
   Kachin State National Congress for Democracy
   Kayah State All Nationalities League for Democracy
   Kayin National Congress for Democracy
   Mara People's Party
   Mon National Democratic Front
   Shan Nationalities League for Democracy
   Zomi National Congress

5. **Main non-ceasefire groups (not at National Convention)*****
   Arakan Liberation Party**
   Arakan Rohingya National Organization
   Chin National Front**
   Hongsawatoi Restoration Party (2001 split from NMSP)
   Karen National Union** (1995-6 talks broke down; resumed 2003)
   Karenni National Progressive Party** (1995 ceasefire broke down)
   Lahu Democratic Front**
   Mergui-Tavoy United Front*
   National Socialist Council of Nagaland (Khaplang faction)
   National United Party of Arakan
   Rohingya Solidarity Organization
   Shan State Army [South] (reformed 1996 after MTA surrender)
   Wa National Organization** (1997 talks broke down)

* Former ally or breakaway group from CPB
** Present or former National Democratic Front member
*** A number of other small groups also exist in name on the borders. Most are affiliated to the National Council Union of Burma or Ethnic Nationalities Council, but they do not have broad or active organization inside the country.
Source: M. Smith, "Ethnic Politics and Regional Development in Myanmar: The Need for New Approaches", in Kyaw Yin Hlaing, Tin Maung Maung Than and R.H. Taylor, *Myanmar: Beyond Politics to Societal Imperatives*, pp. 78–80 (Singapore: ISEAS, 2005).

As a result, the National Convention's revival in reformed shape in the middle of 2004 initially appeared to be another defining moment in the country's transitional landscape. Indeed, the consequences may yet be profound. In particular, the resumption brought to the surface a difference in outlook and strategy between two groupings in Myanmar politics that had existed since the late 1980s. The groupings are informal and the inter-linkages are in some cases tenuous. On the one hand are the groups that have essentially looked to a "political solutions first" process in bringing about reform. This category includes the NLD, some of the electoral ethnic parties (principally the United Nationalities Alliance members) and the non-ceasefire groups, such as the KNU.[23] Such parties were not represented at the National Convention when it started in May. On the other hand are those groups that believe peace and development initiatives must be pursued as an essential parallel to achieving reconciliation and socio-political change that is sustainable. In this grouping have been the military government and ethnic ceasefire groups, as well as many community-based organizations inside the country. Representatives of these organizations and their supporters were at the 2004 National Convention between 17 May and 9 July 2004.

Given the current state of flux, it is impossible at this time to make final judgments about the effectiveness of either strategy in bringing about long-term change. During the past decade both outlooks have had passionate advocates, and both strategies have had some limited impact. In addition, as in any country of "complex emergency", it is possible to single out particular regions, or particular issues such as HIV/AIDS, narcotics or refugees, in order to determine priorities or present very different pictures of events unfolding in the country. The course of developments in Kachin State and Karen State since 1988, for example, has been strikingly different in many aspects.

However, while it may not be possible to determine which strategies or processes will eventually bring reform, it can be acknowledged in ethnic and insurgent politics during the SLORC-SPDC years. For the moment it can be acknowledged that the social imperatives have, in the main, come to take dominance over the political. In particular, it has become clear that in many long-suffering communities the driving priority has become the desire to achieve peace and progress today — not at some indeterminate date in the future through some unclear process.

The scale of these local factors for change has not always been internationally recognized. Indeed, the spread of the ethnic ceasefire movement was not a historical development that was at all predicted in the aftermath of the 1988 downfall of the BSPP government. Rather, it was armed opposition forces, especially those of the ethnic minority National Democratic Front, that initially seemed boosted when thousands of students and pro-democracy activists took sanctuary in their territories following the SLORC's assumption of power. Subsequently, a number of members of parliament-elect from the NLD and other political parties followed them, and, in an echo of U Nu's time with the KNU in the NULF, a new cycle of insurgency appeared to be taking root in the borderlands through such new united fronts as the National Council Union of Burma (NCUB, formed 1992).[24]

In subsequent years, it has often been the borderland activities of such groups, many of whose supporters have since gone into exile, that have received the most international media and humanitarian attention, especially in Thailand. Inside Myanmar, however, the momentum of ethnic and armed opposition groups has generally been steered in a very different direction. From a cautious beginning, that direction has increasingly tended towards participation in peace talks, compromise with the government, and efforts to be included in any Yangon-based process of reform.

Among different ethnic nationality parties, a number of reasons have been advanced for such change. A common factor has been the determination among leaders of ethnic forces, who regard their organizations as the vanguard defenders of their peoples, to be on the inside of any political process during any new period of change. In particular, they feel that they have been excluded too many times before in times of transition, and that it has always been the ethnic minorities who have ended up paying the highest price following earlier periods of upheaval in national politics, notably after 1948 and 1962. The late president of the Kachin Independence Organization (KIO), Maran Brang Seng, explained in July 1990:

> For the KIO, the most important thing is that we become a legal political party during this period of constitutional change. We have already lived through three different periods of government since 1961, so we know what it is like to be forgotten ... But we have the real mass support of the people, so at least we want to get our voice into the historical record. That is our duty.[25]

A related development, quickly noted by ethnic minority leaders, was that after the volatile events of 1988, insurgent movements among the ethnic Burman-majority began to decline rapidly during the SLORC-SPDC era. The CPB, which was mostly Burman-led, became almost defunct following the 1989 ethnic mutinies, while none of the plethora of new armed groups that attempted to form up within the shelter of NDF territories in the late 1980s proved sustainable.[26] Ethnic leaders noted that, in contrast, the NLD, which rapidly became the main focus of pro-democracy sentiment in the country, from its inception in 1988 rejected armed struggle as a means of achieving political change. This non-violent stand — combined with the decisive nature of the 1990 general election result, the country's first in three decades — had strong resonance among veteran ethnic leaders who had watched the epoch-making events during 1988–90 from the hills. Many saw little reason to continue fighting if a reform process was truly about to begin. Moreover, they could not remain immune to growing demands for peace among communities in the front line, demands that had undoubtedly been a major factor behind the CPB's collapse.[27]

Finally, if any doubts remained about the changing geo-political realities, the neighbouring governments of China, India, and Thailand privately made it clear to ethnic nationality leaders that the years of insurgent groups being allowed cross-border access to arms and supplies would be over. With the near-simultaneous demise of the BSPP and the end of the Cold War in the late 1980s, much in this Asian sub-region was about to change. Within a few years, improved government-to-government relations had become the new priority in all the neighbouring countries, exemplified by Thailand's "battlefields to marketplace" philosophy.

Already facing considerable pressures on the internal front, many armed opposition leaders quickly realized that border-world tactics would have to be adjusted if they were not to face even further marginalization in the years ahead. At that moment, therefore, the SLORC's unexpected offer of ceasefires provided an opportune process by which armed opposition groups could enter the country's transitional landscape as "legal" entities, as well as deal with the mounting challenges that they felt gathering all around them.[28]

Against this backdrop, and while government fighting continued against the KNU and its allies in southeast Myanmar, the ceasefires with some of the ethnic groups began. In general, the ceasefire parties came from two main groups. The first group was led by the UWSP and others who had mutinied and left the CPB in 1989. But over the years the ceasefire movement spread to a second important group, including such former allies of the KNU and members of the NDF as the Shan State Army (North), the Pao National Organization (PNO), the Kachin Independence Organization, and the New Mon State Party. In subsequent years there were splits and factionalism, while the SLORC-SPDC also agreed ceasefires with a number of small defector groups from non-ceasefire parties, including from the KNU. This meant that a remarkable twenty-eight ceasefire groups were represented at the National Convention when it resumed in 2004. It is generally considered that about seventeen ceasefire parties have a legacy of some history or political-military substance. By the late 1990s there were only four armed opposition groups of any real size that had not agreed to a ceasefire with the government — the Karen National Union, which resumed peace talks in December 2003; the Karenni National Progressive Party (whose 1995 ceasefire broke down); the Chin National Front (CNF); and the Shan State Army-South (SSA-S) (see Chart 3.1).[29]

By any international standards, the achievement of ceasefires with so many insurgent groups, in one of the most conflict-torn countries in Asia, has to date been unexpectedly smooth and stable. In most cases, there has been no substantive international involvement.[30] It therefore needs to be stressed that a major factor behind the relative ease with which the ceasefires spread, in unpromising circumstances, was their simplicity. Reflecting the "Year Zero" level of governmental outreach in many parts of the country after 1988, the ceasefire terms were, in essence, very basic: the ceasefire groups would be allowed to continue holding their arms and territory, but would concentrate on peace-building and development projects until a new constitution was introduced.

Such terms may have appeared at the time to be skeletal, the result of a strategy quickly put together by a military government that needed to win itself credibility and time. International analysts also argued that the ceasefires were providing a cover for narcotics traffickers to increase production. Certainly, illicit production of opium and, later, methamphetamine accelerated rapidly in both the China and Thai borderlands.[31] However, in many front-line communities themselves, perceptions were rather different. Rather, the lack of local strings in the ceasefire agreements, the *de facto* recognition of autonomy, and the chance to end fighting quickly found popular support.

In addition, if any doubts remained, the clear-cut result of the 1990 election encouraged armed ethnic opposition groups, many of which had close contact with the newly-formed parties in the towns, in their desire to become integral players in any discussions about the country's future. Ceasefire leaders in the northeast of the country were especially encouraged, and, along with the NLD and electoral Shan Nationalities League for Democracy (which won most seats in the Shan state), some of the early ceasefire groups, such as the UWSP and PNO, were represented at the first inception of the National Convention during 1993–96.

The Social Challenges

It was at this point in the early 1990s, as military truces were agreed with more and more groups, that some leaders began to consider more seriously strategies for building peace during the period from the conclusion of the ceasefires (which, by definition, are transitory affairs) to the achievement of the goal of inclusive political reforms. The dilemmas and outlook were summarized after the 1995 ceasefire with the New Mon State Party (NMSP) by its late president, Nai Shwe Kyin:

> We want to establish peace in our country. It is not a time to confront each other because we need national reconciliation. We have reached ceasefire agreements and the next step is political dialogue. We must establish trust. After bloodbaths lasting nearly half a century, we must establish trust with the view that one day reconciliation will come about.[32]

What evolved in the following years was a strategy that ceasefire leaders characterized as "peace through development". Crucially, in many areas this was supported by community-based leaders, including members of the Buddhist Sangha and Christian churches who, in some cases, acted as go-betweens in the peace talks.[33] In the field, many dissatisfactions remained; other than the welcome halt to fighting, the ceasefires had not heralded a dramatic transformation nor altered the political realities. In addition, critics complained that certain armed groups and powerful vested interests were using the ceasefires to enrich themselves by exploiting natural resources between themselves. As in other countries in conflict, the problems of "warlordism" run deep. However, in many front-line areas, long-suffering communities were eager to embrace the peace if it would provide a sustainable platform to introduce real change. In consequence, as the 1990s progressed, this new emphasis on social issues and community-based improvements became an important locomotive in the unexpected stability of the ceasefires.

In recent years ethnic nationality leaders have often expressed frustration that there has not been greater international support, in terms of both humanitarian aid and development assistance, for their long-divided communities as they struggle to rebuild from conflict. For the government's part, after the first ceasefires were concluded in 1989 the SLORC-SPDC initiated a Border Areas Development Programme which was upgraded into the Ministry for the Progress of Border Areas and National Races in 1992. Health, education, and infrastructure projects were initiated in the Ministry's eighteen administrative areas, with a claimed expenditure of Kyats 58,399.34 million (quoted at US$550 million) in its first fifteen years.[34] From the mid-1990s, UN agencies and international non-governmental organizations (NGOs) also gained permission from Yangon to access an increasing number of border and ceasefire areas. However, to date international commitments of aid have been minimal. Indeed official development assistance to the whole of Myanmar was estimated at just US$1 *per capita* in 2001 which contrasted with, for example, US$35 for Cambodia and US$68 for Laos.[35] Given the scale of humanitarian needs, this is a very low figure by any international standards.[36]

As a result, community leaders in Myanmar believe that many international bodies missed an important opportunity in the mid-1990s to support a different kind of socio-economic momentum for change in the country that was offered by the ceasefires. According to Daw Seng Raw, director of the Metta Development Foundation, an indigenous NGO established after the Kachin ceasefires:

> Many ethnic minority groups feel extremely disappointed that in general foreign governments are not responding to the progress of the ceasefires or indeed even understand their significance or context.... It ignores realities in areas long affected by war. To revitalize these communities and bring about real reform, health, social and economic development must run in tandem with political progress.[37]

In recent years, such a view has been supported by an increasing number of international NGOs and humanitarian agencies that take a long-term view of the challenges of socio-political transition in Myanmar. For example, according to a 2004 report by the International Crisis Group:

While the international community focuses on the need for regime change in Yangon, it has tended to disregard the need to integrate ethnic minorities into the broader society and economy. Foreign aid for Border Areas should be seen and pursued as complementary to diplomatic efforts to restore democracy and help unite the long-divided country.[38]

Such an opinion is reflected by different UN agencies. Most recently, Antonio Maria Costa, executive director of the United Nations Office on Drugs and Crime (UNODC), reiterated that humanitarian engagement is needed to support the UN's goals of "democratization and national reconciliation in Myanmar".[39] In particular, he argued that without alternative sources of income, ethnic minority communities dependent on opium cultivation would "remain vulnerable to human rights abuses, human trafficking and forced relocation".[40]

However, it needs to be stressed that in recent years it is not only in Myanmar that the issues of humanitarian aid or intervention in situations of conflict, insurgency and post-insurgency have become questions of deep controversy between governments and international agencies. In such contexts, the provision of aid — whether for humanitarian or development purposes — can become hostage to the different agendas of the various donor countries or to the polarized debates between competing groups in a particular donor country. Recently, for example, a group of US senators called on the United Nations Development Programme and the Global Fund to Fight AIDS, Tuberculosis and Malaria to cease additional funding to Myanmar because of its military government.[41] In contrast, the United Kingdom government, which is also a strong critic of the SPDC, announced in a 2003 change of policy by its Department for International Development (DFID) that it would contribute US$15.7 million to combat the spread of HIV/AIDS in Myanmar. In addition, a new country plan for closer on-the-ground engagement was developed as part of DFID's "Drivers of Change" philosophy, to better target health and poverty-related issues.

As such dilemmas and DFID strategy papers highlight,[42] recent experience in other strife-torn countries of the world suggests that the processes of conflict resolution and effective aid delivery are hardly exact sciences or necessarily prescriptive.[43] It is not uncommon that participants on different sides in a situation of conflict proclaim the same multi-agenda goals of both humanitarian assistance and long-term reform. As Hugo Slim recently commented, in reference to the present transitional crises in Afghanistan and Iraq: "There is often considerable moral overlap of ends between insurgents, counter-insurgents, humanitarian, human rights and development agencies."[44]

This very much remains the case in Myanmar where, for the moment, no general consensus between international donors has been achieved and where the debate over aid has often been contentious.[45]

It must therefore be emphasized that, while engagement with Myanmar through international participation in aid projects is likely to accelerate in the coming decade, at present many internationally-supported aid projects in conflict-affected areas are still in the early stages. On the macro level, the growing body of data gathered in field work since the mid-1990s has only served to confirm the severity of the humanitarian situation in many areas as well as the depths of socio-economic under-performance that became entrenched during the long decades of war and marginalization. According to the UN Development Programme (UNDP), the result of this long-standing cycle of conflict and impasse is a pattern of "human insecurity" that is especially apparent in three "disparities" in the country: "regional and ethnic", "rural-urban", and "gender".[46] In particular, the most worrying statistics in relation to a number of issues, such as treatable or preventable illnesses as malaria, tuberculosis and HIV/AIDS, poverty, malnutrition and illiteracy, come from the ethnic minority borderlands.[47]

Just a few examples follow. According to UNICEF's Child Risk Index, most border regions fall "significantly" below the national average in terms of income poverty and access to health care, education, sanitation and safe water supplies.[48] The highest levels of child malnutrition (between 40 and 50 per cent) are reported in the Chin, Rakhine, Shan and Karen States and in Tanintharyi Division, ethnic minority areas where it is estimated that just one-third of children complete the four basic years of schooling.[49] In the eastern and northern parts of the Shan State, very high maternal mortality rates of over 500 per 100,000 live births have been recorded.[50] And in its 2004 survey, the United Nations Office on Drugs and Crime estimated that there were still 260,000 households in Shan State involved in opium cultivation, earning an average of just US$133 per annum, which, in turn, represented 62 per cent of an average annual income nation-wide of only US$214.[51]

Given this background, it is notable just how much has been achieved in several areas since the ceasefires. As with any post-conflict situation, the results are most immediately apparent in areas where long-standing fighting has halted. Visible evidence of the change is seen in the new towns that since the early 1990s have sprung up in the borderlands, towns such as Laiza, Pangkham and Mongla, for example. Immunization programmes by international agencies in the Wa and Kachin hills have resulted in significant improvements in life expectancy and the health of children;[52] since 1996, crop substitution programmes supported by the UNODC have seen a cumulative reduction of 73 per cent in areas of the Shan State under illicit opium cultivation, with the total crop down to an estimated 370 metric tons in 2004;[53] and in one innovative conservation measure, the world's largest tiger reserve has been established, with the help of the Wildlife Conservation Society, in the former conflict-zone around the Hukawng Valley, near Myanmar's borders with China and India.[54]

Among the local ceasefire and community-based organizations, particular attention has been given to training and education programmes, such as those organized by the Mon Women's Organization in Mon State; Farmer Field Schools, such as at Sadung in Kachin State and at Nong Hkam in the Pao National Organization area of Shan State; and health and teacher-training programmes supported by the Kachin Independence Organization in various locations in the country's far north. During the 2002–03 school year, for example, the New Mon State Party was reported to have administered 187 Mon national schools, with over 50,000 pupils.[55] Similarly, students from the PNO ceasefire area today have access to seventeen government high schools, three of which have been opened in PNO territory since the 1991 ceasefire. In the Pao region, too, farming and business projects have noticeably accelerated, in areas from agriculture to natural resource mining and tourism, as many displaced persons have resettled on their lands. But according to the PNO's veteran chairman, Aung Kham Hti: "The real success of peace is not in trade. Anyone can dig a piece of jade. The real progress has been in the health and education to improve the status of the people."[56]

In the success of such grass-roots approaches (which have sometimes involved both governmental and non-governmental actors), the role played by local community-based organizations has often been vital. In Myanmar, such religious-based organizations as the Myanmar Council of Churches and the Catholic Bishops Conference have long experience of aid and development work, and have international linkages as well. Among ethnic minority peoples, too, local Culture and Literature Associations have historically been active. But in a new development since the ceasefires, a number of indigenous NGOs have also been established, such as the

Metta Development Foundation, Shalom Peace Foundation, and Karen Development Committee, which reflect new attempts at revitalizing communities that are recovering from conflict.

Such energy has not been confined to post-ceasefire areas but is indicative, many aid workers believe, of gradual changes that have occurred in the country at large during the past decade. Indeed a recent unpublished survey by one international NGO estimates that the past decade has witnessed the most rapid expansion of community-based organizations in Myanmar's history. By 2003, there were over sixty indigenous NGOs with offices in Yangon alone. In such activities, some observers see the revival of civil society, without which peace and democratic reforms in the country are unlikely to be sustainable.[57] However, one needs to take care not to run too far ahead in such theoretical analyses. As one senior religious leader admitted at a recent seminar on civil society in Myanmar: "It is an immense challenge ahead of us and we have barely understood some of the terms and concepts used by the UN and other NGOs."

In summary, it remains important not to underestimate the scale of the difficulties that Myanmar still faces in relation to socio-political transition. The socially-based trends manifested in ethnic and ceasefire politics over the past fifteen years do highlight a determination to meet humanitarian needs and address the failures of the past in new ways. Experience to date has confirmed what can be achieved with good will and without the backdrop of war, but the sustainability of many initiatives has yet to be demonstrated, and there remain many questions about the effectiveness of public health and educational outreach, and about the future integration of planning and services.

Meanwhile time is passing, and some influential ethnic minority leaders fear that such continuing issues as poverty, the burgeoning epidemic of HIV/AIDS, and exploitative activities by powerful vested interests (including uncontrolled logging and a corrosive culture of corruption and local rent-seeking) threaten to produce a new generation of grievances, unless movement towards sustainable and accountable transition speeds up — and soon.[58] Indeed, to take one example, UN officials privately estimate that as many as 60,000 people out of a population of 200,000 have moved out of the Kokang ceasefire region after an opium ban was enforced in 2003, due to the lack of food and alternative sources of income. As a result, the adjoining Wa region and nearby territories in Shan State, which are among the poorest areas in

Asia, could be facing an even greater humanitarian crisis when a similar ban is introduced in 2005.

Finally, no picture of the present situation would be complete without emphasizing that around the edges of the ceasefire regions remain areas where conflict has not ended, especially in the areas along the border with Thailand and along the northwest frontiers with India and Bangladesh. From all these areas, reports continue of intermittent fighting, village relocations, forced labour and other human rights abuses, including the indiscriminate use of land-mines and the conscription of child soldiers, in which all sides have been complicit. A litany of human rights violations, "especially in ethnic minority areas affected by counter-insurgency operations", was again repeated by Paolo Sergio Pinheiro, the UN special rapporteur on human rights to Myanmar, in October 2004.[59] Particular abuses he singled out for condemnation included violations of "economic, social and cultural rights" as well as sexual violence, and threats to life and the most fundamental human rights.

The most visible evidence of continuing conflict in Myanmar is the more than 140,000 ethnic-minority refugees in official camps along the Thai border, but the true number of those fleeing conflict (especially ethnic Shans) is estimated by international aid workers to be considerably higher. In 2004, for example, 905,881 "illegal migrants" from Myanmar took the opportunity of changes in Thai immigration policy to register themselves legally for work.[60] But this is only the external face of crisis. Inside Myanmar, the Global Internally Displaced Persons Project estimates that more than half a million people are either in relocation settlements or displaced in the hills.[61] Meanwhile, in the ceasefire areas many communities continue to suffer the long-term socio-economic consequences of earlier displacement.

Thus in early 2004, as the SPDC's road map approached its first hurdle, speculation was high as to whether the National Convention would finally mark the inception of a process towards the end-goal that many parties had long been awaiting — that of political reform. Across the country, the political landscape remained divided, but it was the hoped-for potential for a new beginning that encouraged the KNU to resume peace talks. Indeed government officials told KNU delegates that while a formal ceasefire could not be arranged in time for the KNU to attend the first stages of the National Convention, this would be possible later. Moreover, fuelling hopes in many domestic and international quarters was the growing expectation (encouraged by some government officials) that restrictions on the NLD and other electoral parties would be lifted, thus permitting them to organize and attend the National Convention.

Certainly, after over a decade of ceasefires, many ethnic nationality leaders were focusing on this moment. Many believed that the advance of peace in the ethnic-minority areas over the past decade had helped to provide an essential ingredient of inclusiveness that had been missing in earlier periods of crisis and change. Compromise and political solutions, they reasoned, could now be sought and found. This perspective was summarized by the PNO chairman, Aung Kham Hti: "We have seen the achievement of peace. In this way, the situation in the whole country can become stable. This is not just for the Pao. We must think of all the peoples. Therefore we want the National Convention to succeed and the whole road map to follow through."[62]

The Political Landscape

At the end of 2004, it remains difficult to reach definitive conclusions. As during other critical times in Myanmar's political history, the current landscape is still one of complexity. 2004 saw a succession of rapidly-unfolding events that may not yet have ended. Moreover, while the country remains in a state of supposed transition, it is salutary to recognize that the present incarnation of military-dominated government, in the form of the SLORC-SPDC, has endured longer than the fifteen years of the parliamentary era between 1948 and 1962. The central dilemmas about reform remain. Experience warns that unless political processes are inclusive and a new constitution is drawn up through agreements that have both popular and legitimate support, it is likely that a new cycle of problems will only be stored up for the country to face in the future. This remains the cautionary view of the United Nations which, while continuing to see the SPDC's road map as a process that could bring peace and reform to the country, has repeatedly urged that the National Convention, and a future referendum or elections, must be open to representative parties, witness the release of all political prisoners, and be free from restrictions.[63]

On this basis, it must be said as an initial observation that the road map and the National Convention have proceeded so far without the participation of the NLD and several other parties that won seats in the 1990 general election, while the question of concluding a formal ceasefire with the KNU and other remaining non-ceasefire groups appears to have been put on hold by the SPDC. In addition, doubts about procedures and continuity have been raised in recent months by the unexpected removal of the prime minister and Military Intelligence chief, General Khin Nyunt, along with several other senior officials who had been associated with the public face of the government since the late 1980s.

This has led to intensive domestic and international speculation about future changes in SPDC policy, whether for personal or political reasons. Many analysts believe there will be changes. But as of mid-November 2004, it can be noted that the rising group of new senior officers in the military government, including Generals Shwe Mann, Soe Win, and Thein Sein, have to date insisted that both the road map and ethnic ceasefires are on course as before. This is a message that they have personally taken to a series of ongoing meetings with different organizations, business groups, and ethnic ceasefire parties around the country. In turn, many ceasefire leaders have reiterated their commitment to continuing with both the ceasefires and the National Convention, despite predictions in the international media that both processes could be in for a very unsettled time.[64] In response to these doubts, ethnic veterans privately point out that they have seen many crises before, and, at this time of potential constitutional change, their commitment to putting political ideas into the reform process is unwavering, as long as the opportunities for peaceful reform exist.[65] Too many years of hardship and struggle have been invested for them to change course precipitately at the first sign of uncertainty. Such a view is also shared by the KNU, whose leaders say that, despite the October 2004 interruption in talks, they still intend to explore the possibility of peace at this time. "It's better to keep talking. Both sides are playing a political game now," commented Colonel Ner Dah, the son of General Bo Mya, in a recent interview.[66]

For the moment, until any different news emerges, it is on the detail of recent processes of discussion that analysis has to be based. As during earlier eras of constitutional crisis, a diversity of nationality parties is currently active in Myanmar politics, highlighting the fact that ethnic politics remain far from moribund in the SLORC-SPDC era.

As outlined above, initial hopes had existed that, one way or another, that all ethnic and political parties would eventually become involved in the SPDC road map. This, however, was not to be the case.

During the resumed sessions of the National Convention held between May and July 2004, nationality parties in the country could generally be divided into two broad categories — those ethnic parties that attended the

Convention, and those that did not. In the first category were ethnic ceasefire groups and some of the political parties included in the first stage of the National Convention between 1993 and 1996, while in the absentee category were parties that were either not invited or decided not to attend, as well as the non-ceasefire groups.

Once again, this is not to suggest that these analytical groupings are in any ways formal or concrete.[67] But all groups, in differing ways, had been focusing on the imminence of the National Convention and their response to it. For example, of the electoral parties in the United Nationalities Alliance, only the Shan Nationalities League for Democracy is believed to have actually been invited to the National Convention, but all concurred in the decision that conditions were not acceptable for them to attend once their political ally, the NLD, had decided not to take part.[68] Similarly, although the KNU was still involved in conducting peace talks, it was considered that the KNU could remain informed of discussions at the Convention by other Karen delegates.

Despite such absentees, the unusual importance attached to ethnic nationality questions in 2004 continued to be highlighted in the way that the National Convention was configured when it restarted. Ethnic minority representatives made up over half the 1,088 delegates invited, and also formed a majority in three of the eight National Convention category groups: political parties, national races, and specially invited guests (the other categories are: elected representatives, peasants, workers, intellectuals and public servants). Each of the eight category groups, which elected their own chairmen, listened to submission papers from delegates or groups within their individual categories, which were then debated and reformulated by consensus into a final report from each category. These eight reports are reportedly, in turn, being further reformulated by some of the category chairmen and the National Convention Convening Working Committee into a final version, which will then be added to the "104 detailed basic principles" that were relayed forward from the earlier sessions of the National Convention between 1993 and 1996.

With the National Convention only part-way through its deliberations, the diversity of papers and categories makes it impossible to determine what will be the points of controversy, or what will ultimately become the key conclusions. It is too early to tell, and participants say that, as in any process of debate, different ideas have been put up, with no party expecting that they will get everything their own way.

Nevertheless, from the discussions so far, a number of future trends appear likely, unless there are major or unpredicted changes. The first is that the concept of "power-sharing" with the armed forces in government will be accepted by the National Convention. In essence, this will mean that the six basic principles of the SLORC-SPDC are recognized, that 25 per cent of seats in a future parliament will be reserved for the armed forces, and that control over certain ministries (notably defence and foreign affairs) will remain with the armed forces. It seems that in the context of the country's complex challenges of transition, many parties believe it is worth making these compromises, as a first step, so long as such changes are accompanied by a constitutional guarantee that there will be a return to a civilian system of democratic government involving the sharing of power with other representative parties and interests. "Seventy-five per cent is better than nothing," has been a buzz phrase in recent months, and comparisons about how transition has proceeded have been made with such Asian countries as Thailand or South Korea that have also emerged from long periods under armed forces' influence or government.

The ethnic nationality groups made their views quite clear in this process. In particular, the performance of the ethnic ceasefire groups in the "other specially invited guests" category received most comment and attention at the time. By all accounts, there was a lively debate. It had been of crucial importance to the ceasefire groups that they had the right to choose their own delegates, which they did, and that they had the right to raise any issue, which they also generally did.

In total, eleven papers were submitted by different ceasefire parties or groupings. Most were submitted by small splinter factions that carry little weight,[69] and it was the two joint submissions from the older and larger ceasefire parties that received most attention. The smaller of these was a three-party submission by what are often referred to as the "Wa-Kokang-Mongla" groups (that is, the United Wa State Party, the Myanmar National Democratic Alliance Army, and the National Democratic Alliance Army), while the main submission, presented on 9 June, came from a thirteen-party grouping of many of the best-known armed opposition parties, including such former members of the NDF as the Shan State Army (SSA), the KIO and the NMSP.[70]

Underlying the differences in these two submissions were the differences in the ethno-political backgrounds of these two alliances. The Wa-Kokang-Mongla grouping has its origins in their common CPB past, with each of these groups still practising politburo or central committee systems of party administration — although officially they pursue pro-business and pro-democracy philosophies today. The ethnic autonomous regions in neighbouring China also provide a model, although leaders of all three parties say that their historic rights to independent status should be legally stronger in Myanmar. At the National Convention, however, the main controversy was not about models for autonomy, but about their proposal for sub-states of their own that would, in essence, mean a separation from Shan State. Objections to this delineation came not only from ethnic Shan parties but also from other local minority groups. The proposal appears to have been withdrawn as a result, and it is expected that the Wa-Kokang-Mongla grouping will work more closely with the other ceasefire groups in future sessions.

In contrast, the proposals of the thirteen-party grouping presented an articulate espousal of what are essentially federalist ideas. Indeed, the clarity of these proposals took many observers by surprise, and they were accorded considerable attention, causing members of parties that had stayed away from the National Convention to consider whether they had made the right decision.

These ceasefire proposals are still under review by the National Convention, so no definitive judgments can be attempted. However, according to reports, as the Convention progressed it became clear that there were differences on many points of detail, the result of a divergence in outlook between those espousing a "unitary" system (largely supporters of the military government) and those advocating a union system (supported by the ethnic and pro-democracy parties). Furthermore, the ethnic parties in general want to move more powers away from the armed forces and into civilian sectors of government (for example, nuclear issues should be under "energy" rather than "defence"), while increasing residual powers for the ethnic minority states.

At one stage deadlock ensued, and it seemed that there would be no way to find wording on a number of issues that could be agreed between the nationality parties and the National Convention Working Committee.[71] In the end, however, it was informally "agreed to disagree", with the proposals by the ceasefire groups remaining in the official records, including those ideas that were not included in the final draft. This means that, in theory, they can be revived at a later time if the situation allows.

In essence, there were seven main areas of disagreement, which concerned the extent or definition of the following legal issues in relation to the ethnic states: the legislative powers of the states, residuary rights, state constitutions,[72] ethnic and cultural rights, defence and security, foreign affairs,[73] and resources and taxation. At the same time, nationality leaders point out that compromise was also reached on about thirteen areas of constitutional discussion, such as the right of elected representatives within the ethnic states to choose their own prime ministers, or the right of the states to regulate power generation up to medium-range capacities.

How the remaining differences will be resolved in the future is unclear. There are more issues to be discussed when the National Convention resumes in 2005, including the powers of the executive and judiciary (the 2004 sessions mainly concentrated on the principles for power-sharing in the legislature). But providing that the momentum towards substantive reform and peaceful development is certain, many of the ethnic nationality leaders and ceasefire parties contend that they will continue with the present process. Among such groups, hopes are still privately expressed that other political parties could yet become involved, including the NLD, the UNA parties and the non-ceasefire groups which currently remain as bystanders. These groups, too, are also closely watching developments, and in October 2004 representatives of both the UNA and United Nationalities League for Democracy in Yangon and the mostly-exile Ethnic Nationalities Council on the Thai border urged the ceasefire groups to continue to propose federalist ideas.[74] But for the moment, any influence from such groups remains on the periphery of the central course of discussions.

What does seem incontrovertible now is that, while the future form of democracy in Myanmar remains contentious, in the coming years the country's political map will once again be reshaped, and that as long as peace remains, there will be greater devolution. This means that at the very least there will be new territories designated for nationalities that are not currently recognized in politics. On the basis of population numbers and region, there is likely to be a "self-administered division" for the Wa and "self-administered districts" (or zones) for the Danu, Kokang, Lahu, Palaung, and Pao in the Shan State and also a "self-administered district" for the Naga in Sagaing Division. In addition, it is likely that nationalities will be able to put up a representative for areas where they constitute a sizeable minority in other states or political territories (such as the Pao in Karen State).

However beyond these conjectures, it is premature to make predictions in detail. A number of leaders of different nationalities say that the demarcation of new ethnic territories will not be a problem so long as they represent political inclusiveness and not ethnic separation or marginalization. But other than such local understandings, much still remains to be discussed and achieved.

Conclusion

Huge challenges lie ahead in the accomplishment of socio-political and ethnic reform in Myanmar. The National Convention has yet to be completed, and a referendum on the constitution and future general elections will then have to be held. Both of these events will raise questions about inclusiveness and about the responses of parties that have not so far been involved in the constitutional discussions. During this period, the difficult question of the transformation of ceasefire forces will also have to be addressed, because the current general condition that ceasefire groups have the right to maintain independent arms and territories will only exist until a new constitution is introduced. As in any country in conflict, this will raise the difficult issue of disarming former insurgent groups. But in Myanmar's case this process may be especially sensitive because of the long-standing durability of many of the ethnic struggles, which means that, to maintain confidence, demilitarization will have to run parallel to the implementation of democratic reform.[75]

Even as military transformation is being addressed, the perspectives of different international governments and actors, including neighbouring countries that are critically affected by the stability of Myanmar's borderlands as well as the United Nations and Western governments further afield, will have to be considered. All can play a vital supporting role in alleviating humanitarian suffering and in encouraging and sustaining the processes of reform, provided that they can see the landscape changing.

In the final analysis, however, the course of events must always be determined by the will and actions of the peoples of Myanmar themselves. In this respect, the common calls for democracy, the non-violent stand of political parties, and the ethnic ceasefires of the past fifteen years have shown that national consensus and reconciliation may be possible. Experience is showing that there are other ways to resolve conflict, and, if nothing else, the tragic experiences of the past five decades have proven that no side can unilaterally win or impose its own vision. The ethnic make-up and landscape of Myanmar is too complex and the legacy of past failures too great.

Looking to the future, it is clear that, however the constitution is configured, the essential issues of political rights and equality for all citizens wherever they live in the country are likely to be the main keys to peaceful and constructive socio-political development. After over five decades of struggle, such basic freedoms as the right to security, to development, to ownership of land, to language and culture, to freedom of religion, to health and education, to freedom of expression, and the right to have democratically-elected leaders, will be fundamental if Myanmar is ever to find sustainable peace. Until such issues are addressed, ethnic nationality leaders contend that there will always be grievances.

The dilemmas and challenges were expressed by David Taw, a leader of the KNU peace delegations in 2004:

> Nowadays we are struggling for our identity. This means equal status. That will be enough. If we can achieve this, all the peoples of this country can live very easily together. But now we have come to feel like second-class citizens. It does not matter where you live. In a war-zone, people get killed. And in urban areas, you feel you always face discrimination in both education and job opportunities. This has to be resolved.[76]

In 2003, the UN Special Rapporteur Paulo Sergio Pinheiro stated in a report to the UN Human Rights Commission in Geneva:

> Every political transition in the world is a process, sometimes a torturous and slow one, and it would be unrealistic and naive to expect an instant regime change in Myanmar. Instead of continuing to complain that little has changed … the international community must have its eyes wide open to see the nuclei of change.[77]

The vital question then is whether enough groundwork and confidence-building has been achieved for the country to move on. Since 1988 Myanmar has certainly come a long way. But after so many years of struggle, the consensus is becoming overwhelming that it is time for inclusive reform to truly begin.

Notes

[1]   In this paper, the term "ethnic minority" is used to distinguish non-Burman (non-*Bamar*) nationality groups or identity.

2   For recent reports that highlight different aspects of these challenges, see, for example, International Crisis Group, *Myanmar: Aid to the Border Areas* (Brussels: International Crisis Group, 2004); Transnational Institute, "Drugs and Conflict in Burma (Myanmar): Dilemmas for Policy Responses", in *Drugs and Conflict*, TNI Debate Papers No. 9 (Amsterdam: Transnational Institute, 2003); F. Kahrl, H. Weyerthaeuser, and S. Yufang, *Navigating the Border: An Analysis of the China-Myanmar Timber Trade* (Washington: Forest Trends, 2004); EarthRights International, *Another Yadana: The Shwe Natural Gas Pipeline Project (Burma-Bangladesh-India)* (Washington: ERI, 2004); Burmese Border Consortium, *Burmese Border Consortium Relief Programme: January to June 2004* (Bangkok: BBC, 2004); and Nwe Nwe Aye with Katie Maher, *Field Notes from Myanmar: Developing Children and Young People's Participation in the Border Areas* (Bangkok: Save the Children (UK), 2003).

3   Awareness of the burgeoning importance of regional and border relations appears to be reciprocated by the SPDC. In October 2004, within days of replacing Prime Minister General Khin Nyunt, the SPDC chairman, Senior General Than Shwe, made the first official state visit to India by the country's top-most leader in twenty-four years, to discuss border, counter-insurgency, and bilateral economic issues. *Agence France Presse*, 29 October 2004. Similarly, the new prime minister, Lt-General Soe Win, made his first official trip to China just one week later, to attend the China-ASEAN Business and Investment Summit.

4   M. Rajaretnam (Convener), *Quality of Partnership: Myanmar, ASEAN and the World Community* (Singapore: Asian Dialogue Society, 2003), p. 2.

5   For a history of political and armed opposition movements, see, for example, M. Smith, *Burma: Insurgency and the Politics of Ethnicity* (London: Zed Books, 1999).

6   See, for example, United Nations General Assembly, *Situation of Human Rights in Myanmar: Report of the Secretary-General* (New York: UNGA, 59th session, 16 August 2004), p. 2.

7   *New Light of Myanmar*, 27 February 1998.

8   Ibid., 27 March 2004.

9   Interview with KNU Vice-President, General Bo Mya, 12 February 2004.

10   UN Country Team, Yangon, "A Review of the Humanitarian Situation in Myanmar", unpublished monograph, February 2003, p. 11.

11   "UN warns of child malnutrition in Myanmar", *Agence France Presse*, 14 September 2004.

12   See, for example, J. Silverstein, *Burmese Politics: the Dilemma of National Unity* (New Brunswick: Rutgers University Press, 1980), pp. 185–205; Smith, *Burma: Insurgency*, pp. 71–87.

13   *The Times* (London), 3 March 1962. See also, Smith, *Burma: Insurgency*, pp. 195–

97. In fact, in 1958 Ne Win had perceived communist supporters to be the main threat — not ethnic parties. For new analyses of both the 1962 coup and Ne Win's 'Military Caretaker' Administration (1958–60) that are based on armed forces' sources, see M. Callahan, *Making Enemies: War and State Building in Burma* (Ithaca: Cornell University Press, 2003), pp. 184–206.

14   *Working People's Daily*, 10 January 1990. As in any conflict, the bulk of casualties included civilians, armed opposition troops and supporters, and the many auxiliary or paramilitary formations, but no reliable figures appear in official statistics. However, to give substance to his claim, Saw Maung mentioned that in 1989, within the armed forces alone, there were 28,000 families still receiving pensions for soldiers who had been killed since 1953, and 40,000 for disabled veterans.

15   See, for example, Smith, *Burma: Insurgency*, pp. 258–62.

16   For an eyewitness account of these years, see Chao Tzang Yawnghwe, *The Shan of Burma: Memoirs of an Exile* (Singapore: Institute of Southeast Asian Studies, 1987).

17   Quoted in BBC, *Survey of World Broadcasts*, 2 May 1989.

18   See, for example, *Forward*, 1 April 1969; *Loktha Pyeithu Nezin*, 14 February 1975; and *Botahtaung*, 18 May 1978. On 26 March 1987, for example, in accordance with instructions of the fifth BSPP congress to "eliminate the subversive insurgents", state radio claimed that the armed forces had found 2,538 insurgent bodies during military operations in the preceding twelve months and captured another 463 alive.

19   "From the UN Secretary-General", UNIC/Press Release/233-2004, 17 August 2004.

20   See, for example, Zarni and May Oo, *Common Problems, Shared Responsibilities: Citizens' Quest for National Reconciliation in Burma/Myanmar* (New York: Free Burma Coalition, 2004).

21   See, for example, Aye Aye Win, "Hundreds Register for the NC, but NLD Undecided", *Associated Press*, 13 May 2004.

22   Interview with Dr Tu Ja, 27 July 2004.

23   The links between such groups, in institutional terms, are complex. The NLD and UNA parties, for example, are linked by such bodies as the 1998 Committee Representing the People's Parliament and the 21-party United Nationalities League for Democracy. Armed opposition groups such as the KNU are, in turn, allied in the 28-party National Council Union of Burma with the NLD "Liberated Areas", Members of Parliament Union and other parties or activists that lobby for recognition of the 1990 general election result in the international community.

24   See, for example, Smith, *Burma: Insurgency*, pp. 406–11, 434–35, 440–44.

25 Interview with Maran Brang Seng, July 1990. For a perspective of his unfolding views as revealed in a series of interviews between 1987 and 1992, see M. Smith and L. Jagan, "Maran Brang Seng: In his Own Words", *Burma Debate*, Vol. 1, No. 3, 1995, pp. 17–22. It was in a July 1990 interview that Brang Seng, while welcoming the 1990 election result and the NLD victory, first mentioned the concept of a "National Convention" so that "all parties can put up their ideas" in an inclusive process of dialogue and reform.

26 The most active, the All Burma Students Democratic Front, commemorated its sixteenth anniversary on 1 November 2004, but, following splits and retirements, it is a shadow of its initial size.

27 Interview with UWSP chairman, Bao You-Xiang, 15 March 2003.

28 The designation "legal" has caused some problems during the different ceasefire processes. The expression "to enter the legal fold" has been preferred by the SLORC-SPDC to describe the transition of armed opposition groups to a *de facto* status of political recognition and peace. However, the leaders of some armed opposition groups, notably the KNU, have resisted this term because they argue that their parties have never been "illegal" in the first place.

29 The reasons given by SPDC officials for the failure to hold talks or achieve ceasefires with the SSA-S and CNF are that the SSA-S is considered a breakaway group from an existing ceasefire group, the Mong Tai Amy, while the CNF's struggle only really began in the post-1988 period. It is thus considered an opponent of the SLORC-SPDC, unlike parties such as the KNU and KNPP whose struggles were "inherited" from other eras of government.

30 The one exception in some respects has been the New Mon State Party (NMSP), where there was some involvement of Thailand, including in relation to questions of access and continuing humanitarian aid.

31 See, for example, B. Lintner, "Drugs and Economic Growth in Burma Today", in *Burma/Myanmar: Strong Regime Weak State?*, edited by M. Pedersen, E. Rudland and R. May (Adelaide: Crawford House, 2000), pp. 164–94; L. Kean and D. Bernstein, "The Burma-Singapore Axis: Globalizing the Heroin Trade", *Covert/Action Quarterly*, Washington, Spring 1998.

32 *Reuters*, 2 October 1996.

33 Peace go-betweens include Rev. Saboi Jum of the Kachin Baptist Convention, the Catholic Bishop Sotero in Kayah State, and the Karens, Rev. Saw Mar Gay Gyi of the Myanmar Council of Churches and Professor Tun Aung Chain of Yangon University.

34 *New Light of Myanmar*, 26 September 2004. See also, Lt-Gen. Thein Han (Director General of BADP), "Human Resource Development and Nation Building in Myanmar: Unity in Diversity", in *Human Resource Development and Nation*

Building in Myanmar, produced by the Office of Strategic Studies (Yangon: Ministry of Defence, 1997), pp. 215–29.

35   UN Country Team, *Myanmar: A Silent Humanitarian Crisis in the Making* (Yangon: 30 June 2001), p. 2.

36   In *per capita* terms, the international aid budget for refugee or exile groups in Thailand has been much higher. For example, the proposed 2002 budget for the 138,117 refugees recorded in Thai camps was US\$12.5 million. Burmese Border Consortium, *BBC Relief Programme: July to December 2001* (Bangkok: Burmese Border Consortium, 2002), p. 1.

37   Seng Raw, "Views from Myanmar: An Ethnic Minority Perspective", in *Burma: Political Economy under Military Rule*, edited by R.H. Taylor (London: Hurst & Co, 2001), pp. 161–62.

38   International Crisis Group, *Myanmar: Aid to the Border Areas*, p. i.

39   UNODC, "UN confirms steady reduction in opium cultivation in Myanmar", Press Release, 11 October 2004.

40   Ibid.

41   US Senator Sam Brownback, "Brownback, Gregg, McConnell Call on Global Fund to Cease Funding Burma", Press Release, 5 October 2004.

42   Department for International Development, *Drivers of Change* (London: November 2003) and *Which Aspects of Governance Matter Most for Growth and Poverty Reduction?* (London: August 2003).

43   See, for example, M. Smith, "Ethnic Conflict and the Challenge of Civil Society in Burma", in *Strengthening Civil Society in Burma: Possibilities and Dilemmas for International NGOs*, edited by T. Kramer and P. Vervest for Burma Center Netherlands & Transnational Institute (BCN/TNI), (Chiengmai: Silkworm Books, 1999), pp. 20–25.

44   Hugo Slim, *With or Against? Humanitarian Agencies and Coalition Counter-Insurgency* (Geneva: Humanitarian Dialogue Centre, 2004), p. 11.

45   See, for example, International Crisis Group, *Myanmar: the Politics of Humanitarian Aid* (Brussels: International Crisis Group, 2002); also, International Crisis Group, *Myanmar: Aid to the Border Areas*. For a counter view, see, for example, D.S. Mathieson, "The ICG, Burma, and the Politics of Diversion", *The Irrawaddy*, Vol. 12, No. 9 (October 2004).

46   UN Working Group, *Human Development in Myanmar: An Internal Report* (Yangon: UNDP, 1998), pp. 11–13.

47   For an overview of the human legacy of conflict, see for example, M. Smith, *Burma/Myanmar: the Time for Change* (London: Minority Rights Group, 2002), pp. 21–28.

48   International Crisis Group, *Myanmar: Aid to the Border Areas*, p. 3.

49   Ibid.

50 The source for this figure is the Ministry of Health, as quoted in: *Review of the Humanitarian Situation in Myanmar*, UN Country Team, pp. 32–33.

51 UN Office on Drugs and Crime, '2004 Myanmar Opium Survey — Results at a Glance', Press Release, 11 October 2004.

52 For example, from 2001 to 2004, an international NGO, Health Unlimited, completed a whole-course immunization of over 50 per cent of children under two years of age in eleven Wa districts (total population 160,000) with the cooperation of the Wa, Myanmar, and Yunnan health authorities. For the experience of another international NGO in Myanmar, World Concern, see D. Tegenfeldt, "International Non-Governmental Organizations in Burma", in *Burma: Political Economy under Military Rule*, edited by R.H. Taylor (London: Hurst & Co, 2001), pp. 109–18.

53 UN Office on Drugs and Crime, "UN confirms steady reduction in opium cultivation in Myanmar", Press Release, 11 October 2004. Weather changes are also a factor, especially during 2003–04.

54 Alan Rabinowitz, "Valley of Death", *National Geographic*, April 2004, pp. 102–17. For other local conservation efforts between 1999 and 2003, see Lasi Bawk Naw, *Biodiversity, Culture, Indigenous Knowledge, Nature and Wildlife Conservation Programmes in Kachin State, Myanmar* (Myitkyina: YMCA, 2004).

55 International Crisis Group, *Myanmar: Aid to the Border Areas*, p. 13.

56 Interview with Aung Kham Hti, 15 September 2004.

57 See, for example, Kyaw Yin Hlaing, "Burma: Civil Society Skirting Regime Rules", in *Civil Society and Political Change in Asia: Expanding and Contracting Democratic Space*, edited by M. Alagappa (Stanford: Stanford University Press, 2004), pp. 389–418; and the essays by D. Steinberg, M. Smith, Z. Lidell, and M. Purcell in *Strengthening Civil Society in Burma: Possibilities and Dilemmas for International NGOs*, edited by T. Kramer and P. Vervest for Burma Center Netherlands & Transnational Institute (BCN/TNI).

58 See, for example, Global Witness, *A Conflict of Interests: The Uncertain Future of Burma's Forests* (London: Global Witness, 2003).

59 *Statement by Mr. Paulo Sérgio Pinheiro: Special Rapporteur on the Situation of Human Rights in Myanmar* (New York: UNGA, 59th Session, 28 October 2004). p. 4.

60 Burmese Border Consortium, *Burmese Border Consortium Relief Programme: January to June 2004*, pp. 2–7.

61 Global IDP Project, *Myanmar (Burma) Country Report* (Norwegian Refugee Council, 1 July 2004).

62 Interview with Aung Kham Hti, 15 September 2004.

63 See, for example, "From the UN Secretary-General", UNIC/Press Release/233-2004, 17 August 2004.

64 See, for example, "Myanmar leader assures turned-in armed groups of no policy change", *Xinhua News Agency*, 7 November 2004; G. Peck, "Ethnic Peace May Be in Jeopardy in Myanmar", *Associated Press,* 22 October 2004.

65 Interviews, 26 October, 2 November, 6 November 2004.

66 S. Montlake, "Burma's disorientated rebels", *BBC World Service*, 8 November 2004.

67 See note 23.

68 See, for example, Kyaw Zwa Moe, "'Game Over' if NC Proceedings Not Changed, Says Ethnic Leader", *Irrawaddy News Alert*, 7 May 2004. The decision of UNA parties was also made on the basis of other alliances, including the United Nationalities League for Democracy and the Committee Representing the People's Parliament.

69 MTA Homein Region Group, Ex-KNU Phayagon Special Region Group, DKBA and Haungthayaw Special Region Group, Burma Communist Party (Rakhine Group), Kayinni National Development Party Dragon Group, Kayinni National Unity and Solidarity Organization, Mon Splinter Nai Saik Chan Group. Another individual paper was submitted by the Pao National Organization, which had been active in the earlier National Convention, 1993–96.

70 The full list is: Shan State Army (North), New Democratic Army-Kachin, Palaung State Liberation Party, Kachin Defence Army, Kachin Independence Organization, Kayan National Guard, Karenni Nationalities People's Liberation Front, Kayan New Land Party, Karenni National Progressive Party (Splinter, Hoya), Shan State Nationalities People's Liberation Organization, New Mon State Party, Shan State National Army and Mon Armed Peace Group (Chaungchi Region).

71 The National Convention Working Committee argued that certain expressions or ideas were contrary to the existing "104 detailed basic principles".

72 Military government officials reportedly do not want individual state constitutions since there could then be fourteen in the country: seven for the ethnic states and seven for the divisions.

73 Because the ethnic states adjoin neighbouring countries, minority leaders want special rights in this sphere.

74 For example, "Ceasefire groups must insist on equal rights say Burmese ethnic leaders", *Democratic Voice of Burma*, 1 November 2004; "Burma's Ethnic Nationalities Council held meeting", *Democratic Voice of Burma*, 31 October 2004.

75 Ceasefire leaders, however, believe that there are a variety of ways in which the issues of demilitarization can be achieved, ranging from the creation of new political parties to different kinds of military or policing authorities.

76 Interview with David Taw, 6 September 2004.

77 UN Wire, 12 March 2003.

II

Perspectives on the Economy and on Agricultural Development

4

Burma's Economy 2004: Crisis Masking Stagnation

Sean Turnell

In 2004 Burma's economy was convulsed in a monetary crisis. Triggered by the collapse of the country's nascent private banking system the previous year, this latest drama has deeper roots in, and to some extent disguises, the longer-term malaise that has characterized Burma's economy for four decades.

Burma's economic stagnation, not readily identifiable from its official statistics, has a myriad of causes, including a policy-making process that is erratic, arbitrary, and usually counter-productive. Over and above policy, however, Burma lacks the fundamental institutions that history tells us are necessary for a functioning market economy. Principal amongst these institutional absentees is a regime of enforceable property rights.

In the following section, the state of Burma's economy in 2004 will be assessed, beginning with an exploration of some relevant "numbers" — data that highlights the damage wrought by Burma's latest monetary crisis, and data that casts doubt on the narrative of economic success suggested by the country's official statistics. Next, the author examines some of the ostensible causes of the latest crisis, highlighting macroeconomic and other policy failures. It is suggested that these are but symptoms of a more profound malaise which is founded in the failure of Burma's government to establish a credible regime of private property rights. The absence of these rights presents the principal obstacle to private capital formation in Burma, not least as a consequence of the extent to which "money" itself is compromised.

Burma's Economic Performance

Burma has not published a full set of national accounts since 1999. However the country's Central Statistical Office (CSO) does supply certain data, including its estimates of economic growth, to multilateral institutions such as the Asian Development Bank (ADB). Such data paints a rosy picture of Burma's economy, as Table 4.1 indicates.

If the CSO's numbers are indeed an accurate description of Burma's economy, then the country must assuredly be riding an economic miracle of epic proportions. Growth rates such as those shown in Table 4.1 are almost unprecedented, with the exception only of the (doubtful) experiences of China today and the Asian "tigers" of selected memory. The figures would seem to be proof of an economy that is not only growing rapidly but, as the growth rates for 2003 and 2004 imply, also one that is extraordinarily resilient to misfortune — including the latest near-collapse of its financial system.

Alas, however, Burma's official statistics bear little relation to the reality of the country's economic performance. Subject to almost every conceivable obstruction to statistical best practice — from the low pay, scant resources and corruption of Burma's civil service, to the existence of a "black" or

TABLE 4.1
Claimed Annual GDP Growth Rates (% p.a.), Burma, 1999–2004

	1999	2000	2001	2002	2003	2004*
	10.9	13.7	11.3	10.0	10.6	10.0

*estimate.
Source: Asian Development Bank, *Asian Development Outlook 2004*, and *Asian Economic Monitor 2004*, based on data supplied by Burma's CSO.

shadow economy that stalks the recorded one, to the propaganda usefulness of "good news", and to plain wishful thinking — Burma's official statistics can only be regarded as suspect and more than usually requiring of a methodology founded on asking the question: *cui bono?*[1] Of course, this does not mean that constructing an alternative, more reliable, statistical narrative of Burma's economic performance is easy or even possible. The lack of reliable information out of the country necessarily precludes precision whosoever should claim it, and this author can only but be in agreement with Dapice, that economic analysis of Burma can only be "a series of more-or-less informed speculations rather than a standard exercise in processing data".[2]

Yet, the difficulty of crafting a more realistic account of Burma's economic situation should not allow a complacent acceptance of the country's official statistics by default. Such complacency seems entrenched in certain multilateral agencies, but thankfully a vanguard of scholars and commentators are committed to what must at times seem the Sisyphean task of getting to the truth of Burma's economy.[3] These scholars have adopted a number of approaches — which Bradford insightfully groups under the labels of "internal" and "external" critiques.[4] The "internal" critiques attempt to match the claimed growth numbers for Burma's economy with other statistics — such as energy usage, land under cultivation, calorie intake, and so on — that should corroborate the official story of growth if, indeed, it is accurate. "External" critiques, by contrast, examine Burma's growth performance vis-à-vis what the examples of other countries, and history, tell us is reasonable.[5]

Neither internal nor external critiques of Burma's growth performance, however, are favorable to the claims of its official statistics. Even the Asian Development Bank, an organization not noted for publicly questioning the data of its members, implicitly employed an internal critique to Burma's official data when it noted that the country's claimed growth numbers for 2002 were inconsistent with data on the use of certain factors of production — including electricity production (which actually fell), crop acreages, fertilizer and pesticides application, and the consumption of oil and natural gas (all of which were stagnant).[6] More systematically, Dapice critiqued Burma's growth claims by focusing upon electricity production.[7] He noted that from 1990 to 2000 the generation of electricity in Burma increased by an average of 7 per cent per annum. Employing the well-established rule of thumb that in developing countries such as Burma, electricity generation invariably grows by 1.5 to three times the growth rate of real GDP, he calculated an implied growth rate for Burma across the decade of something in the order of 2.3 to 4 per cent per annum. The official statistics claimed 6 per cent average annual growth over the same period.[8] The rice sector likewise came under Dapice's lens, and his finding that the growth of this critical item in the Burmese diet lagged behind the rate of population growth over the 1990s meant that it was likely "that hunger is increasing" in the country, notwithstanding the official figures indicating rapid growth. In its *Country Reports* and *Country Profiles* the Economist Intelligence Unit (EIU) has long expressed doubt over the official numbers provided by Burma's relevant authorities. The EIU implicitly employs an internal critique such as those above to provide "alternative" growth numbers for Burma, as in Table 4.2.

The EIU's methodology is not spelt out in its publications, and contains what must necessarily be subjective assessments of whether information is plausible or not. Given the singular lack of plausibility of much of the official data coming out of Burma, "informed speculations" such as the EIU's are as good as can be reasonably hoped for.

Banking Crisis Damages Burma's Economy

In late 2002, a series of failures amongst certain "private finance companies" (which for the most part were little more than gambling syndicates and "ponzi" schemes) caused a crisis of confidence in Burma's financial arrangements.[9] Although these firms were not legally authorized deposit-taking institutions, they presented a tempting investment opportunity for Burmese seeking a non-negative return on their funds.[10] Such temptation

TABLE 4.2
EIU Estimates of Annual GDP Growth Rates (% p.a.), Burma, 1999–2004

	1999	2000	2001	2002	2003	2004*
	10.9	6.2	5.3	5.3	−1.0	−0.9

*Forecast
Source: Economist Intelligence Unit, *Country Report: Myanmar (Burma)*, August 2004.

had an irrational side, in that the promised rates of return were far too high to be credible, but there was a rational side as well, in that the interest rates that Burma's (authorized) banks can pay on deposits are capped at 9.5 per cent per annum, which is well below the country's inflation rate (estimated by the IMF at 57.1 per cent in 2002), meaning that putting money in the bank was a (certain) losing proposition in Burma.[11]

The crisis in Burma's private finance companies quickly spread to the country's nascent (and hitherto fast-growing) private banking sector — a contagion perhaps unremarkable given the country's history of periodic monetary and financial crises. Long lines of anxious depositors formed outside the banks, a phenomenon that rapidly swelled into an archetypal "bank run". From this moment on, the response of the relevant monetary authorities in Burma, principally the Central Bank of Myanmar (CBM), was (if unintentionally) almost wholly destructive. Late and inadequate liquidity support to the banks by the CBM was overwhelmingly negated by the imposition of "withdrawal limits" on depositors that escalated into an outright denial to depositors of access to their money. Even worse, loans were "recalled" with little consideration given to capacity to repay. More potent breaches of "trust" in banking would be difficult to imagine. With a full-scale banking crisis now in play, there followed the usual symptoms of such events — bank closures and insolvencies, a flight to "cash', the creation of a "secondary market" in frozen deposits, the cessation of lending, the stopping of remittances and transfers, and other maladies destructive of monetary institutions. By mid-2003 the private banks had essentially ceased to function. In 2004 selected banks reopened, some of the largest closed completely, and an anaemic recovery began.[12]

According to Burma's official statistics, however, the bank crisis of 2003 did little damage to the country's economic performance. The estimates of the Central Statistical Office for 2003 and 2004 (see Table 4.1) show growth rates in excess of 10 per cent prevailing. The Economist Intelligence Unit (EIU), on the other hand, ascribes negative growth for Burma during these years (Table 4.2), principally as a consequence of the banking crisis. It is true, of course, that the number of enterprises affected *directly* by Burma's banking crisis is relatively low, but their economic importance — as employers, traders, and participants in the most modern and productive sectors of Burma's economy — is more significant than perhaps their numbers suggest.

The banking crisis allows us another avenue through which to critique Burma's official story of growth, since (as with energy usage) there exists a parallel set of data related to the experience, from which we can draw. This data set consists of the monetary information the Central Bank of Myanmar provides to the International Monetary Fund, and which the latter publishes each month. This data is subject to many of the problems that confront users of other statistics relating to Burma, but these may, arguably, be less severe. Banks, and central banks, owe their *raison d'être* to the aggregation of numbers, and they have ample incentives for "getting them right". Financial numbers are also less politically sensitive than those for most other sectors of the economy.[13] They are not widely understood, seldom reported upon in the press (both inside and outside Burma), and there is little in the way of an informed constituency needing to be appeased or deceived.[14] Burma's financial statistics cannot be regarded as the "truth', but they might just be a useful tool in helping us move toward this elusive quantity.

The financial statistics provided to the IMF are unambiguous in pointing to the depth and scope of the damage wrought on Burma's economy by the 2003 banking crisis. By far the greatest damage, however, was visited upon the private sector — both as borrower and lender. As the first column of Table 4.3 indicates, bank lending to the private sector in Burma has taken a grievous blow from which it has yet to recover. Private sector lending, the lifeblood of a capitalist economy and a primary source of the working capital of the firms within it, fell a precipitous 45 per cent from its peak immediately before the banking crisis (fourth quarter, 2002) to the latest quarter for which we have reliable information (first quarter, 2004). Certainly some private-sector lending before the crisis was unproductive (especially in underpinning various inflation-hedging schemes) — but it is nevertheless true that it is only upon the adequate provision of capital to the private sector that any hope for Burma's future prosperity can be entertained. Joseph Schumpeter observed many years ago that the "essential function of credit" was to enable "the entrepreneur to ... force the economic system into new channels".[15] In Burma today, these channels are decidedly sclerotic.

Such then, was the effect of the Burma's banking crisis on private sector *liabilities*. But on the assets side of the private sector "balance sheet', matters are no better. The banking crisis saw "demand" deposits in Burma's

TABLE 4.3
Selected Banking Statistics, 2000–2004
(Kyat billions)

Selected Quarter/Year	Loans To Private Sector	Demand Deposits	Time Deposits
Q1 2000	199.0	82.2	235.9
Q1 2001	303.9	139.6	351.9
Q1 2002	476.9	231.3	465.6
Q4 2002	609.1	290.5	541.3
Q1 2003	482.8	177.1	415.9
Q2 2003	396.2	135.0	371.5
Q3 2003	368.1	80.3	395.8
Q4 2003	342.5	82.9	386.3
Q1 2004	333.4	112.6	414.2

Source: Table derived from: IMF, *International Financial Statistics* (Washington, D.C.: International Monetary Fund, 2004).

banks also fall precipitously — by 73 per cent from the fourth quarter of 2002 to a low point in November 2003. They have recovered somewhat since but, as at the first quarter of 2004, "demand" deposits remain at only 38 per cent of their 2002 peak. Time and fixed deposits are down 24 per cent from the fourth quarter of 2002, meaning that overall the value of private sector "wealth" in Burma's banks has been reduced by an astonishing 37 per cent in the wake of the banking crisis.[16]

Estimating the Short-Term Economic Costs of the Banking Crisis

What can we say about the costs of Burma's 2003 financial crisis to the economy as a whole?

Economists typically estimate the costs of banking crises in two — admittedly rather rough and ready — ways. One way, a "broad" measure, attempts to estimate the *macroeconomic* costs of a crisis by determining any deviation from trend GDP. Among the numerous objections that could be raised against this measure is its implicit *ceteris paribus* (other things being equal) assumption. The second way, narrower but usually more precise, attempts to measure the fiscal costs of a crisis — the increase in government expenditure that is incurred in bailing out banks, guaranteeing deposits, reforming and restructuring financial institutions, and so on.[17]

Measuring the broad macroeconomic costs of Burma's latest financial crisis is even more problematic than might normally be the case in such situations. Not only are there the universal *post hoc, ergo propter hoc* (after this, therefore because of this) issues noted above but, as has also been noted, we cannot regard Burma's macroeconomic statistics as being in any way reliable. Great caution is therefore required. Nevertheless, caution duly noted, we can use imperfect but more reasonable alternative estimates, such as those supplied by the EIU, to come up with something that it is at least indicative.

Using ten years of EIU economic growth data for Burma (1993–2002), we calculate a "trend average" real rate of growth of GDP of 6.3 per cent per annum. Accordingly, and once more using the EIU's estimates for Burma's GDP growth, but for 2003 and 2004, the macroeconomic costs to Burma of the banking crisis are around 7 per cent of GDP in *each* of these years. Given the higher absolute value of GDP in 2003, it was in this year that the impact was felt more. In absolute terms, we estimate the banking crisis cost Burma in lost output around 560 billion *kyat* in 2003, and 550 billion *kyat* in 2004. Such losses are large by any estimation — indeed, as a proportion of GDP, they are considerably larger than the median output losses experienced in the thirty-three systemic banking crises that have taken place across the world over in the last three decades.[18]

Measuring the *fiscal* costs of banking crises is usually substantially easier than estimating lost output, and considerably more accurate. The reason for this is simply because, unlike output costs, the fiscal costs of a banking crisis do not need to be "estimated'; rather, as expenditure of government and/or the appropriate monetary authorities, they could be expected to appear in the accounts of the relevant bodies. This is not the case for Burma, however, since, shrouded in mystery as their actions remain, we still do not really know the extent of financial support given by Burma's monetary authorities to the distressed banking system. As noted by this author in 2003,[19] much fanfare was made in the middle of the crisis regarding a 25 billion *kyat* loan to three of the worst affected banks, but doubts as to whether this actually took place have not entirely gone away. In the end, IMF statistics reveal that the Central Bank of Myanmar made about 165 billion *kyat* available to banks at the peak of the crisis in the first quarter of 2003, but some 70 billion of this had been repaid by the first quarter of 2004.[20]

Burma's Macroeconomic Environment

Poor banking practices were the proximate cause of Burma's financial crisis of 2003, but such practices took place in a macroeconomic environment that was hardly conducive to the proper functioning of financial intermediaries. Among banking malpractices most frequently reported, for example, were procedures through which banks lent money to their customers in order to enable them to pursue various inflation-hedging strategies — including investing in the "private finance companies" and speculating in gold and real estate. Such procedures were extraordinarily risky for the banks, since they depended on the "bubble" inherent in each of these strategies, and bubbles are well known for their tendency to burst, as all ultimately did, but they would not have been pursued in the systemically-damaging way they were if it had not been for the fact that chronic inflation would otherwise have impoverished the prudent minded.

Unfortunately, high and persistent inflation is but one of a number of macroeconomic problems that beset Burma. Others include an unstable "dual" exchange-rate regime that rewards rent-seeking behaviour and promotes corruption, a current account position that is usually deeply in deficit, negligible foreign exchange reserves, chronic underemployment, foreign debt arrears, and a policy-making environment that is arbitrary and often irrational.[21] All of these woes, however, have an important root cause — the large and persistent budget deficits that are run up by Burma's central government. In the latest year for which we have data on Burma's fiscal position, the 2000–2001 financial year (that is, April 2000 to March 2001), the revenue of the central government accounted for little more than 60 per cent of its spending.[22] There is little reason to believe this situation has improved (see Table 4.4), and what efforts have been made to increase the taxation revenue of the central government have only added to the chaos and confusion that always seem to accompany policy-making and policy implementation in Burma.

One typical illustration of this was the announcement by Burma's Ministry of Finance and Revenue in June 2004 of a new flat-rate tax of 25 per cent on imports, to replace a differentiated series of duties ranging from 2.5 to 20 per cent.[23] This could be seen as a sensible attempt to bring

TABLE 4.4
Lending to Government and the Private Sector, 1994–2004
(Kyat millions)

Year	Bank Lending to Private Sector	Central Bank Lending to Government
1994	28,262	116,131
1995	45,956	142,023
1996	75,346	182,431
1997	115,506	214,392
1998	155,761	281,383
1999	188,649	331,425
2000	266,966	447,581
2001	416,676	675,040
2002	609,101	892,581
2003	342,547	1,262,588
Q1/2004	333,360	1,364,703

Source: Table derived from: International Monetary Fund, *International Financial Statistics.*

coherence to Burma's rates of duty, but the announcement was accompanied by another which declared that the exchange rate used to calculate the value of imports (and upon which the duties were levied) would also rise, from a staggered rate of US$1 = 100–180 *kyat* (for different commodities) to US$1 = 450 *kyat*. Taken together, these comprised two significant revenue enhancing measures (to the extent they were not evaded), but the effect was rather ruined by the chaos that ensued in Burma's cross-border trade as a consequence of the abrupt and arbitrary nature of the announcements (after an initial effort to keep the rate rises a secret) and of their implementation.[24] The change in the dutiable exchange rate was itself a sensible development — at US$1 = 450 *kyat*, at least it sat in the middle of the divide between Burma's official fixed exchange rate of around US$1 = 6 *kyat*, and the prevailing "market" exchange rate of over 1,000 *kyat* to the US dollar. However, the change provided yet another element of uncertainty regarding the value of Burma's currency, while not removing the obvious incentive for corruption created by the application of differential exchange rates.

In the absence of adequate revenue, the Burmese regime has reverted to the device time-honoured in application but universally ill-starred in its effects — monetization. Simply, the Burmese government borrows from the central bank (effectively "prints money') to cover its budget shortfall. The monetization of the budget deficit in Burma is shown in Table 4.4, as indicated by the Central Bank of Myanmar's lending to the central government. Not only has this item been consistently growing since a supposedly pro-economic reform regime came to power in Burma, but it also dwarfs the financial resources elsewhere committed by Burma's financial system (public and private) to the private sector.

Table 4.5 juxtaposes the government's "money-printing" with the inflation numbers that are one of its symptoms.

The Importance of Property Rights

In recent decades, the necessity of establishing clearly-defined and enforceable property rights as a central pillar of an economic development strategy has come to be recognized by economists, development specialists, and policy-makers. Property rights have two critical elements. First, they grant to the individual owner exclusive entitlement to use their property as they see fit (subject to the proviso that this does not infringe on the rights of others), and to enjoy the fruits of this use. Second, they grant to the owner the right to dispose of, sell, or otherwise transfer those rights at will.[25] The first element provides the basis of the incentives to work, to produce, to save, to invest, and to conduct all those other activities that collectively provide the motor of the capitalist economy. The second element

TABLE 4.5
Government Borrowing from the Central Bank and Consumer Price Inflation
(% change per annum, 1999–2003)

	1999	2000	2001	2002	2003
Govt. Borrowing from CBM	17.8	35.0	50.8	32.2	41.4
Consumer Price Inflation	18.3	2.6	21.1	57.1	36.6

Source: Calculations by author based on data in: IMF, International Financial Statistics.

is just as important, since it provides the *means* through which capital can be created. Clearly-defined property rights — and their expression in formal legal documentation — have been the basis of collateralized lending for investment in the industrial world for two centuries. Hernando de Soto, the Peruvian economist who has done perhaps more than anyone else to underline the importance of this "second element" of property rights, described its capital-creating mechanism in his seminal book, *The Mystery of Capital*, thus:

> In the West ... every parcel of land, every building, every piece of equipment or store of inventories is represented in a property document that is the visible sign of a vast hidden process that connects all these assets to the rest of the economy. Thanks to this representational process, assets can lead an invisible, parallel life alongside their material existence. They can be used as collateral for credit. The single most important source of funds for new businesses in the United States is a mortgage on the entrepreneur's house. These assets can also provide a link to the owner's credit history, an accountable address for the collection of debts and taxes, the basis for the creation of reliable and universal public utilities, and a foundation for the creation of securities (such as mortgage-backed bonds) that can then be rediscounted and sold in secondary markets. By this process the West injects life into assets and makes them generate capital.[26]

The "representational process" celebrated by de Soto above scarcely functions in Burma. As shall be examined below, it is implicitly undermined by events such as the 2003 banking crisis, during which the relationship between physical property and its abstract representation was severed in significant ways. But the representational process is also *explicitly* undermined in Burma. Various laws, but chiefly the *Land Nationalization Act* of 1945 (as amended 1953), have the effect of prohibiting the pledging of land as collateral.[27] Such laws, of course, negate the ability of entrepreneurs to raise capital in ways commonplace in the United States and elsewhere. Physical property in Burma is left purely in its "material existence" and is assuredly not a device, in conjunction with a properly functioning financial system, for the introduction of "life" into assets, or for self-replication into capital.[28]

Property Rights in Burma's Banking Collapse

An inescapable conclusion from Burma's banking crisis of 2003 is that the country's relevant authorities were unable, or unwilling, to protect the property rights of participants in the financial system. Most obviously this was the case with respect to the holders of bank deposits in Burma. This cohort had the rights to their property — their monetary assets — violated in multiple ways, including the complete denial of access to it at critical moments. Such assets ceased even to be useful as the means of exchange, as remittances and transfers ceased, and as established tokens (credit, debit cards and the like) were disavowed.[29] Perhaps even more damaging were the violations of the property rights of borrowers whose loans were recalled by the banks concerned, acting at the explicit direction of the CBM — arbitrarily withdrawing working capital and undermining businesses that had entered into supposedly binding and dependable contracts. Of course, with a number of the private banks, including two of the largest, now seemingly permanently closed, a substantial number of depositors have effectively "lost" their money.

The importance of a credible regime of property rights for banking and financial systems hardly needs to be stressed — financial assets such as deposits are, after all, little more than notations on paper (not even on paper in the case of electronic banking products) that are merely claims on the issuer, an abstract representation of the real assets and resources into which they are meant to be redeemable. They are symbolic, backed up by nothing other than the trust their holders are willing to invest in the corporate entity that issues them. In the developed financial markets of the world this trust has been hard won. As Drake notes: "Those who decide ... to hold financial assets as wealth need the reassurance, which law and custom confer, that it is safe to do so".[30] Of course, "law and custom" have seldom conferred such safety in Burma, and the 2003 banking crisis is but the latest reminder of this fact.

Failure of the Fundamental Financial Asset: "Money" in Burma

The most obvious function of money is as a medium of exchange. A more efficient substitute for barter, it is in this role that money allows for the division of labour — famously, one of the factors that Adam Smith posited as partially explaining the "wealth of nations". But money, especially in its modern form, is much more than simply a means of exchange. As a store of value, money allows for "inter-temporal" decision-making by economic agents. Participants in an economic transaction do not need to instantly consume the products of their exchange — rather, money allows consumption to be postponed, brought forward and more generally "liberated" from its initiating transaction. In a practical sense, this allows for saving, for investment, and for the longer-term consumption decisions that people make. Finally, money is a unit of account. Often overlooked, it is this virtue that makes possible the calculation of relative prices, debts, wages, and profits — the signals that allow for the "progressive rationalization of social life".[31]

It is when we stop to consider the nature of money that the importance of property rights becomes apparent. Once valued because it was a commodity of intrinsic worth (gold and silver, for instance), modern money is merely a socially-constructed "promise to pay". In its most recognizable form — that is, as embodied in a nation's currency — this promise is made by the state.

Currency is at the peak of the money hierarchy in terms of its widespread acceptability, but it is, of course, only a component — and in modern economies with a proper functioning financial system, an increasingly small component — of what we regard as "money". The major component of money in modern financial systems is that created by financial institutions — claims against them (in the recognizable forms of deposits, credit cards, and so on) that are transferable and, as such, widely accepted for payment.

Burma has failed to establish credible money at every level of this hierarchy. The currency, which has been weakened by chronic inflation, a collapsing exchange rate, and successive "de-monetizations" (four in total — two in 1964, and then in 1985 and 1987), functions as a low-value medium of exchange, but scarcely as a store of value and unreliably as a unit of account.[32] In purchasing power, one *kyat* today is unlikely to be worth one *kyat* tomorrow. Money in its other forms, as the liabilities of Burma's financial institutions, has all the problems of its currency of denomination, but — as the 2003 crisis reveals — with that extra uncertainty that the standing of these institutions themselves may be dubious.

The failure to create reliable money in Burma is important for a host of reasons, many of which have been discussed above. But more than anything else, the failure to create reliable money in Burma means the country is greatly inhibited in its ability to generate internal sources of financial capital. Much angst is exercised amongst Burma watchers that the country is without much in the way of foreign investment or external aid. Yet such avenues are *not* the most important sources of national capital accumulation. From the United Kingdom as "first-mover" in the industrial revolution to the Asian "tigers", internal capital accumulation through the creation of claims against a country's own financial institutions have been the dominant pool from which capital is financed.[33] The mechanism by which this pool is formed is the simple "money creation" process much beloved by students of elementary macroeconomics, but seemingly forgotten thereafter. This process describes the way that banks take in deposits, lend them out again, take in new deposits from the recipients of the spending created by the loans, in turn lending these out again — and thus on and on. Deposits beget lending, lending begets deposits; bank-created money of the sort described above is created and, with it comes greater production, greater consumption, and a growing economy. Of course, the story has added complexities — prudential reserves siphon off portions of new deposits, lending depends on the supply of credit-worthy borrowers, and other institutional barriers limit infinite money creation. Nevertheless, the core of the story, that banks create money (claims upon them), holds true. The fact that Burma's government allowed the formation of private banks from 1992 (under *The Financial Institutions of Myanmar Law, 1990*) demonstrates that the regime at least partially understood this point.

As Collignon notes,[34] the recognition that domestic financial systems create money in this way discredits the idea that the principal problem facing countries such as Burma is that of a "financing gap" which must be filled by external borrowing or aid. Instead, such a gap can be "filled" by a country's own financial system — so long as it is able to function in the ways indicated. In terms of a role for government then, a principal objective should be ensuring that the right institutions are in place to allow this to happen. This is not to say that a country such as Burma is not in need of foreign investment, nor that foreign investment could not play a positive role in the country's economic development. There are certain goods and services, certain types of expertise, that can only be sourced offshore and secured through financial resources beyond the domestic financial system to create. Nevertheless, it is true that the means through which Burma can realize its potential, as implied by its substantial physical endowments, are largely in its own hands.

Conclusion

In his major work, *The Wealth and Poverty of Nations*, which concerns what history demonstrates are the primary determinates of the wealth of nations, the eminent economic historian David Landes lists seven "institutions" that are essential for the state to guarantee. The state must:

- secure rights of private property, the better to encourage saving and investment;
- secure rights of personal liberty; that is, secure them against the abuses of both tyranny and private disorder (crime and corruption);
- enforce rights of contract, explicit and implicit;
- provide stable government — not necessarily democratic government, but government that is itself governed by publicly-known rules (a government of laws rather than men);
- provide responsive government, one that will hear complaint and make redress;
- provide honest government, such that economic actors are not moved to seek advantage and privilege inside or outside the marketplace;
- provide moderate, efficient, un-greedy government. The effect should be to hold taxes down, to reduce the government's claim on the social surplus, and to avoid privilege.[35]

It is a sobering fact that in 2004 Burma's economy exhibits scarcely *any* of the institutional attributes above. The monetary crisis that enveloped Burma throughout 2003 and 2004 had a number of causes explicable in terms of poor policy and other phenomena of the country's immediate circumstances but, as this chapter has attempted to argue, its causes were inextricably bound up with institutional failures that have been apparent for many decades. Principal amongst these institutional malfunctions has been the failure of governments in Burma to establish a reliable monetary system. Money, as a construction of the state and of the banking system, is that set of transferable financial claims that allows the creation, aggregation, and efficient allocation of a country's capital. As a "claim', money only has value to the extent that people have trust that it is ultimately redeemable in real goods and services. In Burma, such trust has been seriously undermined. To restore trust in Burma's financial institutions, and in its economic institutions more generally, remains the country's most important challenge.

Notes

[1]   For a first-hand account of the corruption and distorted incentives inherent in the collection of official statistics in Burma, see Alison Vicary, "The state's incentive structure in Burma's sugar sector and inflated official data: A case study of the industry in Pegu Division", *Burma Economic Watch*, No. 2 (2004), pp. 15–28.

[2]   D. Dapice, *Current Economic Conditions in Myanmar and Options for Sustainable Growth*, Global Development and Environment Institute Working Paper 03-04 (Medford, MA: Global Development and Environment Institute, Tufts University, 2003), p. 14.

[3]   Sisyphus was the mythical King of Corinth condemned by Zeus and the other Olympian gods to spend eternity pushing a large stone up a hill, only to have it roll back to the bottom again just before his objective was achieved.

[4]   W. Bradford, "*Fiant fruges?* Burma's *sui generis* Growth Experience", *Burma Economic Watch*, No. 2 (2004), pp. 6–14.

[5]   Such an *external* critique of Burma's claimed economic growth is beyond the scope of this chapter. For a recent effort aimed squarely at this end, see Bradford, "*Fiant fruges?* Burma's *sui generis* Growth Experience".

[6]   Asian Development Bank, *Asian Economic Monitor 2004* (Manila: Asian Development Bank, 2004).

[7]   Dapice, *Current Economic Conditions in Myanmar*, pp. 14–15.

[8]   Calculated from data in Asian Development Bank, *Asian Development Outlook 2004* (Manila: Asian Development Bank, 2004).

[9]   For a detailed account of Burma's 2003 banking crisis, see S.R. Turnell, "Myanmar's Banking Crisis", *ASEAN Economic Bulletin*, Vol. 20, No. 3 (December 2003), pp. 272–82. Ponzi schemes pay extremely high returns to their members out of the capital of *new* members. They must ultimately fail when the supply of new members dries up.

[10]   That is, these schemes were not authorized under the *Financial Institutions of Myanmar Law 1990*, the law under which banks and other financial institutions are authorized in Burma.

[11]   International Monetary Fund (IMF), *International Financial Statistics*, various issues (Washington, D.C.: International Monetary Fund, 2004).

[12]   The largest and third-largest of Burma's private banks, the Asia Wealth Bank and Myanmar Mayflower Bank respectively, were particularly hard hit and seem likely never to re-open. Both banks have subsequently been named as (narcotics) money-laundering institutions by the United States Treasury, and their operations subject to an enquiry set up by the Burmese Government. For more details, see S.R. Turnell, "Burma Bank Update', *Burma Economic Watch*, No. 1, 2004, pp. 19–29. Since the 2003 crisis, the Kambawza and Myawaddy

Banks have emerged as the dominant players in Burma's private banking system. Eliminating malfunctioning and unsuitable banks is difficult in any jurisdiction, and although wholesale collapse is hardly an optimal way of going about "weeding out" institutions, it may be that the collapse of the Asia Wealth and Mayflower Banks is not all bad news for Burma.

13 Instructive in this context is the way in which the monetary authorities in China seem to enjoy a high degree of latitude in openly criticizing the performance of the country's state-owned banks and other financial institutions.

14 There was, for instance, great confusion in the press coverage of Burma's 2003 banking crisis, including amongst media outside the country. Within Burma there was only one press conference held by the Central Bank of Myanmar during the whole of the crisis period (on 11 February 2003). See Turnell, "Myanmar's Banking Crisis", p. 275.

15 J.A. Schumpeter, *The Theory of Economic Development: An Inquiry into Profit, Capital, Credit, Interest and the Business Cycle* (Cambridge, Mass.: Harvard University Press, 1934), p. 106.

16 IMF, *International Financial Statistics*.

17 G. Hoggarth, P. Jackson, and E. Nier, "Banking Crises and the Design of Safety Nets", *Journal of Banking and Finance*, Vol. 29 (2005), pp. 143–59; E.J. Frydl and M. Quintyn, *The Benefits and Costs of Intervening in Banking Crises*, IMF Working Paper 00/147 (Washington D.C.: International Monetary Fund, 2000); D.G. Mayes, "Who Pays for Bank Insolvency in Transition and Emerging Economies?", *Journal of Banking and Finance*, Vol. 29 (2005), pp. 161–81.

18 In their global survey of banking crises from 1977 to 2002, Hoggarth and his colleagues estimated a median output loss from a systemic banking crisis of 2.4 per cent of GDP. They calculated such losses, as we have here, as the deviation in the rate of GDP growth over the crisis period from its pre-crisis ten-year trend. Their survey included the 1997 Asian financial crisis, as well as others across a myriad of other countries and regions. See Hoggarth, Jackson and Nier, "Banking crises and the design of safety nets', p. 153.

19 Turnell, "Myanmar's banking crisis", p. 276.

20 We cannot say that the remainder — 95 billion *kyat* — is unrecoverable, since the data collection from which our analysis of the CBM's actions are drawn includes items unrelated to any "rescue package". See IMF, *International Financial Statistics*.

21 In recent years, exports of clothing and textiles from Burma (to Europe and the United States primarily) have been growing strongly. This will be hindered, and probably reversed, by the effects upon the global market in clothing and textiles of the ending of the Multi-Fibre Agreement (MFA) from 1 January 2005. Under the MFA, countries were allocated clothing and textile export

"quotas" in the largest consumer markets. These quotas have hitherto protected manufacturers such as Burma from efficient large-scale producers in China and elsewhere. It is widely expected that, freed from quota ceilings, producers in China will quickly erode the share of more marginal producers such as Burma. As such, Burma's external position is likely to come under further pressure in the near term. For an introduction to the MFA and the significance of its ending, see the website of the World Trade Organization and, in particular, <http://www.wto.org/english/tratop_e/texti_e/texintro_e.htm>. Accessed 25 July 2005.

22 Economist Intelligence Unit, *Country Report: Myanmar (Burma)*, August 2004 (London: Economist Intelligence Unit, 2004), p. 9.

23 No warning and no reasons were given for the increases, which came into effect from 15 June 2004.

24 The initial secrecy is also typical of policy-making in Burma. This author has calculated that, if fully applied, these two measures would mean the "average" importer bringing goods into Burma faced an increase in duties payable of around 56 per cent. This outcome was bad for the importers and provides a ready explanation for the panic buying that took place in June, but it was potentially a boon for the government's budget. The press release announcing the changes, and the reports of the panicked reaction that followed, can be found at a number of news sites, including <www.burmanet.org>.

25 G.P. O'Driscoll, "Property Rights: The Key to Economic Development", *Policy Analysis*, No. 482 (August 2003), p. 8.

26 H. De Soto, *The Mystery of Capital: Why Capitalism Triumphs in the West and Fails Everywhere Else* (London: Bantam Press, 2000), pp. 6–7.

27 Additional laws that similarly inhibit the raising of finance capital in Burma include the *Transfer of Immoveable Property (Restrictions) Law 1987* (as amended from the original 1947 legislation), which explicitly denies the ability of foreigners to lend against land as security, and the *Money Lenders Act 1947*, which effectively limits the term on loans in Burma by various injunctions upon the amount of total interest payable on a loan. Of course, all of these laws are consistent with an important clause in Burma's original 1948 constitution, which states (Section 30, Chapter III) that "[t]he State is the ultimate owner of all lands". See, Government of Burma, *The Constitution of the Union of Burma* (Rangoon: Superintendent of Government Printing and Stationary, 1948). Burma's constitution is currently suspended, but it remains the legal base upon which Burma's existing property laws are based.

28 Among studies examining ways to improve agricultural productivity in Burma, there is near unanimity about the important role that can be played by establishing private land title. See, for example, Asian Development Bank,

Asian Development Outlook 2003 (Manila: Asian Development Bank, 2003); J. Copland, "The Agricultural Sector and The Role of International Assistance in Promoting Agricultural Reform in Myanmar", Paper presented to the Myanmar/Burma Update 2004 conference, held at the Australian National University, Canberra, 18–19 November 2004, published as Chapter 7 in this volume; H. James, "Cooperation and Community Empowerment in Myanmar in the Context of *Myanmar Agenda 21*", *Asian-Pacific Economic Literature*, Vol. 17, Issue 1 (May 2003), pp. 1–21; T. Kurosaki and others, *Rich Periphery, Poor Center: Myanmar's Rural Economy under Partial Transition to a Market Economy*, Discussion Paper Series, No. d03-23, Institute of Economic Research, Hitotsubashi University (Kunitachi City, Tokyo: Institute of Economic Research, 2003); World Bank, *Myanmar: Policies for Sustaining Economic Reform*, Report No. 14063 (Washington D.C.: World Bank, 1995). An instructive example for Burma in this respect might be Vietnam. Vietnam introduced private land title in 1995, leading to an almost instantaneous increase in investment on the land, increased yields and various other efficiencies. For details, see Q.T. Do and L. Iyer, *Land rights and Economic Development: Evidence from Vietnam*, World Bank Policy Research Working Paper Series, No. 3120 (Washington D.C.: World Bank, 2003), http://ssrn.com/abstract=445220.

[29] Meanwhile another set of "tokens" emerged — in the form of "tickets" issued by banks that allowed depositors daily or weekly access to a portion of their funds. Functioning not unlike ration cards, these tickets acquired real value and, as such, a market in them quickly developed. See Turnell, "Myanmar's Banking Crisis", p. 275.

[30] P.J. Drake, *Money, Finance and Development* (Oxford: Martin Robertson, 1980), p. 34.

[31] G. Ingham, *The Nature of Money* (Cambridge, UK: Polity Press, 2004), p. 4.

[32] Burma's government seems to have learnt the lessons of past demonetizations, and has been at pains at various times (such as when a new note is introduced) to reassure the public that such measures will not be repeated. Nevertheless, in monetary matters, fear is a difficult emotion to dispel. Details of the 1987 de-monetization, which was to have dramatic political repercussions, are outlined in D.I. Steinberg, *Burma: The State of Myanmar* (Washington D.C.: Georgetown University Press, 2001), pp. 131–32. For further information on the earlier demonetization episodes, see Mya Maung, *The Burma Road to Poverty* (New York: Praeger, 1991). The author is grateful to Trevor Wilson for his insights on the extent to which the lessons of the past demonetizations are seared into the collective memory of various monetary actors in Burma.

[33] The importance of this point, in the specific context of Burma, is made with great verve and authority by S. Collignon, "Human Rights and the Economy

of Burma", in *Burma: Political Economy Under Military Rule*, edited by R.H. Taylor (London: Hurst and Company, 2001), pp. 90–4.

[34] Ibid., p. 91.

[35] D.S. Landes, 1998, *The Wealth and Poverty of Nations* (New York: W.W. Norton, 1998), pp. 217–18.

5

The Status of the Agricultural Sector in Myanmar in 2004

Kyaw Than

As everyone knows, Myanmar still remains mainly reliant on agriculture, which constitutes the principal pillar and foundation for Myanmar's future all-round development. Now the population of the country stands at 53 million, and about 70 per cent of the people live in the rural areas, engaged mainly in the agriculture, fisheries, and forestry sectors. For food security and economic development, the Myanmar Government gives priorities to the performance and production of these important sectors.

To raise the human development index, aiming to improve the education, health and economic well-being of 36 million rural people is of vital importance.

In agriculture, especially in the crop sector, more than sixty kinds of crops can be grown throughout the country. These can be classified into seven groups: namely, cereals, oilseeds, food legumes, industrial crops, kitchen crops, plantation, and horticultural crops. The total crop sown area in Myanmar covers 41.32 million acres (16.72 million ha.).

Every effort is made to encourage rice production so as to meet the demand of both increasing local consumption and foreign exports.

Normally rice has been grown as one crop a year, in the monsoon season, but with the introduction of the summer paddy program in 1992–93, rice is being sown throughout the year. So in 2003–04, the total sown area of summer paddy reached 2.736 million acres (1.107 million ha.). For several reasons, the average yield of rice, at 3.42 tonnes per hectare, is still low compared with yields achieved by neighbouring countries. So it is evident that there is a strong need for Myanmar's agriculture to make further improvement, in order to catch up as much as possible with the high yields pertaining among some Southeast Asian nations. The most significant shortcomings in agriculture at present include: the non-optimum yields of some major crops; the inadequacy of inputs such as chemical fertilizers and other agro-chemicals; lack of good quality seeds; and inadequacy of post-harvest technology and farm mechanization services.

In regard to irrigation systems, Myanmar is rich in water resources. Of the annual total volume of 876 million acre-feet of water flowing into all rivers and streams, only 6 per cent has been put to use at present. Many irrigation works are being implemented with the aim of increasing water utilization, mainly for agriculture development.

A total of 289 irrigation projects were completed by the year 2002–03, covering an area of around 1.4 million hectares. The total investment costs more than *kyats* 65 billion. The number of dams constructed after 1988–89 to date is 164. The number of pumping irrigation structures, completed after 1988 to the present is 265.

The Situation of Agro-based Industry

In Myanmar, traditional agro-based industries have long existed and have gradually developed over time, but these agro-industries are scattered all over the country. They can be categorized on the basis of ownership, and can be grouped as state-owned, private-owned, or co-operatives.

The major agro-industries are rice, edible oil, sugar, textile, jute, and rubber. In the publication *Industrial Development in Myanmar: Prospects and Challenges*,[1] T. Kudo identified a number of constraints against improving agro-industries including:

1. Policy and strategy;
2. Infrastructure;
3. Transportation and communication;

4. Power and energy supply;
5. Technology and services;
6. Institutional arrangement and capability;
7. Co-ordination and co-operation;
8. Finance and Investment.

By improving agro-based industries, the problems of rural unemployment and rural poverty can be solved to some extent. In the agriculture sector, favourable conditions exist for the establishment of new agro-industries in the area of crop production, upgrading the existing processing and other post-harvest facilities, and expansion of downstream industries using advanced modern technologies.

Agricultural Education

Agricultural education, agricultural research, and agricultural extension are the three important areas for agricultural development. In agricultural education, the formal system involves ten agricultural high schools (AHS), seven state agricultural institutes (SAI) and one agricultural university. The agricultural high schools have an important role in educating rural youth of poor families. Educating such persons will improve the prospects for the employment of trained groups of low-level service personnel, especially in remote areas. However, some of these schools have been closed down, for two main reasons — inefficient performance and low student enrolment. The schools were also facing a shortage of trained teaching staff and farm facilities.

There are seven state agricultural institutes responsible for vocational agricultural education. The vocational agricultural education system is in a better situation, because there are job opportunities for diploma certificate holders, and they have a good chance to go on to higher-level agricultural education at Yezin Agricultural University (YAU).

For higher agricultural education, there is only one centre in Myanmar, Yezin Agricultural University, which was established in 1924. Between 1924 and 2004, the university has turned out 7,083 graduates, as well as 107 Master of Agricultural Science graduates. A doctoral program was initiated in 2001. Most of the graduates have gone into jobs in the departments and enterprises of the Ministry of Agriculture and Irrigation.

Human Resources Development at Yezin Agricultural University

About 52 per cent of staff members at YAU have post-graduate degrees from various foreign countries. The rest of the staff will be equipped with postgraduate degrees within two to three years. In this connection, YAU is currently working in close scientific co-operation with some foreign institutions and organizations to create better conditions for the teaching and research activities of its academic staff and students.

International Collaboration

At the present time YAU has signed MOUs with ten international institutions to promote activities for staff development, staff and student exchange, and joint research programs. We are in the process of collaborating with ten other universities and research institutions. About 180 fresh graduates are being sent annually to Arava Co Ltd in Israel for eleven months of on-the-job training and to undertake an agricultural business studies diploma course.

Agricultural Research

Myanma Agriculture Service (MAS) is the biggest organization within the Ministry of Agriculture and Irrigation. It coordinates agricultural research and extension in the country, and under it are various research institutes and divisions, such as:

1. Central Agricultural Research and Training Centre (CARTC);
2. Vegetable and Fruit Research and Development Centre (VFRDC);
3. Plant Protection Division (PPD);
4. Land Use Division (LUD).

The Central Agricultural Research Institute (CARI) has been upgraded as a separate Department of Agricultural Research (DAR) with a Director-General as head. The Seed Division (SD) has also been given separate status. There are other research stations or units under other departments that conduct various kinds of research, such as the Agriculture Mechanization Department (AMD), Myanma Sugarcane Enterprise (MSE),

Myanma Cotton and Sericulture Enterprise (MCSE), Myanma Perennial Crops Enterprise (MPCE), Myanma Jute Industries (MJI), and the Yezin Agricultural University (YAU).

Under the breeding program of the Department of Agricultural Research (DAR), sixty-two varieties of rice, seven varieties of OPVs, and four varieties of hybrid maize, four varieties of groundnut, four varieties of sesame, fourteen varieties of food legumes, two varieties of cotton, four varieties of jute, and four varieties of sugarcane have been released for farmers.

The research approach and research priorities are mostly targeted towards increasing the productivity of individual crops.

Agricultural Extension

The agricultural extension approach and methods are very important for effective transfer of technologies to farmers. The linkages between research and extension need to be strengthened. Also, in setting up the extension programs, attention should be given to differences in socio-economic and agro-ecological conditions. The following problems have been encountered in carrying out agricultural extension services:

1. Poor technical knowledge
2. Extension resources
3. Market for farm products
4. Finance for farmers, and
5. Working environment.

Agricultural extension officers need relevant training to improve their knowledge and skills. CARTC offers different kinds of training to various service personnel, including extension officers, such as pre-service training, in-service training, on-the-job training, and training workshops. Some 2,089 trainees attended various training programs at CARTC during the five-year period 1995–2000. Similar kinds of training were also provided at DAR, PPD, and LUD.

Rural Development

In the case of improving rural development, the government is attempting to solve the rural poverty problem through implementing various policies such as agriculture-based development policy, agricultural price reform policy, macro-price reform policy, technology development policy, credit policy, irrigation policy, marketing policy. and integrated rural development policy.

There is a relatively high incidence of poverty in the marginal agricultural areas such as dry zone and hilly regions of Myanmar. Common characteristics of these marginal areas are a high rate of degradation of natural resources, unreliable rainfall, lack of proper irrigation systems, and other problems. It is vital to strengthen the current Integrated Rural Development Projects in these marginal areas in order to achieve sustainable agricultural productivity and improved equity, and for promoting stability.

The Fishery Sector

In regard to the fishery sector, Myanmar has a 2,800-kilometre-long coastline, with abundant fish and shrimp resources. There is huge potential for aquaculture and marine fisheries, but there are insufficient processing facilities and trained personnel.

The Forestry Sector

In the forestry sector, Myanmar still retains a substantial coverage of valuable forests. However, due to agriculture expansion, shifting cultivation, urbanization, and the use of fuels by households, deforestation has been estimated at around 15,000 hectares annually. The Forest Department has been carrying out re-afforestation at the rate of 30,000 hectares annually.

Like other developing countries, Myanmar faces environmental deterioration in various forms, depending on the particular agro-ecological zone. Due to deforestation, soil erosion occurs in many of the hilly and mountainous regions. Unsustainable farming practices, such as the practice of slash-and-burn cultivation, are major threats for environmental degradation. As a result, environmental protection programs are very essential for combating poverty amongst the rural population.

International Assistance

Compared to other developing countries, Myanmar has received relatively little international assistance; multilateral development agencies and bilateral agencies have provided only limited funds and assistance. But 2004 was encouraging for the agricultural sector as the OPEC Fund has agreed to provide US$12.3 million funding for a project on oil seed production. Since 1980, very little or no international aid or funding has been received for agricultural education, although Myanmar is an agricultural country.

Conclusion

Myanmar knows well the importance of agricultural and rural development, which is a key to social, economic, and environmental reform in Myanmar. The country is undertaking this heavy work-load mainly through its own efforts. With the help of international assistance, the development process would be more efficient and productive in the agricultural sector.

Note

[1]   T. Kudo (ed.), *Industrial Development in Myanmar: Prospects and Challenges* (Chiba, Japan: Institute of Developing Economies, 2002).

6

Sustainable Agricultural and Rural Development: Pathways to Improving Social, Economic and Environmental Conditions in Myanmar

Myo Win and Graeme Batten

"Anything can wait but not agriculture" — Pandit J. L. Nehru

"Do not underestimate their [farmers'] knowledge and skill. Most of them are not lazy. They know the economic side of crop selection and operation. There are only a few points which they need advice from experts" — U Ba Tin (1980)

Introduction

Sustainable agricultural and rural development are the foundation for developing agro-based industries, and are positive pathways for solving many of Myanmar's current issues and challenges related to rural poverty, unemployment, human development, and associated malnutrition and rural urban drift.

In a recent Human Development Report (HDR) of the United Nations Development Program (UNDP)[1] Myanmar ranked 131st out of 175 countries in terms of the Human Development Index (HDI). The HDI is the average value of three other indices: Life Expectancy Index (LEI), Education Index (EI,) and GDP (gross domestic product) Index (GDPI). Myanmar's LEI, EI and GDPI indices are 0.53, 0.72 and 0.39 respectively, resulting in HDI of 0.549. By comparison the HDI for Australia was 0.939 and for Luxembourg 1.0.

Based on GDP Index alone, Myanmar falls into the "least developed countries" category but on the Education Index measurement, it falls into the "developing countries" category. The final HDI for Myanmar sits between Low Human Development (0.440) and Medium Human Development (0.684) category.

The economic growth of a country not only improves human development; it also creates opportunities for widening people's choices. For an agricultural country like Myanmar, development strategy will obviously have to focus on agriculture. Agricultural development and a rise in agricultural productivity can be achieved through agricultural education, research, and extension, but above all, funding and investment from local and international sources are needed.

About 75 per cent of the total population resides in rural areas and is principally engaged in the agriculture, livestock, and fishery sectors for their livelihood.[2] In order, therefore, to improve the HDI for Myanmar, improvements in the rural HDI, which reflect rural health, rural education, and rural economy, will be required.

The key players for achieving this are the government, the opposition, ethnic groups, urban and rural people, agricultural entrepreneurs, international investment companies, and aid organizations. For more than fifteen years Myanmar has not received significant assistance from the international donor community for the agriculture sector. Lack of such investment has been the main weak point in rural economic development.

Myanmar is a country of 676,578 square kilometres (measuring approximately 925 km from east to west, and 2,090 km from north to south) and is located between 92°10' and 101°11'E longitude, and between 9°32' and 28°31'N latitude. The population is 52.4 million (2003) with an annual growth rate of 1.84 per cent.[3]

The agriculture sector contributes 45.1 per cent of GDP, 18 per cent of total export earnings, and employs 63 per cent of the labour force. As mentioned above, three-quarters of the total population resides in rural areas and is principally engaged in agriculture. In 2001–02, 15.8 million hectares was utilized for various crops; the reserve forest covered 13.9 million hectares, with 19 million hectares of other forest area.[4]

Rice is the staple food of Myanmar and the sown area in 2002–03 was 6.48 million hectares, with an average yield of 3.42 tonnes per hectare. Myanmar usually produces over twenty million tonnes of rice per year, and is the seventh-largest producer of rice in the world. It also has the highest rice consumption of any country in the world, at 211 kilograms (kg) per head per year.[5] Rice consumption for Thailand and Vietnam are 101 kg per head per year and 170 kg per head per year respectively, indicating a reduction in the consumption of rice due to the availability of alternative staple foods. Reduced rice consumption is also an indication of the level of economic growth of a nation.

Myanmar is rich in water resources. Annual rainfall ranges from 750 mm in the alluvial lowlands of the central region to 1,500 mm in the eastern and western mountains and to 4,000–5,000 mm in the coastal region. Only 6 per cent of the total surface water resources of 1,081 cubic kilometres per annum are being utilized at present. The total ground water potential is approximately 500 cubic kilometres per annum. Three parallel chains of forested mountain ranges run from north to south separating the country into three main river systems: the Ayeyarwady or Irrawaddy (2,170 km long) and its tributary the Chindwin (960 km); the Sittaung (298 km); and the Thanlwin or Salween (1,274 km). The total area of the fertile valleys between these rivers covers 50,000 square kilometres. In 2001–02, the area of irrigated land was 18.8 per cent of the net sown area. In 2002 the total number of dams and reservoirs was 628 (including 146 major dams).[6]

These data indicate the vast land and water resources of Myanmar, which are the two major requirements for agricultural development.

At present, agricultural development in Myanmar has three main objectives:

- to achieve a surplus in paddy (rice) production;
- to achieve self-sufficiency in edible oils;
- to step up the production of exportable pulses and industrial crops.

Food Security: A Key to Stability, Peace and Prosperity

For a developing country like Myanmar, food security is the key to peace and stability, and the foundation for economic development. Rice is the most important crop in Myanmar, therefore it is the driving force for the development of the nation. Although there has been an increase in rice production, this increase seems to be lagging behind population growth, with the result that there is a shortage of rice, especially when the weather is unfavourable.[7] Besides rice, improving the production of other food and industrial crops and related agro-based industry is the key to solving problems such as rural unemployment, rural poverty, associated malnutrition, and rural-urban drift.[8]

Food security strategies adopted by Myanmar include:

- transforming wasteland into new cropping land;
- expansion of irrigated cropping area;
- increased use of high-yielding varieties, quality seeds and technology;
- increased use of farm machinery;
- encouraging entrepreneurial skills and innovative abilities of farmers.[9]

Reducing poverty calls for rapid economic growth that is aimed at helping the poor and that is based on efficient competitive markets. There should be a balanced division of responsibilities between the state, the private sector, and civil society. Myanmar potentially has the physical capability to match Thailand as a dominant rice exporter, but its progress has been restricted by a lack of fertilizers, lack of access to quality seed, lack of appropriate agricultural machinery and skilled farm labour, and the limited amount of capital available for farmers.[10] Without international trade and investment, progress towards achieving food security will be slow.

Agricultural Development

Agriculture plays a significant role in Myanmar's national economy, and further development will depend on the level of national and international investment. Recently the Ministry of Agriculture and Irrigation (MOAI) adopted a policy and strategy of allowing freedom of choice in agricultural production and encouraged private sector participation in commercial crop production. It remains to be seen whether the policy will be implemented in every State and Division. It should also be noted that unless the amount of foreign direct investment increases significantly, progress will be slow. Foreign Direct Investment (FDI) for Myanmar at US$0.14 billion is small compared to US$3.2 billion for Indonesia and US$4.6 billion for Malaysia.[11] A considerable amount of this investment is going into the agricultural sector, but the full potential production is still not being realized.

The success or failure of sustainable agricultural development depends on effective and appropriate agricultural education, agricultural research, and agricultural extension, all of which will in turn depend on effective macro-agricultural policy and market-oriented agro-based industries. These three areas of development must be well coordinated in all projects. Agricultural projects should cover not only cropping but also livestock and fishery development, since most farmers are involved in all three areas.

Agricultural Education

In Myanmar, there are ten agricultural high schools, seven state agricultural institutes, and one agricultural university (Yezin Agricultural University or YAU). Few students have the opportunity to attend university, and due to inefficient performance, low student enrolment numbers, and shortage of teaching staff and farm facilities, some of the agricultural high schools have had to close down. Students would be encouraged to remain in agricultural high school and state agricultural institute courses if the curricula contained more rural-based vocational agriculture, animal husbandry, and rural craft. Better education will not only support better rural economic growth but will also counter the drift of rural youth to urban areas.

The enrolment in state agricultural institutes is satisfactory because there are opportunities for the graduates to get jobs within the government, and also the option for entry into higher agricultural education at YAU.

Formal education in agriculture, along with the agricultural research farms, started in 1914. Agricultural education at college level began in 1924, with the establishment of the Burma Agricultural College and Research Institute at Mandalay which offered a three-year diploma in agriculture. The first agricultural degree course was offered in 1938 at Mandalay University. Under an initiative of UNDP and the Food and

Agriculture Organization (FAO), the Agriculture Faculty was moved to Yezin in 1973 and established as Yezin Agricultural University (YAU). The first postgraduate course was offered in 1978.[12]

As YAU is the only centre of higher learning in agriculture, every effort must be made to improve and update its resources and its funding for capital and operating expenditure. The annual capital expenditure allocated to the University, which has 197 teaching staff and 1,300 students, is insufficient for such an important institution, especially for the teaching facilities there. The University has highly-qualified, internationally-trained staff but most of them are now in their fifties and near retirement age. One good incentive would be to extend the retirement age for academics. There are also a significant number of well-qualified and enthusiastic younger staff, and every effort should be made to nurture them to become the leading educators and researchers for the future. It is perhaps true that agricultural education has not suffered as much as other sectors in terms of the decline in quality of education being provided, but without a substantial increase in investment, the risk is that it will fall behind international and regional standards. Considerable injection of funding is urgently needed from international organizations for improving the library facilities and laboratory equipment, and for consumables.

Yezin Agricultural University has the potential to play a pivotal role in agricultural development in Myanmar. It has the basis to link with international organizations to enhance technology, and it must also lead the training program for regional agricultural research and advisory staff.[13]

Agricultural Research

A developing country like Myanmar does not have the time or money to engage in a "theoretical knowledge hunt" in agricultural research. Agricultural research must be farmer-driven, involving participation by farmers and collaboration between researchers and farmers who are looking for practical solutions to their problems. Agricultural research should also focus on improving the productivity of the crops that the poor consume most. Researchers using new agricultural technologies need to target the areas where the largest numbers of poor people live.[14] It is important for researchers to be aware of the interaction between the new technologies and rural livelihood assets such as human capital (farming knowledge, education, available labour, etc.), natural capital (water, land, forests, soil fertility, etc.), financial capital (credit, insurance, savings), physical capital (tools, roads, water-pumps, etc.) and social capital (neighbours, local farmer organizations, etc.).[15]

The agricultural research institutions in Myanmar operate under the Myanmar Agricultural Service (MAS), which in turn comes under the Ministry of Agriculture and Irrigation. The major research centres are:

1. Agricultural Research Department (ARD). It is the core research department for research in Myanmar. ARD has nineteen research farms and fifteen divisions of research activities including rice, other cereals, legumes, farm machinery, seed bank and plant pathology.
2. Vegetable and Fruit Research and Development Centre (VFRTC). It conducts research and germ plasm collection of fruits and vegetables.
3. Yezin Agricultural University (YAU). The research activities of the university are related to postgraduate programs and significant amount is done in collaboration with ARD.
4. Other government departments, which are responsible for individual crops such as cotton and sugarcane, also have research and development programs.

Agricultural research in Myanmar is centrally planned and managed, which puts constraints on achieving profitable returns, but the MOAI is looking into restructuring for a better model.

Collaboration and the dissemination of research information between different departments need to be opened up. Because crop production, crop processing and storage come under the supervision of different ministries, there is a need to have a common forum for the exchange of ideas. The Myanmar Academy of Agricultural, Forestry, Livestock and Fishery Sciences (MAAFLFS), which is an independent group of retired agricultural scientists, plays an important role as a medium for such collaboration. Its activities would also benefit enormously from much greater interaction with international experts in these areas, and its leadership is keen to proceed in this direction.

Myanmar's research organizations have a number of agricultural, livestock, and forest research projects which are funded by international organizations such as FAO and UNDP, universities from Asian countries, and the Australian Centre for International Agricultural Research (ACIAR).

At present ACIAR is financing two projects in Myanmar, one on rodent control and another on Newcastle disease in poultry (see Chapter 7).

Agricultural Extension

Agricultural extension means the transfer of knowledge and solutions obtained from agricultural education and research to the farmers in the field. It is important to find local ways of strengthening the links between scientists and farmers that exist even in a developing country such as Myanmar. Information or knowledge transfer through extension programs is more effective if farmers participate directly in the process of problem-solving using a Participatory Extension Approach (PEA). This means facilitating participation in a bottom-up problem-solving approach. The key players will be not only the government extension officers but also the farmers, local community, local administrators, and non-government organizations (NGOs).

Traditional agricultural extension started in Myanmar in 1927, about the same time as Myanmar produced its first Diploma in Agriculture graduates from Mandalay Agricultural College. The "training and visit" approach and the "selective concentrative approach" in the 1970s were top-down approaches and mainly aimed at "technology transfer". Those methods did not cater for "participation, decision-making, leadership, and ownership" of farmers.[16]

The Agricultural Extension Division (AED) is one of the largest branches of the Myanmar Agricultural Service with about 1,200 staff, of which 1,000 are agricultural university graduates. The ratio of extension agents to farmers is about 1:500.

The Central Agriculture Research and Training Centre (CARTC) regularly trains personnel of AED but the participatory training for farmers needs to be improved.

The Plant Protection Division (PPD) runs training in integrated pest management (IPM) and the Land Use Division (LUD) runs training courses for farmers in soil conservation, soil survey, soil and water testing and analysis.

UNDP/FAO and NGOs have implemented a number of human development and extension projects in the dry zone, in Shan State and in Ayeyarwaddy Division.

For the agricultural extension programs in Myanmar to be successful and effective, the major objective would be the alleviation of rural poverty by increasing their net income from agriculture. We suggest that extension activities be aimed at obtaining information and demonstrating best management practices for local conditions in areas such as:

- fertilizers and plant nutrient management;
- crop rotation and crop management;
- farm machinery and tools;
- water management;
- soil management;
- agricultural chemicals;
- farm budget management;
- irrigation and drainage;
- soil conservation;
- post harvest operations;
- marketing.

Although these topics are being researched and information is being extended, progress would be more effective with financial and technical support from developed countries.

Agricultural Projects

An agricultural project, whether big or small, and whether at village or district level, is the amalgamation of agricultural education, research, and extension. Agricultural projects are the building blocks of agricultural development, which is the pathway to a country's economic growth.

Except for small village-level projects (less than US$50,000) operated by non-governmental organizations and civil society organizations (CSO), Myanmar needs support from developed countries for major projects in agricultural training, and for education infrastructure such as laboratories and research facilities.

For any major project to be successful, it is important that reliable data and information should be gathered. Projects should, therefore, be long-term — operating for a minimum of ten years — and built step-by-step from shorter-term projects of one to three years. Project outcomes should be profitable for farmers, and should have the potential to increase economic growth. One important outcome of such projects should be a reduction of poverty, which in turn would foster peaceful and stable communities, and could ultimately lead to democracy.

Carefully-planned agricultural projects should be seen by the international community as important humanitarian assistance. Food is more important than health, since health depends on food. Of the thirty-five international NGOs at present operating in Myanmar, only six have agriculture and rural development programs among their activities.[17] International aid donors and policy-makers should consider the positive impact agricultural development plays in strengthening peace through food and poverty reduction in conflict-prone regions of Myanmar, and re-think their programs to give more support to agricultural assistance.

Rural Development

Rural development programs in Myanmar are being carried out by the Myanmar government to improve the rural economy. Some of the notable rural development programs and projects include the following:[18]

1. the development of border area and ethnic groups, by the Ministry of Border Areas and National Races and Development Affairs;
2. the National Program for Nine Districts Greening, by the Ministry of Forestry (MOF);
3. the National Program for Development of Irrigation and Rural Water Supply, by MOAI;
4. the Model Mechanized Farming Village Project, by MOAI;
5. the Contract Farming System in Livestock and Fisheries, by the Ministry of Livestock and Fisheries (MLF);
6. the Rural Credit Scheme, by MOAI;
7. environmentally-sustainable food security and micro-income opportunities in some deteriorating ecosystems, by MOAI, UNDP/ FAO, MOF, MLF, and the Ministry of Cooperatives;
8. capacity-building and empowerment of women and self-help groups through micro-credit and social mobilization, by MOAI and the Centre on Integrated Rural Development for Asia and the Pacific, funded by the Government of Japan.

At the Fourth ASEAN Meeting on Rural Development and Poverty Eradication held in Singapore on 7 October 2004, the Minister for Progress of Border Areas and National Races and Development Affairs reported on the implementation and successes of five key rural development activities in Myanmar:

- rural roads;
- rural water supply;
- rural education;
- rural health;
- rural economy.[19]

These programs are indicators of the government's commitment to rural development programs using the limited resources which the country can afford. However, greater injection of national and international funding is needed to have more impact on reducing rural poverty and increasing food security.

Infrastructure

The construction of additional storage dams (for irrigation), roads, and bridges have been significant improvements that support increasing cropping area and the transport of farm produce.

Recent infrastructure developments in Myanmar include:

- Roads constructed and upgraded: 45,000 km of earthen road, 2,692 km gravel roads, and 489 km of tarred road constructed, and 3,030 roads in border areas upgraded;
- Bridges: 43 large bridges, 661 small bridges, 16 suspension bridges in border areas;
- Dams: as of 2004, 155 dams have been built and commissioned, and there are 34 dams under construction. Of these, 118 dams are located in the dry zone area of Sagaing, Bago, Magway and Mandalay Divisions.[20]

These achievements are frequently publicized by the government, reflecting their desire to demonstrate the progress that has occurred during their term of office. These changes do constitute a basic improvement in infrastructure and provide the foundation for increased, more reliable production, transportation, and distribution of agricultural and food products. Other priorities for infrastructure that is essential for supporting agriculture include provision of processing and storage facilities for agricultural crops, and improvement of the railway transport system. The government of India is involved with some projects to upgrade the rail transport system that could be of benefit to the agriculture sector.

Farm Family

The majority of farmers in Myanmar are small-scale farmers, having less than four hectares per family. The relatively high costs of agricultural inputs such as fertilizers, farm machinery, and fuel have limited the production potential of the average family farm. Net income of farm families is often further eroded by poor marketing, interventionist export policies, and the poor transport system.

By adding value to their farm product (for example, by processing), and with additional small livestock and fish farms, rural families could generate additional income to support their overall performance. We suggest that there are many opportunities to further enhance incomes in rural areas by encouraging agro-based cottage industries; for example, tourism; food preservation; handicrafts; tailoring, weaving and knitting; growing fruit trees and horticulture.

In addition to national and international investments in rural electrification, and the present development in rural roads, the removal of sanctions by Western nations — especially those being enforced through multilateral agencies — is essential to speed up this rural development.

Rural Youth

The future of rural development of any country depends on how well young men and women in rural areas are educated and trained. In Myanmar a considerable number of young people, especially in rural areas, need help in their education and vocational training. They have great potential to help in alleviating rural poverty and enhancing rural development and food security.

It is important to give job or trade opportunities to those whose academic levels are low and who have failed to gain entrance into either state agricultural institutes or Yezin Agricultural University. This problem could be overcome by creating income-generating agricultural and rural development projects and businesses. These should focus not only on field operations but should also cover all aspects of processing, storage, transportation, marketing, and entrepreneurship.

The needs and challenges for rural youth are greater than ever. In most developing countries, youth represent more than 50 per cent of the total rural population.[21] Their potential impact is tremendous; with adequate education, training, and support they could become active partners contributing to food security through sustainable development. Significantly, in Myanmar one of the few matters on which all political parties agree is the need to pay greater attention to the needs of youth.

Agri-business opportunities and entrepreneurship training for rural youth are worthwhile investments for rural development. It is a way to eradicate rural poverty and create productive farmers and farm businessmen. While male youths have the opportunity to enter military service or the police service, females tend to rely on jobs in factories producing textiles and other goods, mainly for export. Here, again, sanctions are limiting job opportunities.

Rural Health

Young children and pregnant mothers in rural areas are most vulnerable to health-related problems, and the situation is exacerbated by poor nutrition and remoteness from hospitals or health clinics. Health problems in rural communities are one of the main constraints on improving agricultural productivity and enhancing food security. The Myanmar Maternal and Child Welfare Association (MMCWA) has been achieving some success in providing maternal and child-care services and social welfare.

Another source of support comes from UNICEF (United Nations Children's Fund) and international NGOs. All thirty-five NGOs operating in Myanmar have a rural health component in their program. Using both field-based clinics and mobile clinics, the programs focus on nutrition, malaria, HIV/AIDS education, home-based care, tuberculosis, and sexually-transmitted diseases.

Availability of clean drinking water and of good sanitation are essential to solving health problems related to water. There are ongoing projects by UNICEF and international NGOs in those two areas. For more than thirty years Australia has been helping the development of better rural water supplies, especially in the dry zone, working mainly through UNICEF.

Credit must also be given to local Myanmar doctors and nurses, who do an enormous amount with scarce resources. Both Western and traditional medicines are used to treat ailments, but the rural population relies more on traditional medicines. Aid should be directed to projects which aim to identify, collect, preserve, and cultivate sources of the traditional medicines. One such project is headed by Daw Khin Win Myint at the Institute of Forestry, Yezin.

Markets

Maximizing a profit or minimizing the loss from farm produce depend on the market and on marketing strategies. In Myanmar there are some situations in which farmers do not bother to make an extra effort or to use inputs such as fertilizers on a particular crop because it has insufficient market value to make a profit. For example, a farmer may use his expensive and limited supply of fertilizer on his vegetable crop rather than on his paddy field, even though the latter is showing signs of low nitrogen, because the cash return from the vegetable crop is larger and can be realized more quickly than with rice. The farmer will have even more advantage if his farm is less than a day's journey from a city.

When deciding which crop to grow, the farmer's decision is influenced by factors such as transportation costs, fluctuating market demand, government policies, fertilizer costs and availability, and the risk of poor-quality products deteriorating before reaching the distant market. New road-works and bridges are helping to increase the marketing options for farmers by reducing the time between harvest and consumption.

Maximizing the farmers' profit margin needs information and business guidance at local, national, and international level. Farmers will respond quickly if they have access to better and more timely information about market conditions for their crops, but this calls for innovative measures to overcome gaps in communication infrastructure.

Sustainable Agricultural Development and the Environment

The current accelerated development and expansion of land under irrigation in Myanmar will inevitably result in land and water degradation problems. Land degradation includes soil erosion, salinization, rural tree decline, soil nutrient depletion, soil structure decline, soil biological decline, soil acidification, and rising water tables. The final stage of land degradation is a barren unproductive land. With an increasing population to feed, the country cannot afford to allow such degradation to occur. During a recent visit to Myanmar, we observed that some of these problems have already started to occur.

New development projects in Myanmar have environmental protection programs built into them. This is not only a responsibility of the government; the whole community must actively take part in such programs. At the local level there is now greater awareness about these problems, but a more concerted approach, through appropriate education and training, legislation and regulation, by the central government is needed.

The lessons and experience gained through the "Land Care" movement in Australia would be a good model to introduce to the intensive farming areas and the highland areas in Myanmar.

International Aid: A Role for Australia

International trade and market opportunities for developing countries are likely to be enhanced as a result of the Doha Development Agenda for world trade, where the major focus of negotiation is agriculture. Since 1 July 2003, Australia has provided tariff- and quota-free entry and a preferential trade system for goods from the least developed countries. Myanmar is a member of the World Trade Organization, and it has been suggested that Myanmar could become an important export destination for Australian goods in the long term if economic development, political stability, and the inflow of tourists lead to demand for high-value food products.[22]

One of the important roles of Australian aid in helping a developing country is to support investment in health, education, agriculture, and public infrastructure. Australia's international aid policies focus on assisting developing countries to reduce poverty and achieve sustainable economic development.[23]

Generally, the international aid agencies give preference to humanitarian assistance that focuses on health and education. Food security and agricultural development should be in the forefront of humanitarian assistance, because many health problems arise from food shortages and poor nutrition.

An intensive agricultural development program, with education, research, and extension as the main components leading to the improvement of agribusiness, could lay the foundations for sustained improvement in social, economic, and environmental conditions in Myanmar. The authors' optimism is based on an appreciation of the skills and enthusiasm of key agriculturalists in Myanmar, who are eminently capable of implementing worthwhile projects. However, the agricultural sector in Myanmar needs the support and financial backing of the international community to develop up-to-date agricultural education and training programs, to build essential infrastructure, supply equipment, and promote human resource development.

The Case of Charles Sturt University and Myanmar

Actions such as the signing of an MOU between Yezin Agricultural University (YAU) and Charles Sturt University (CSU) in 2002 demonstrate that collaboration between Myanmar and foreign agricultural organizations, in Australia, Europe, and Asia, is already occurring, despite some international barriers. It is time for the international community to work with Myanmar to help it develop a productive, viable, and sustainable agricultural sector.

In early 2004, Ms Tamara Jackson and Ms Jennifer Hardwicke, two of CSU's top final-year agricultural students, visited YAU and attended a few YAU classes. They commented in their internal report that the lecturers were highly committed, the subject content was more comprehensive than for similar subjects delivered in Australia, and that the coursework was studied in more depth. The weaknesses they noted were in the laboratory and library facilities.

Staff from CSU who have visited Myanmar concluded that Yezin Agricultural University has a wealth of potential at all levels; there is excellent leadership, and a capable and enthusiastic staff, many with experience and linkages gained from postgraduate training in Europe, USA, Asia, and Australia. Younger staff members are very willing to invest in their own futures if the opportunity is available.[24]

Active collaboration between CSU, YAU, and the various sections of MOAI would be enhanced by international support, which underpins exchanges of staff and students between the two countries and provides some essential equipment for undergraduate training and postgraduate research.

In the first instance there should be a focus on increasing rice production (yield per hectare) and water use efficiency (yield per megalitre of water). These goals are relevant in both Myanmar and Australia, and the collaboration would create a synergy that would benefit both nations. While there are many new water storages in Myanmar, careful use of this "new" water is essential if crop production is to be maximized and environmental damage minimized. Optimum utilization of the new facilities will require many well-trained and highly motivated staff. Improvements in the profitability of rice farmers would have flow-on effects to their rural communities.

CSU has considerable expertise in rice production, teaching, and research, and so is in a strong position to develop and deliver undergraduate subjects and short training courses in conjunction with YAU and MOAI staff. It would also be logical for CSU to be involved in the supervision of postgraduate projects. We envisage post-graduate students undertaking research and study involving time spent in each country, to enhance the learning experience and to establish linkages for future expansion of the program. It is also important to note that CSU has strong links, through the rice industry and the Cooperative Research Centre (CRC) for Sustainable Rice Production, with experts in the fields of rice genetics, agronomy, weed and pest control, low-cost crop assessment, fertilizer management, cold tolerance, sustainability, eating quality, storage and marketing, and economics.

For the best long-term gain, we suggest that a balance of basic and practical projects is essential at the postgraduate level. CSU has already been approached by several excellent candidates willing to undertake postgraduate projects in the fields of rice, water, and pathology.

Conclusions

Myo Win offers the following observations on the real situation of Myanmar's agriculture and rural development.

1. *Finance and capital.* Myanmar farmers know how to achieve higher yield and quality but lack finance or the capital to buy the best

seeds, fertilizers, pesticides, herbicides, and farm machinery. In the 1940s and the 1950s, rice farmers were doing well with 1.5 tonne-per-hectare yields, because there was no need for fertilizers or expensive agricultural chemicals. Cattle manure was sufficient to maintain the fertility of paddy fields. The problems came when high-yielding varieties that required more inputs were introduced, and the majority of farmers could not afford the additional costs.

2. *Agricultural knowledge and skill*. Most Myanmar farmers have sufficient local knowledge and skill in crop production. However, increasing population and increased demand for imported items have brought pressure to produce more food for local consumption and for export. The use of high-yielding varieties, as well as being more costly, requires higher inputs and special management technique skills.

3. *Agricultural and Rural Development*. By 2001 it was possible to see the big leap in agricultural activity and development that had taken place along the Ayeyarwaddy River basin. The construction of dams, bridges, roads, and irrigation canals in recent years had increased cropping areas. Farming of more kinds of livestock (particularly ducks) and of fish are carried out during the summer season, which traditionally was a period between crops.

4. *International aid and investment*. In most of the agricultural areas, basic infrastructure, such as roads and water storages for irrigation, have been built, but there is still a need for international aid and investments in agro-industries. Removing sanctions and providing aid are a long-term investment strategy for agricultural and rural development in Myanmar.[25]

5. *Future Challenges*. In line with the future challenges identified by the United Nations Commission on Sustainable Development, Myanmar's future food security and improvement of farming systems need to consider the following items.[26]

   - improving information for early warning forecasting systems for food and agriculture;
   - improving information on the trading system at both national and international levels;
   - the need for diversification of agricultural crops for both local consumption and export;

- improving post-harvest processing and storage, and transportation to markets;
- creating non-farming employment opportunities for the rural poor;
- the adoption of participatory agricultural extension for the transfer of environmentally acceptable technology and know-how to farmers;
- developing cooperation among agriculture, horticulture, and livestock units, and inland fisheries, for capacity-building, education, and research and development;
- all development programs must follow natural resource planning and conservation principles to prevent soil and water degradation;
- the agriculture sector in Myanmar has the potential to be the engine for rapid and sustained national economic growth, poverty reduction, and the generation of surplus for reinvestment in infrastructure and industrialization.

Graeme Batten offers the following comments on the opportunities for collaboration between Australia and Myanmar.

1. There is a willingness by staff at CSU and YAU and within the Ministry of Agriculture and Irrigation to collaborate;
2. Collaboration will promote leaning opportunities for both countries;
3. The window of opportunity is closing as senior staff retire and young, less-well trained and less-experienced staff must replace them;
4. International exposure for Myanmar staff and visits by CSU staff to Myanmar are essential to enable Myanmar to develop more productive, water-efficient agriculture in the future;
5. Some of the technology applied in Australia may not be suitable in Myanmar, especially where many small holdings are the norm, and it will have to be adapted, using local knowledge and experts;
6. CSU staff have experience in tropical and arid zone agriculture, especially rice production, through projects with several Asian countries and strong links with the International Rice Research Institute;
7. The best way to advance agriculture is to learn together, after pooling each other's knowledge, enthusiasm, and experiences.

Notes

This paper was based on our experience gained during our recent visits to Myanmar. We would like to thank U Tin Htut Oo, the Director General of the Department of Agricultural Planning, Ministry of Agriculture and Irrigation (DAP-MOAI) and his staff for their hospitality during our two visits in December 2002 and February 2004. We would also like to thank Professor Dr Kyaw Than, Rector, and his staff at Yezin Agricultural University for looking after us during our both visits to YAU.

Special thanks also go to Professor Yi Yi Myint and Daw Khin Oo of YAU for looking after CSUs' two final-year agricultural students, Ms Tamara Jackson and Ms Jennifer Hardwick, during their 2004 visit to YAU. Their visit and meeting with young future Myanmar farmers and agricultural scientists have given them a great impression of the people and of the potential of the country.

Finally, we thank Mr Trevor Wilson for his valuable assistance in preparing this paper.

[1]   Mr. Bertie Ahern, T.D., "Global Launch of the 2003 Human Development Report", Government Buildings, Dublin, 8 July 2003, United Nations Development Programme, Human Developments Report 2003. Available at: http://www.undp.org/hdr2003/taoiseach.html; accessed 22 June 2005.

[2]   Kan Zaw, "All-round Development in Myanmar", Seminar on Understanding Myanmar, held at Yangon ICT Park, 27–28 January 2004.

[3]   Myanmar Ministry of Foreign Affairs web site, www.mofa.gov.mm, 2004.

[4]   Kan Zaw, "All-round Development in Myanmar"; Department of Agricultural Planning, Ministry of Agriculture and Irrigation (DAP-MOAI), *Myanmar Agriculture at a Glance* (Yangon: Department of Agricultural Planning, Ministry of Agriculture and Irrigation, 2003).

[5]   J.L. McLean, D.C. Daw, and G.P. Hettel, *Rice Almanac: Source Book for the Most Important Economic Activity on Earth*, 3rd edition (Los Banos: International Rice Research Institute in association with CIAT, FAO and WARDA, 2002).

[6]   DAP-MOAI, *Myanmar Agriculture at a Glance*.

[7]   "Burma: Reconciliation in Myanmar and the Crises of Change", Conference Report, Washington DC, 21–23 November 2002.

[8]   Tin Htut Oo and Toshihiro Kudo, *Agro-based Industry in Myanmar: Prospects and Challenges*, Joint Studies on Economic Policies in ASEAN and Neighboring Countries (ASEDP) No. 67 (Tokyo: Institute of Developing Economies, Japan External Trade Organization, 2003).

[9]   K.B. Young, G.L. Cramer, and E.J. Wailes, *An Economic Assessment of Myanmar's Rice Sector: Current Developments and Prospects*, Research Bulletin 958, Arkansas Agricultural Experimental Station, Division of Agriculture, University of Arkansas (Fayetteville, Arkansas: Arkansas Agricultural Experimental Station, 1998); DAP-MOAI, *Myanmar Agriculture at a Glance*.

[10] Young, Cramer, and Wailes, *An Economic Assessment of Myanmar's Rice Sector.*

[11] Tin Htut Oo and Kudo, *Agro-based Industry in Myanmar: Prospects and Challenges.*

[12] Kyaw Than, "Current Status and Potential of Agricultural Education in Myanmar", Paper given at Australian Conference on Engineering in Agriculture, Charles Sturt University, 26–29 September 2002.

[13] G. Batten and Myo Win, "Report on a visit to Myanmar and the signing of an Agreement for Academic Collaboration between Charles Sturt University and Yezin Agricultural University", Charles Sturt University internal report, 2002.

[14] R. Meizen-Dick, M. Adato, L. Haddad, and P. Hazell, *Science and Poverty: An Interdisciplinary Assessment of the Impact of Agricultural Research* (Washington D.C.: International Food Policy Research Institute, 2004).

[15] Department for International Development (UK), "Sustainable Livelihoods Guidance Sheets" (London: Department for International Development, 2001).

[16] Khin Mar Cho and H. Boland, "Toward a Sustainable Development in Agriculture: An Analysis of Training Needs for Potential Extension Agents in Myanmar", Paper given at conference on International Research on Food Security, Natural Resource Management and Rural Development, Deutscher Tropentag, Gottingen, 8–10 October 2003. Available at: http://www.tropentag. de/2003/abstracts/full/233.pdf; accessed 22 June 2005.

[17] *Directory of International Non-Government Organizations (international NGOs) and Red Cross Movement Organizations Working in Myanmar*, compiled by International NGOs, Yangon, August 2004.

[18] Daw Naw Jenny Loo, "Country Paper: Myanmar", in *Non-Farm Employment Opportunities in Rural Areas in Asia*, edited by Tongroj Onchan, Report of the APO Seminar on Non-farm Employment Opportunities in Rural Areas, held in the Philippines, 24–29 September 2001 (Tokyo: Asian Productivity Organization, 2004). Available at: http://www.apo-tokyo.org/00e-books/ AG-05_Non-FarmEmployment/00CoverTOCFore_Non-Farm.pdf; accessed 22 June 2005.

[19] *New Light of Myanmar*, 8 October 2004.

[20] Conference Report, "Myanmar Road to Democracy: The Way Forward", Paper given at Seminar on Understanding Myanmar, held at Yangon ICT Park, 27–28 January 2004.

[21] S.T. Mancebo, F.M.L. Tuquero, and M.S. Hazelman, *Best Practices for Education and Training or Rural Youth: Lessons from Asia* (Bangkok: FAO-UN Regional Office for Asia and the Pacific, 2003).

[22] S. Bhaskaran and S. Fahey, *Australian exporters urged to target Myanmar*, Short Report No. 32 (Canberra: Rural Industries Research & Development Corporation (RIRDC), 1998). Available at: http://www.rirdc.gov.au/pub/shortreps/ sr32.htm; accessed 22 June 2005.

[23] A. Downer, "Australian Aid: Investing in Growth, Stability and Prosperity",

speech given by Hon. Alexander Downer, MP, Minister for Foreign Affairs, Parliament House, Canberra, September 2002.

24 G. Batten and Myo Win, "Report on a visit to Myanmar and the signing of an Agreement for Academic Collaboration".

25 J.H. Badgley (ed.), *Reconciling Burma/Myanmar: Essays on US Relations with Burma*, NBR Analysis, Vol. 15. No. 1 (Seattle, WA: National Bureau of Asian Research, 2004).

26 United Nations, "Sustainable Agricultural and Rural development: Trends in National Implementation", Report of the Secretary General to the Economic and Social Council, Commission on Sustainable Development, Eighth session, 24 April–5 May 2000, E/CN.17/2000/5. Available at: http://www.un.org/documents/ecosoc/cn17/2000/ecn172000-5.htm. Accessed 22 June 2005.

7

The Agricultural Sector and the Role of International Assistance in Promoting Agricultural Reform in Myanmar

John Copland

In Myanmar, the rural sector plays a dominant role in the economy and agriculture, based on Myanmar's rich natural resources, and is a major potential growth engine in overall national development. An overview of the agricultural sector will highlight the potential for international technical assistance, assistance that will need a strong humanitarian focus.

There is a wide range of agro-climatic zones in Myanmar, ranging from an equatorial zone in the south, a densely populated humid zone at the Irrawaddy [Ayeyarwady] River delta, merging in the centre to an extensive "dry zone" that is surrounded by mountain ranges and a high plateau in the east. The agricultural sector (which includes crops, livestock, fisheries and forestry) involves 75 per cent of Myanmar's population of an estimated 51 million people; it accounts for 40 per cent of gross domestic product (GDP) and two-thirds of all employment. In contrast, industry contributes only ten per cent of GDP. Consequently, changes and reforms in the agricultural sector are of national importance. The agricultural sector will continue to have a dominant role in the development of Myanmar.

Overview of the Agricultural Sector

Myanmar has abundant land and low labour costs, which give the country a comparative advantage in a number of sub-sectors, such as crops, livestock, and fisheries. Of Myanmar's 68 million hectares of land-mass, almost 18 million hectares are classified for agricultural production, and just 60 per cent of that is currently exploited. Forestry accounts for 50 per cent of the land area. Under the constitution of Myanmar, all land ownership rests with the state. Farmers have security of tenure, which is inheritable, but land rights cannot be sold or transferred. The most recent census (1993) indicates that 80 per cent of holdings are below 2 hectares and only 3 per cent are bigger than 8 hectares. In 1991, to encourage industrial agriculture, the government gave thirty-year leases of large blocks (2000 hectares each) to companies and individual investors.

Agriculture (cultivation of crops) is dominated by paddy rice production (21.5 million tonnes), oilseeds (2.1 million tonnes), and pulses (leguminous plants such as peas, beans and lentils) (2.9 million tonnes), all figures being for 2001–02. Rice is grown on 40 per cent of all cultivated land nation-wide, and centres on the delta region, although a policy of encouraging regional self-sufficiency and of increasing irrigation infrastructure has expanded rice production in other regions. The national irrigated area has doubled since 1988 to two million hectares, with only 10 per cent of irrigation water coming from groundwater services. Rice yields are lower than in other countries of the region, but higher than in Cambodia and Thailand. Two other crops are of major importance: oilseeds (including sesame, groundnut, and sunflower seeds) and pulses (including mung bean, black gram, and pigeon pea). There have been limited yield increases in oilseed production. Rice and these crops account for 75 per cent of all sown areas in the country. Horticulture, cotton, rubber, and sugarcane are of significance.

Livestock production is extensive, and traditional methods are still mainly used, although there are some commercial-scale piggeries, poultry farms, and dairy farms in peri-urban areas around Yangon and Mandalay. Large draught animals play an important part in crop production.

Fisheries are dominated by a large marine-capture supply, while the state issues fishing rights for inland fisheries. Aquaculture is not well developed.

Support for the agricultural sector is provided through the Ministry of Agriculture and Irrigation (MOAI) and the Ministry of Livestock, Breeding and Fisheries (MLBF) which have around 75,000 and 8,000 personnel respectively. There are several State Economic Enterprises, including the Myanmar Agricultural Development Bank and Myanmar Livestock and Fisheries Development Bank, each controlled by the relevant Ministry. Extension services are dominated by the Myanmar Agricultural Services of MOAI, with 14,000 field staff, which looks after crops, provides the research base and seeds, and operates around sixty farms. The MLBF has a much smaller number of field staff and is mainly focused on animal health. There is limited fisheries extension capacity in Myanmar.

There is no comprehensive agricultural policy statement available, but several public declarations have been made. The basic role of agriculture in contributing to national development is a key Myanmar national economic objective, as is the effective evolution of a market-orientated economic system. Although the national policy of moving towards a market-orientated system was declared in 1989, there still remain vestiges of central planning, such as the setting of production targets for key crops, control of credit, and the complexity of international trade permits, as well as a policy of aiming for self-sufficiency. This has resulted in a diminished role for local communities in determining local priorities — for example, watershed protection, involvement in income-generating activities such as raising small livestock, or relevant technology transfer.

Most controls on domestic markets have been lifted and there is an effective traditional marketing system. At the wholesale level, however, the lack of market infrastructure causes problems, often because there are post-harvest losses of crops that either cannot be transported in a timely fashion or stored adequately. In isolated areas, such as, for example, where other crops have been substituted for opium poppies, the lack of markets has limited the benefits of the crop substitution policy. Without markets for the new crops, the livelihood of former opium farmers is not as profitable as it was in the past.[1] Agricultural standards and related legislation need to be developed and further strengthened.

Since 1980, the agricultural sector investment and financing profile has decreased by an estimated 40 per cent to 14 per cent of overall investment.

Strong support for water resources and irrigation, which occupy 3 per cent of total land area, reflects government priorities. The Myanmar Agricultural Development Bank is the only formal source of financing for small farmers and levels of loans are low, often covering only 10 per cent of production costs.

The performance of the agriculture sector has been uneven and the rural poverty profile may be rising. The increasing number of landless rural householders, currently estimated at around 30 per cent of all rural householders, is becoming a matter of significant concern. However, if the GDP growth profile is used as an indicator, the agricultural sector must have experienced significant overall growth in recent years. The contribution of livestock to overall agricultural GDP is estimated to be 20 per cent.

Outlook for the Agricultural Sector

Current Agricultural Production

Crop production contributes 45 per cent of GDP and 18 per cent of export earnings, and employs some 63 per cent of the national labour force. The priority crops are paddy, oilseeds, pulses, and industrial crops such as cotton and sugar. As the use of fertilizer is low, there is growing concern on the one hand about the removal of vital nutrients from the soil (soil nutrient mining), and, on the other, about imbalances caused by adding nutrients. Limited use of improved seed varieties means crop yields are not as great as they could be. In the dry zone, efficiency of irrigation water use is an issue. River-pumped systems supply 45 per cent of all irrigation water. Intensification of crop production will increase farm incomes in the short to medium term, but for intensification, expansion, and diversification of crop production to occur, changes need to be made in land and irrigation policies, in the delivery and conduct of extension services, in communication of information about market signals, in provision of infrastructure to provide access to markets, and in supply of inputs. At the same time, efforts need to concentrate on the high value crops where Myanmar has a comparative advantage.

The livestock sector supports crop production by providing draught power and natural fertilizers. Pigs and poultry are the species most widely held, and are especially significant among the landless householders and poorer members of rural communities. Commercial livestock production is carried out on a relatively small scale and is underdeveloped. Traditional low-input livestock production using a natural feed base is the norm. Foot and mouth disease (FMD) of ruminants and pigs is the disease of greatest economic importance, followed by Newcastle disease in village poultry. Extension capacity is limited due to lack of trained staff and transport for field activities. With some exceptions, all components of the agricultural sector have limited data sets for planning purposes.

The fisheries sector provides two-thirds of animal protein in the diet of people. Capture fisheries provide the main supply of fish. Marine resources are now considered to be fully exploited, and new growth will probably come from aquaculture and inland fishing resources.

Agro-processing often operates below full capacity due to electricity shortages and old equipment. Utilization rates in the public sector are around half that of the private sector.

Constraints on Agricultural Development

Technical constraints are of major significance for the development of agriculture. In all agricultural sectors there is a lack of appropriate technology packages for smallholders. Research and extension programmes often do not match the needs and priorities of rural communities because there has been a top-down approach in the past. The low level of use of improved seed varieties, due to the lack of seed multiplication capacity in the public sector, is an important factor, and is compounded by the lack of significant private sector seed multiplication. A major constraint for the intensification of all facets of agriculture is the lack of available finance for high-value and high-input activities.

The limited resources available to the livestock sub-sector compromises the development of an improved animal health and production status. The presence of animal diseases such as foot and mouth disease constrains export of livestock products.

Agro-industry, as with other industries, suffers severely from the lack of suitable infrastructure support, such as modern equipment in agricultural institutions (both for research and for agro-processing), adequate electricity supplies for processing, transport facilities, support and training for staff, and an effective national wholesale marketing system.

There are also important policy constraints, such as the controls on the Rural Financial System, the absence of tradeable land rights, controls on crop production and restrictions on trade, the impact of state economic enterprises on the market system, and the limited role of local communities in their own resource management.

One policy issue that impacts strongly on the agricultural sector is that farmers only have cultivation rights to the land they occupy; they have no legal right to sell the land, to use land as a collateral asset, or to lease or dispose of land rights to other farmers, thus preventing consolidation of farms. The strict control of the conversion of rice lands for other use, such as for aquaculture, is a major constraint on the development of freshwater aquaculture. Other important policy constraints relate to rural financial services, international trade complexities, and directed production.

Financial constraints on agriculture are significant. The general economic environment in Myanmar, with distortions in exchange rates, a high rate of inflation, and an underdeveloped banking sector, all combine to limit development of the agricultural sector.

Human and institutional constraints also hamper development. The number of landless rural households is large (30 per cent) and a significant proportion of smallholders (37 per cent) own less than two hectares. Public sector staff are often under-utilized and lack sufficient resources to undertake their responsibilities. The government's research and extension system, which focuses on commodities, has limited impact on the mixed-farming systems practiced by smallholders, and hampers significantly growth in all sub-sectors.

Opportunities for the Agricultural Sector

Agricultural growth provides the most opportunities for poverty reduction, as long as the poor are deeply involved in the decision-making process. This is particularly the case in Myanmar with its predominantly rural economy. An advantage for Myanmar is also its low population density, as compared with other Asian countries. There are good opportunities for Myanmar to produce value-added goods and services which would provide employment opportunities and a better quality of life for the rural community. The cost of distortionary or restrictive policies is often greater than the cost of technical limitations, and if the technological and policy constraints could be reduced, the prospects for Myanmar's agricultural sector would be encouraging.

The Vital Role of International Assistance in Reforming Myanmar's Agriculture

Current and Potential International Assistance to the Agricultural Sector

Myanmar receives some international assistance for agricultural development, but not nearly enough given the economic importance of the sector, its significance in poverty alleviation, and the vital role such assistance can play in achieving much-needed reforms. The following list of international donor support to Myanmar is likely to be incomplete.

Multilateral Development Agencies

Agencies of the United Nations have provided long-term assistance to Myanmar's agricultural sector, often with the Food and Agriculture Organization (FAO) as the main implementing agency.

- The FAO Bay of Bengal Programme links Myanmar with all countries sharing the marine fisheries resource.
- UNICEF supports capacity building, widespread support for rural health support and an area development focus with participating NGOs. The programme budget is US$63 million over five years.
- The United Nations Development Programme (UNDP) focuses on grass-roots community development and on education and community development projects in remote areas. An important project has been the Human Development Initiative Project. There are two other possible new projects, one in community development and the other in rural micro-finance. UNDP has supported microfinance projects for several years.
- The United Nations High Commissioner for Refugees (UNHCR) supports an Agricultural and National Resource Management Project in Rakhine State which is implemented by FAO.
- The World Food Programme (WFP) has been providing assistance to refugees involving support of agricultural activities for the last ten years.

Other multilateral agencies that provide assistance to Myanmar include the following.

- The International Office for Epizootics (OIE) through the OIE South East Asian Foot and Mouth Subcommission is supporting sub-regional control of Foot and Mouth Disease programme involving Myanmar, Thailand, and Malaysia.
- The South East Asian Fisheries Development Centre (SEAFDEC) provides training research activities on marine and freshwater activities and linkages to Asian fisheries scientists.
- The Asian Development Bank (ADB) has been active in investigating investment opportunities in Myanmar.
- The OPEC Fund has agreed to support a project on oilseed and oil palm research, seed and material multiplication, farmer extension, processing, and policies. An estimated US$15 million has been allocated to the project. The OPEC Fund is also considering support with finance for two other projects, one on agricultural education and training, and a second on water resource management and small scale irrigation.

Multilateral Research Agencies

The Consultative Group for International Agricultural Research (CGIAR) has several research institutions relevant to Myanmar. The involvement of the CGIAR research institutions has been small-scale in the past, but is now increasing. The agricultural research institutions that could assist or are assisting Myanmar are listed below:

- The International Rice Research Institute (IRRI) based in the Philippines, has several large donor-funded projects throughout Asia, including in Laos and Vietnam. This Institute is the premier rice research institute in the world and has a mandate to improve rice production in Asia. Given the importance of rice in Myanmar, IRRI could assist with the technological, social and policy issues that relate to rice production in mixed-farming systems. The identification and multiplication of appropriate improved rice varieties that suit the smallholder farming system would have a major positive impact. IRRI has the world rice germplasm bank.

IRRI also has an active training programme which would enhance the human resource capacity in research and extension in Myanmar.

- The International Water Management Institute (IWMI), based in Sri Lanka, has an Asian focus in improving the management of irrigation systems. Again, given the considerable investment in irrigation systems by the Government of Myanmar, IWMI could provide useful assistance in training staff, design of irrigation systems, and efficient water management strategies for existing irrigation systems. Efficient water management would have national significance.
- The International Crops Research Institute for Semi Arid Tropics (ICRISAT), based in Hyderabad, India, and has the mandate for research on pulses. Linkages to ICRISAT would provide access to improved germplasm, management practices and post-harvest systems.
- The Centre for International Tropical Agriculture (CIAT), although based in South America, has an increasing profile in Southeast Asia and has a regional office in Laos. The Centre's emphasis on improving smallholder farming systems, including livestock, makes its expertize highly appropriate for the large majority of smallholders in Myanmar. CIAT is following up opportunities to increase activities in Myanmar.
- The World Fish Centre (WFC) based in Malaysia, has a mandate for developing sustainable fish management techniques, with a strong emphasis on environmental issues. Given the importance of fish as a supplier of animal protein in Myanmar, and the extensive marine and freshwater resources, WFC could make a positive contribution to the welfare of coastal, landless, and small householders.
- The Centre for International Forestry Research (CIFOR), which is based in Indonesia, has a mandate for research and development of tropical forests. Myanmar has around 50 per cent of its land-mass still forested, a major natural resource that is envied by many other Asian countries. CIFOR could assist with the sustainable management of this rich asset.
- The International Food and Policy Research Institute (IFPRI), based in Washington, may be able to provide some important policy options relevant to the agricultural sector.

There are other CGIAR centres, but their relevance to the Myanmar agricultural sector seems limited.

Bilateral Agencies

Bilateral official development assistance (ODA) has declined since the 1990s, and in 2000 amounted to US$22 million for all sectors. Countries that have provided the most support for Myanmar in agriculture are Japan, the People's Republic of China, India, Singapore, Thailand, and Israel.

Encouraging Reform in the Agricultural Sector to Improve Rural Welfare

This section provides a number of examples of instances in which assistance to Myanmar's agriculture sector has contributed directly to reform and has as a result improved rural welfare.

Two examples of assistance at the national level, and one of assistance at the international level, are given.

Crop Production: Pulses

The area of land used for production of pulses has increased greatly, from 501,000 hectares in 1985 to 2,700,000 hectares in 2001. In 2002, they were the main export crop. This increase can be attributed to several factors: pulses are subject to a much lower level of state control than other crops, so smallholders are able to respond to market signals, and demand for the product has been strong; the market for pulses and beans has been passed to the private sector, with the right to export without state intervention; and, as legumes, the nitrogen fixing ability of pulses and beans provides "built in" fertilizers input for the mixed farming system, something that is of particular importance given the limited use of fertilizers in Myanmar. In addition, the cultivation of pulses is flexible enough to fit with a range of mixed farming systems, and pulses require less water than other crops. All these factors together mean that pulses and beans provide reasonable returns for farmers, and have noticeably improved the income generation capacity of smallholders.

Fisheries: Marine Exports

A similar positive growth and trade situation exists in capture fisheries, which are mainly in the private sector. While export of marine products has increased, there is a risk that marine fisheries will expand their capacity beyond maximum sustainable yield. There is an important role for the Government of Myanmar in fishery management: it has a legitimate and important responsibility for the public good to manage Myanmar's natural resources.

Smallholder Farmers

The Human Development Initiative Project of UNDP has shown that small farmers can substantially increase their production of paddy, pulses, beans, and small livestock by an overall 30–50 per cent when they have access to credit, appropriate extension assistance, and the necessary inputs such as improved seeds and pest control. What this project has demonstrated is important, because it highlights the considerable potential of the rural community to respond with success to government and development interventions geared to smallholders. The impact of the UNDP project is now being magnified by the formation of new groups in the project areas.

Australian International Assistance in the Agricultural Sector: Two Case Studies

This section provides examples of Australian international assistance in the agricultural sector that are encouraging behavioural change and increasing rural incomes.

Crop Production: Ecologically-based Management of Rodents in Rain-fed Cropping Systems in Myanmar

Rice production is a major priority of the Government of Myanmar. Two strategies for increasing rice production are used: intensification of cropping, and increasing the area under production. Although the production of rice in rain-fed areas has increased, the level of pre- and post-harvest losses due to damage by rodents caused the Ministry of Agriculture, in mid-2002, to identify reducing rodent impacts in agriculture as an important priority. The rain-fed lowland cropping system suffers the highest losses from rodents, and these pests have the greatest impact amongst the poorer communities, which have neither the economic capital to absorb chronic losses or sporadic acute losses, nor the knowledge-base or living conditions to minimize these impacts. Rodent losses in pre-harvest rice range from 5 to 10 per cent in normal years, but losses in rain-fed rice can surge to 80 per cent and above, causing serious hardship for householders. Experience in other ASEAN countries has indicated that farmers believe that they have less opportunity to control rodents compared to other rice pests such as insects. Myanmar has limited expertize in rodent biology and control management.

Technical training is one of the major themes of the Australian project. The objectives focus mainly on the biological knowledge required to develop ecologically-based methods of management of rodent pests, and one objective has a strong sociological component that will enable us to quantify the knowledge, attitudes, and practices (KAP) of Myanmar farmers in relation to rodent management, which in turn will assist with the planning and implementation of the project. At the end of the project, a study will be made to measure its social impact.

The objectives of the project are:

- The collection of basic biological data on rodents at two scales:
    (i)   a detailed study of rodent taxonomy, habitat use, and population dynamics at two rural localities in the lowland rainfed environment in Myanmar;
    (ii) a geographically broad-ranging taxonomic and habitat survey of the rodent pests of the other major cropping environments in Myanmar;
- The experimental assessment of the applicability of existing technologies of rodent control (developed in irrigated lowland rice systems in southeast Asia). This work will be conducted primarily on-station under controlled experimental conditions;
- The assessment and analysis of an eighteen-year historical dataset on rodent damage to diverse cropping systems that is available;
- The assessment of current knowledge, attitudes and practices of Myanmar farmers to rodent damage and managements using a farmer-participatory research (FPR) approach in the dominant lowland rainfed rice-growing environment.

The methodology is based on testing the attitudes of the farmers' responses to the importance of rodents and to a range of rodent control strategies, such as an integrated trap barrier system, bund management, and judicious use of pesticide and traditional control methods. Depending on the outcome of the first and second objectives, novel methods of rodent control will be introduced into one of the village communities in the third year as a pilot study, to gauge its suitability for broader adoption. The sociological and economic (benefit-cost) impact of these activities will be monitored against the baseline survey. In the last six months, project staff will work closely with the policy and extension sections of the Myanmar Agricultural Service to develop protocols for best practice for managing rodents in rainfed lowland environments. Farmer groups in at least two regions will review whether these protocols are practical and likely to be adopted.

The Myanmar Agricultural Service (MAS) through its Plant Protection Division, the lead institute, will collaborate with the Central Agricultural Research Institute and the Yezin Agricultural University. The three-year project received about AUD$400,000 from the Australian Centre for International Agricultural Research (ACIAR), with the Division of Sustainable Ecosystems of Australia's Commonwealth Scientific and Industrial Research Organization (CSIRO) as the implementing agency.

Six months prior to the end of the project, there will be a major workshop for farmers and local extension staff involved in the village-level study in order to present key outputs to extension staff and farmer representatives drawn from other regions. MAS officials involved in developing national policy for rodent management will be invited to attend this workshop. The project will be linked regionally with a network of rodent scientists and extension specialists who have been trained during previous ACIAR and Australian Agency for International Development (AusAID) projects in southeast Asia, and with the IRRI Rodent Ecology Work Group.

The project highlights the following issues:

- The essential involvement of the rural community in the primary definition of the rodent problem, selection of possible interventions, and adoption of management strategies within the context of a mixed farming system;
- The importance of having sufficient biological knowledge to develop integrated pest management strategies; for example, taxonomic information on the several rodent species in Myanmar;
- Developing the spirit of collaboration between the Ministry of Agriculture and Irrigation institutions that could lead to future synergistic opportunities;

- Improved income generation for smallholders, if an effective control methodology is established;
- The provision of "on the job" training for MAS staff and postgraduate students at Yezin Agricultural University will consolidate and update the technical knowledge-base of agricultural scientists and extension officers on one of the most serious rice production constraints relevant to poor farmers;
- The linkage and integration of Myanmar scientists into international rodent networks will be beneficial and enhance sustainability;
- The project could provide a national strategy on rodent control that will have positive impacts on national food security and export potential.

Livestock Production: Improved Village Poultry Production Through Control Of Newcastle Disease Epidemics

The priorities of the livestock sector stated by the Government of Myanmar are:

- Integrated development in the livestock sector;
- Self-sufficiency in livestock products and production of exports for surplus;
- Intensification of research and development activities;
- Socio-economic development of householders in the livestock sector.

Although the strategy to achieve these objectives was not clearly articulated, these sector priorities were of paramount importance to ACIAR when selecting which livestock project to support.

It is estimated that 30 per cent of householders are landless, that about 23 per cent of the rural population lives below the poverty line, and that about 40 per cent lives close to that line. Food alone costs 60–70 per cent of total expenditure, leaving little disposable income for other requirements such as education, health, and shelter. Income-generation and food security are of central importance to these householders.

The overall objective of the project to control Newcastle disease in village poultry is to improve food security and income-generating opportunities for rural communities in Myanmar.

Village poultry are spread throughout Myanmar. Poultry are a source of income and provide high-quality dietary protein for village householders. However, it is a low output animal husbandry system because there are severe losses due to epidemics of Newcastle disease, often twice a year, during the monsoonal changes. According to the 2001–02 census, the total chicken population in Myanmar is estimated to be 48 million. Of these chickens, approximately 40.8 million (85 per cent) are village chickens and the remainder are commercial layers and broilers. The consumption of poultry meat and eggs is widely accepted in Myanmar.

Village poultry production requires only a small investment of capital, thus providing opportunity for the rural poor. Women and children are often the main keepers of poultry. One bird is sufficient for one family meal and no long-term storage is required. There is a functional market system for the sale of poultry through middlemen and there is a constant strong demand for poultry meat and eggs. Another advantage is the ability to store eggs for several days without refrigeration in village environments. Eggs are a flexible source of high-value protein, small in size, with acceptable prices and reasonable shelf-life. Poultry can be kept by landless householders and peri-urban dwellers. The labour inputs of village poultry are not high, with the feed-base mainly household scraps, rice bran, and what the birds can scavenge from the environment. Poultry production responds quickly to improved animal disease control. There is a choice for village poultry keepers of either improving their food security by consuming the eggs and poultry meat or by increasing their income by sale of the meat and eggs.

The technology for control of Newcastle disease is relatively robust with the ACIAR developed I2 Newcastle disease vaccine which is a thermo-tolerant live vaccine. The vaccine does not need to be kept all the time in a fridge (cold chain) and has a longer shelf-life than other Newcastle disease vaccines in tropical environments. However, as a biological agent, it does require careful storage and handling. Myanmar, through an earlier FAO project, currently produces large numbers of I2 Newcastle disease vaccine doses, estimated to be around 40 million per year. Vaccine production is expected to increase to 60 million a year as regional vaccine units start production.

The project objectives are:

- To enhance the production, quality, and distribution of thermostable Newcastle disease vaccine in Myanmar;
- To develop appropriate extension materials to enhance sustainable

usage of Newcastle disease vaccines and to improve the capacity of government staff in extension methodologies;

- To improve the capacity of government staff to diagnose the major diseases of village poultry;
- To determine the major constraints to the production of village poultry in Myanmar, and to specifically evaluate the impact of Newcastle disease and the effect of vaccination;
- To characterize genetically field isolates of Newcastle disease virus from Myanmar and to confirm the efficacy of I2 vaccine against these isolates.

The two-and-half-year project received about AUD\$400,000 from the Australian government. The main partners are the Livestock Breeding and Veterinary Department of the Ministry of Livestock and Fisheries and the University of Queensland.

The methodology for achieving the objectives is strongly focused on integrating a two-way linkage between the Livestock Breeding and Veterinary Department of the Ministry of Livestock and Fisheries with the State or Division livestock staff and the project villages, some of whom have nominated village livestock field staff. All the villages were selected on the basis of being representative of the traditional village in terms of size, location (away from townships), and willingness to be involved in the project. Some selected villages were already involved in varying degrees with current national Newcastle disease control activities. The responses and reactions of villagers to all aspects of the project have been positive.

A major first task was to identify the major constraints to village production in Myanmar, as formal data on village production constraints was limited. Monthly data on poultry production from 307 households were collected. An analysis of the data confirmed that the two major constraints were mortality in adult birds due to Newcastle disease and poor survival of chickens up to 6 weeks of age.

Monthly chicken mortality fluctuated at around 10 per cent, with peaks of up to 50 per cent, usually associated with the monsoonal climate changes. The causes of the mortality were predation of chicks by birds (32 per cent), rats (31 per cent), snakes (17 per cent), dogs (15 per cent), cats (2 per cent) and other causes 2 per cent. Malnutrition of chickens was also noted as a constraint to survival by decreasing their "escape reflex" that would help protect them from predators. Among adult poultry Newcastle disease caused high losses.

Analysis of the data clarified two strategies for sustainable poultry production. The first is confinement and supplementary feeding of chickens, and the second is vaccination of adults and growers with I2 Newcastle disease vaccine. The chickens are confined at night to reduce predation, allowed out to scavenge during the day, and are fed local broken rice as a food supplement. These strategies have been integrated into householder activities in order to reduce the labour inputs and to facilitate adoption of the technology. The preliminary results have indicated a marked reduction of predation and reduced loss of adults from Newcastle disease.

Based on the findings of the project, appropriate extension material has been developed for householders throughout Myanmar.

To support vaccine quality, several workshop and training sessions have been conducted with laboratory and field staff. These sessions have helped build the linkages between central and field livestock officers. A number of Myanmar staff were able to visit Laos for a refresher course on vaccine production. Essential laboratory support has been provided to the vaccine and diagnostic laboratories. The Australian project team from the University of Queensland assists in the implementation of the project and provides the training sessions.

This project highlights the following achievements:

- Government extension and animal health officials have a stronger understanding of the needs and priorities of village householders. This has national significance for the Livestock Breeding and Veterinary Department;
- The livestock research and extension team understands better the smallholder mixed farming systems and the competitive calls on householders' time and funds. There is a growing appreciation of the cultural and socio-economic environment for the development of appropriate technical assistance;
- A viable link and two-way interactions between the Livestock Breeding and Veterinary Department and the Vaccine Production Unit has been established. The negative impact of vaccine failures in the field and the need for quality control were highlighted, and the responsibilities and roles of all parties involved in the delivery of vaccine to householders has been strengthened;

- The limited formal field data about village poultry, which can be used as a planning tool throughout Myanmar, have been upgraded;
- The project provides opportunity for the landless and for women to be involved in income-generation, with reduced risk of losses from Newcastle disease over which they had no control in the past;
- Staff of the Livestock Breeding and Veterinary Department have been able to make contacts with other ASEAN scientists as a result of a visit to Laos;
- A cost-recovery system for supply of vaccines to rural communities, a concept that has been tested in other poultry projects in Africa, has been developed;
- Overall food security has improved for householders involved in the project.

The implementation of this poultry disease strategy has national benefits for Myanmar:

- It demonstrates the relevance of an integrated research and extension system at the village, state, and central levels for improving smallholder livestock production. This experience is applicable to other major diseases such as FMD;
- The establishment of an epidemiological village data-bank provides a model for planning programmes at the village, tract, division, and national levels of animal health and livestock extension activities. The epidemiological skills can also be used to monitor other animal diseases;
- It demonstrates the importance of establishing research and extension priorities relevant to rural householders in order to enhance their adoption and sustainability. The spill-over of benefits from this project has significant potential to enhance existing practices nation wide.

Conclusion

Myanmar has a rich natural resource base in the agricultural sector, a relatively low population density, low-cost labour, and rural communities receptive to technical improvements such as animal disease control. The agricultural sector has grown in the last few years; pulses and marine fisheries are major growth areas. The constraints to greater development are a lack of rural credit, an effective commodity-based research and extension system, and complex export and trade policies and mechanisms. Macro-economic factors such as exchange rates, the role of banks in the agricultural sector, and infrastructure deficiencies in areas such as rural electrification, transport and markets, hamper growth. International technical assistance in the agricultural sector would enable Myanmar to develop these national assets further and to reduce poverty among the rural majority.

Myanmar has received limited international assistance over the last ten years, mostly through United Nations agencies such as UNDP, FAO, and WFP. Japan, the People's Republic of China, India, Singapore, Israel, and Thailand have provided bilateral support. International assistance has indicated that if there are appropriate extension and marketing systems, a 30 per cent increase in rural incomes can be achieved on a wide scale. Selected CGIAR institutions, such as IRRI, ICRISAT, CIFOR and others, have the potential to increase their assistance to facilitate a more productive and sustainable national rural development programme.

The realignment of research and extension approaches and methodology in a mixed farming system is important for improving food security in Myanmar. Some major benefits common to the two ACIAR projects described above include building linkages between research and extension relevant to smallholders and landless householders, and providing scientists with training for disease and rodent control through models that can be replicated in other areas. These two projects provide a model for linking the research system to farmers, generating income for poor households, assisting women and disadvantaged rural communities such as the landless, and improving food security. The projects provide opportunities for scientists from Myanmar to link with ASEAN counterparts. These two projects, and similar international technical assistance, make a national impact on food security and poverty reduction.

Note

[1]   A. Ashayagachat, "WFP calls on Burma to ease travel curbs", *Bangkok Post*, 16 September 2004.

References

Ashayagachat, A. "WFP calls on Burma to ease travel curbs". *Bangkok Post*, 16 September 2004.

Asian Development Bank. *Outlook for 2003*. Manila: Asian Development Bank, 2003.

Asian Development Bank. *Key indicators for 2003*. Manila: Asian Development Bank, 2003.

Asian Development Bank. *Myanmar Economic Update, 2001*. Manila: Asian Development Bank.

ESCAP. "Assessment of Water Resources and Water Demand by Users Sectors". In *Water Resources and Water Demand by User Sector in Myanmar*. New York: United Nations, 1995.

Food and Agriculture Organization and Government of Japan. *Review of Forestry and Related Legislation, Policies and Practices and Their Impact/Implementation on Sustainable Forest Management and on the Model Forest Approach to SFM In Myanmar*. 2002.

U Khin Win. *A Century of Rice Improvement in Burma*. Los Banos: International Rice Research Institute, 1991.

Ministry of Agriculture and Irrigation. *Myanmar Agriculture in Brief, 2000*.

Ministry of Livestock and Fisheries (personal communication.)

Ministry of Agriculture and Irrigation (personal communication)

Livestock Breeding and Veterinary Department (personal communication.)

Food and Agriculture Organization website.

United Nations Development Programme website.

III

Perspectives on National Reconciliation and Civil Society Development

8

Civil Society and Legitimacy: The Basis for National Reconciliation in Burma/Myanmar

David I. Steinberg

Introduction

The concept of *civil society* is now an internationally fashionable topic of academic discourse. Its original popularity in Western intellectual circles, where civil society is considered as a requisite for a democratic society, has been enhanced as this theme has been picked up in non-Western states: theorists from many countries reexamine their histories to determine whether civil society had historic roots in their own cultures and, if so, in what forms it may have existed.[1] Thinking about civil society is thus a growth industry. Although both the term itself and the institutions that we call civil society have profoundly important and positive connotations in many societies, especially in the West, this is not universally true. In some states the concept is not generally known. In China, for example, "civil society" has been considered in official circles a pejorative term, one that implies anti-state activities and threats to the monopoly of political power held by the Chinese Communist Party. It has thus often been considered anathema by the regime.[2]

Why specifically might one be interested in civil society, however defined, and why in Myanmar?[3] The social science literature is replete with illustrations of its importance, at least in the American context, and now more broadly. De Tocqueville, writing over one hundred and fifty years ago, pointed out that the interest and phenomenon of private Americans coming together to pursue some common purpose at the local level were singular enough to warrant comment, as this was rare in the Europe of his time. More modern literature stresses four aspects of civil society that have substantial impact on governance.

The first is that when people group together to resolve problems or promote common interests, a degree of limited trust, also called *social capital*, is created that is related to the purposes of the group — that is, to goals characteristic of and generated by such association.[4] This trust, so goes the theory, may then be translated over time into political trust, and thus societies that have such organizations are likely to have more representative and stable governments, while societies that lack a vigorous civil society sector usually have political problems, often in relation to the legitimacy of their governments. This proposition may appear overly simplistic, but there seems to be some anecdotal evidence in its favour, although it would be difficult to quantify in any meaningful sense temporally and across cultures.

The second aspect of civil society relates to pluralism. It is obvious that where civil society is active, pluralism is more prevalent, and pluralism is one essential ingredient of the democratic process. Even if such organizations have been proscribed at a level of national influence or are in part controlled nationally by the state, at a local level they can affect how power is distributed there and mitigate the excesses of over-centralized administrations, making them more responsive to local needs. In other words, civil society organizations can encourage elements of good local governance by insisting on appropriate state performance levels and even encouraging the state to adhere to its own pronounced regulations, such as on the environment or social issues. Although in highly authoritarian or centralized states civil society organizations, even at local levels, may be viewed by governments with a degree of anxiety or suspicion, in fact they may be supportive of some of the state's goals and strategies, if not its tactics.

The third positive aspect of civil society is that a medley of such organizations, each concentrating on a common problem, indirectly encourages broad diversity of interests and discourages orthodoxy — the bane of democracy. The question of orthodoxy (see below) is related to the concept that power is personalized, as is loyalty, and that information is power, and so the media and communications should be under state control or censorship.

The fourth is that civil society groups, especially at the local level, can help supply needed goods and services that the state either cannot or will not provide, or that the state intentionally ignores or considers outside of its purview.

We will explore below how civil society, through support of good governance, may assist in the process of legitimation of any regime, either by helping to make up for deficiencies in the supply of basic goods and services (for example, health, education, micro-credit, and so on), or because the very existence of such non-governmental groups imparts either internal or external legitimacy to a government. Civil society organizations may also help provide an expression of identity, and thus at least localized legitimacy, to various ethnic minorities.[5] Civil society organizations could also help the reconciliation process by highlighting issues that need to be addressed in the negotiations necessary for reaching compromise or concluding peace, and by facilitating understanding of majority-minority relations among the minorities themselves.

It is important to note here that the term "civil society" has no indigenous equivalent in Burmese, indicating that as a concept it is relatively new and probably not well understood.[6] The Myanmar government does not use the term; only Aung San Suu Kyi has mentioned it, and that rarely. But if — or better, because — there is no specific Burmese term for the concept, in the Confucian tradition of the rectification of names we need to define our terms before we can apply the concept of civil society in some meaningful way to the Burma/Myanmar context.

No account of civil society should regard its development as a panacea for the ills either of society or of the political process. The very concepts of "power", "authority", "hierarchy", and "orthodoxy", which we will discuss at the close of this essay, that affect the formal institutions of governance, also affect civil society organizations institutionally and through their personnel, since such concepts are essentially primordial values. Although it is likely that these forces can be at least somewhat mitigated by the private nature of the organizations, civil society groups cannot be considered as the *deus ex machina* that will alone transform society into a democracy, however necessary they may be to the democratic process.

On the Rectification of Names and Terms

Civil society is basically defined as those organizations — local, national, or international — that are autonomous and/or independent of government and the state. They transcend the individual and the family, and are collective, organized, and have some continuity. They operate in the space, often constricted, between the state and the individual.

This is, however, obviously too sweeping a definition, as no organization in any modern state is completely devoid of links to the government at some level or other. Minimally, organizations may have to be registered or incorporated (in Myanmar under the *Companies Act* or under other legislation),[7] or taxed or not taxed, but at some level most organizations are accountable to the state in some manner, or are subject to local or national legal strictures, provisions, or scrutiny, or even intentional indifference. In each society, the classification of civil society will have to take into account the particularities of the power structure, the political system, traditional patterns of control and authority, economics, and the cultural environment. Most broadly, the term "civil society" might encompass businesses, non-profit firms, international private organizations, political parties, the media, and other groups.

In Myanmar, it may be appropriate to categorize a variety of organizations in order to clarify the distinction between civil society organizations and other groups. One might develop seven separate classifications for organizations outside nominal governmental institutions, only the last of which, in the contemporary Myanmar context, we will define as civil society. These seven categories are:

1. State entities, including the state economic enterprises — the public sector, including state-owned or controlled industries, corporations, and businesses;[8]
2. Publicly-supported and controlled, but ostensibly somewhat autonomous, citizens' organizations, such as the Union Solidarity and Development Association (USDA) and a host of other groups that serve state needs and objectives. These are also sometimes

known as GONGOs — government organized (or owned) non-governmental organizations. The leadership of these organizations is generally chosen by, or in some way responsible to, some government entity;

3. The private for-profit sector — the business community;
4. Recognized non-state-sponsored political parties;
5. The media, which in Myanmar are completely under state censorship or authority;
6. Organized groups that are, or have been, in rebellion against the authority of the state;
7. Civil society organizations — those groups that have some reasonable autonomy of action, choose their own leadership, are not for profit, and are essentially privately funded.

Within this last category, civil society organizations can be distinguished according to other characteristics: first, whether an organization is a national, regional, or local body; second, whether an organization is based on membership, or whether it is a body such as a foundation, that has a board and staff, and provides assistance to other groups; or third, whether an organization operates its own programmes but does not seek popular participation in its governance.

Another relevant distinction should be made among three different types of programme that civil society groups pursue:

1. Representational groups (such as non-profit chambers of commerce);
2. Advocacy groups (for example, environmental organizations);
3. Service or programme-oriented groups (focusing on, for example, health, education, training, poverty alleviation, or other activities).

When organizations of this third category are based at the local level, in villages or urban ward areas, and involve membership or popular participation, they are sometimes called "community based organizations" (CBO).[9] Advocacy organizations at local levels may be termed "social movement organizations" (SMO), and because much of their advocacy has been outside the political pale, until recently they have been ignored.[10]

Excluded from this list are movements that have been, or may yet be, politically powerful, but that are at present ephemeral in structure or purpose. In the Myanmar context, these might include amorphous student movements, since the state has outlawed student organizations, and demonstrations by members of the *sangha* (Buddhist clergy) against perceived inequities or insults. The authorities have strong fears concerning the potential for these groups to cause trouble for the state and to instigate pro-democracy activities.[11]

Excluded also from this organizational list are foreign organizations, although their influence may be profound. Foreign private business investment, religious organizations with international connections, groups run by resident aliens, and international NGOs, some of which can be exceedingly important in the development of civil society, should be separately considered (see below). So, too, civil society groups that operate across Myanmar's frontiers, most often in Thailand, are a separate category, even though some perform cross-border services and activities.

In other countries, the business sector and political parties may be grouped as part of civil society, but in many states they operate under stringent regulation, so that their activities are not autonomous. Civil society organizations may also be temporally defined. In South Korea under dictatorial governments, the private sector was dependent on the state, and could not act autonomously; it should not have been considered as an element of civil society, although the situation changed after political liberalization. We have excluded the Myanmar business sector because it is weak in a country where credit is manipulated by the state and where such activities are carefully monitored and controlled by the government.[12]

In Myanmar, anomalies abound. How should one consider the Church of England — which has an official link with the state through a state-approved ideology but which operates with considerable local autonomy? What about the *sangha* in Myanmar, where the structure and hierarchy, as well as the registration of monks, are controlled, but where there is considerable latitude for local action at the village level, and where popular participation in religious rituals is a form of civil society activity? These issues indicate that civil society, even at the theoretical level, must be defined by each analyst according to the culture studied and the purposes of any particular scrutiny.

The State and Civil Society in Myanmar

In 1999, this writer wrote, "Civil society died under the Burma Socialist Programme Party (BSPP); perhaps more accurately, it was murdered".[13]

Was this statement accurate, and is it true today? There is no doubt that a vigorous civil society had existed in the colonial period, even though certain political groups were proscribed.[14] Under the civilian hegemony of the Anti-Fascist People's Freedom League (AFPFL), considerable latitude existed for the formation of private organizations, which included institutions such as schools and nationally important groups. The AFPFL ran its own stable of mass organizations, to ensure support for the government, and although there were laws (some dating from the British period) that were restrictive of some political activity, and political arrests seemed sometimes arbitrary, there is no doubt that civil society flourished, as did a major political opposition, even under the unified period of the AFPFL (until 1958). It may be argued that the British ban on political activity, which was imposed for much of the colonial period, in fact encouraged the growth of civil society through ostensibly religious organizations that had a nationalistic agenda — such as, for example, the Young Men's Buddhist Association. The media, although subject to considerable governmental influence, was relatively autonomous and vigorous in its independent judgment about state policies and activities, and some newspapers often expressed views that were in alignment with those of the opposition left-wing political party — the National Unity Front, the above-ground arm of the Burma Communist Party.

Following the military coup of 1962, as Ne Win forced the country into its socialist straitjacket, businesses and most organizations (for example, private schools) were nationalized, forced into the service of the state, or politically neutralized. It is true that some locally autonomous organizations, such as church groups and the Young Men's Christian Association (YMCA) and the Young Women's Christian Association (YWCA) continued to function, but they were most circumspect in their activities and statements. This is not to say that at some local levels people did not form some groups that served their needs, but these seemed to have been informal means to deal with very local problems. Advocacy groups were co-opted, neutered, or eliminated. In that sense, then, the above quotation is accurate for registered advocacy organizations.

The exception to this pattern was the *sangha*, which for years the government had tried to control by registering all monks, because insurgents and criminals could quietly don a yellow robe and essentially become immune to identity or arrest. It was not until 1980 that the state succeeded in registering the *sangha*.[15] Even then, with the hierarchy and organization firmly under the control of the state, at the village level people did gather together to perform religious rites and social activities in an autonomous manner. In that sense, because it was part of the mainstream of Burmese culture, some civil society activities and groups continued to function and were important in the society.[16] Kyaw Yin Hlaing and Brian Heidel have demonstrated that even in that dour period, at local levels, and often surreptitiously, there existed organizations that were not ephemeral and that operated beneath the government's ideological radar screen.

Organizations that purported to have some national influence or advocacy role, however, were taken over in the service of the state. Eventually, after some dozen years of rule by decree, during which all political activity was banned except for the formation of the Burma Socialist Programme Party, which operated under military domination and control, the constitution of 1974 mandated a single-party mobilization system that virtually destroyed any possibility for the existence of an independent media, an influential private for-profit business sector, or a non-profit sector (except for established religious organizations that came under increasing intelligence scrutiny).

During the 1988 "Rangoon spring", the period of late July–early August and before the coup of 18 September 1988, when state authority eroded and then virtually disappeared, there was a flowering of all kinds of independent civil society groups and media outlets that reflected a release from the stringency of authoritarian rule.[17] This was, however, short-lived.

Since that time, under the SLORC and the SPDC, there has been a growth in NGO activities of various kinds; both indigenous NGOs and international NGOs have mushroomed. Heidel estimates that there are some 214,000 community-based organizations throughout the country, and he believes that in per capita terms Myanmar rates highly in comparison with similar states in the region. He has conducted the only survey undertaken so far, and although this is admittedly incomplete, he extrapolates from the groups he has consulted. He believes that there are some 270 indigenous NGOs in the country. Of these, 48.1 per cent are religious, 23.7 per cent are parent-teacher associations, and 20.9 per cent are social groups.[18] Another list specifically indicates that there are sixty indigenous NGOs in Yangon that conduct activities in other areas.[19] Religiously oriented NGOs have been a vital element in civil society.

Although Christian groups have predominated, Buddhist, Muslim, and Hindu philanthropic organizations have continued to exist and service the needs of their clientele.

Although Heidel's research has revealed that civil society has been expanding even under the auspices of a government that has been rigid in many ways, political advocacy groups at a national level are still essentially proscribed. The BSPP and successive military regimes have in effect prevented the development of such advocacy organizations. The political, social, and legal restrictions on the operation of such groups are still in place and are substantial. As Zunetta Liddell observed, "Overall, the prospect for the development of civil society in Burma is grim."[20] Yet, because the state has not succeeded in supplying needed goods and services to the population, poverty and deprivation have increased; and as they have increased, so has the need (and opportunity!) for various programmatic NGOs grown. Indigenous organizations have been supplemented by NGOs from abroad.

Returning to the author's quotation at the beginning of this section, it must now be asserted that only the advocacy groups have been "murdered", and even among them, many have existed virtually underground. However, this situation may be evolving.

Beyond the Fringes: International Non-governmental Organizations

International NGOs play a special role in Myanmar. Those with resident in-country staff number in the dozens and operate in a wide variety of fields, including health, education, agriculture, micro-credit, and rural development.[21] They are of varied nationalities and some operate under UNDP auspices.[22] They supplement state-provided services, or offer services that the state has found it impossible to provide or that the state has, for whatever reason, ignored. In some sense, these groups both assist the people to improve the quality of their lives and the state to achieve some of its longer-range social plans.

Some international non-governmental organizations strive to influence Burmese nationals who have fled the country as well as those who have remained behind. These include international humanitarian organizations (often that have some religious affiliation) that work both internally and externally to supply social services; expatriate Burmese advocacy groups bent on "regime change" in Myanmar; and international human rights advocacy organizations. Each has its own perceived niche and role.[23]

The government has been often suspicious of international NGOs, and rather than create a transparent and generally applicable set of administrative rules under which each might operate its own programmes, the state has dealt with each separately. This writer in 1994 attempted to convince the SLORC that such a set of rules would be in the interests of all concerned, including the Burmese people, but to no avail.[24] As a result, some NGOs operate under memoranda of understanding (that is, an official, written mandate to operate) and some on the basis of verbal assurances.[25] This reduces the effectiveness of such groups, which must spend inordinate amounts of time dealing with bureaucratic regulations that are often unclear and may be subject to inconsistent interpretation.

In addition to their value in supplying goods and services, international NGOs also provide a counterpart, and role model, for the local organizations through which they work and for local staff. Thus, indirectly but importantly, they assist in building local civil society organizations, and they train individuals who may have a key role in the local context (and sometimes in an international context) and who can carry on the work through indigenous groups at some future date. In this way the international NGOs may be helping lay the groundwork for some form of national reconciliation.

Expatriate advocacy groups are devoted to the re-establishment of civilian rule in Myanmar and the retirement of the military from the political arena. Most do so through supporting recognition of the results of the May 1990 elections — that is, the installation of the NLD as the government in power. Although there has been some attrition of the vehemence of this position as the years have passed, these organizations (often supported by other international organizations, such as the Soros Open Society programme and the US Congress) still engage in strong media campaigns through their own media outlets, which have proliferated, as well as through the established international media.

Some among them believe that the National Convention to draft a new constitution (which began in 1993, and after several starts, resumed in December 2005) provides perhaps the last chance to influence military policy and a new government, and have therefore advocated joining that process toward national reconciliation. Others have strongly disagreed, and the debates between various groups have been vigorous and vituperative.[26] Should a new civilian or "civilianized" government come into power, be stabilized, and be generally accepted internationally, these organizations would likely lose the most.

International human rights organizations have characterized the Myanmar government as one of the world's most repressive regimes. They have attempted, with considerable success, to mobilize international public opinion in support of their aim of getting the military regime to step down. The cause has struck a chord among the international community, in part because the situation of the country is presented simplistically and without ambiguities, in part because of the parlous state of the Myanmar people, and in part because it is believed that regime change is possible. Yet, if one looks at history, the BSPP period was as authoritarian as the present (or even more so), but was less subject to international scrutiny, because the society was essentially closed to external contacts, because the international public and private mechanisms for monitoring human rights were less developed,[27] because the massacres of 1988 had not taken place, and most importantly, because there was no iconic figure like Aung San Suu Kyi with whom to identify. These factors have changed the nature of Burma/Myanmar's foreign relationships, and especially of its relationship with the United States.

The importance of the NGO communities working on the periphery should not be ignored.

> Although their [indigenous and international NGOs and their local staffs] access to the most needy rural populations (including internally displaced persons) is highly restricted, and the political aspects of their programmes are usually obscured by a humanitarian-welfare gloss, these pioneer NGOs have played an important role in the development of civil society networks, under the most difficult and repressive of conditions.[28]

Legitimacy and Civil Society

Policy-makers — both those concerned with humanitarian assistance and the plight of the poor, and those concerned with either the withdrawal of the present military government or its continuation — have to make a judgment, which often is not articulated, concerning the roles of both indigenous and international NGOs in Myanmar. For those who believe that the present military regime should withdraw, change, or evolve into something else, the operations of both types of NGO provide added legitimacy to the government. As Alagappa has indicated,[29] one of the elements that contributes to the legitimacy of a government is the provision of basic and appropriate services to the populace (what he terms the "performance" criterion). In this respect, the present government of Myanmar has failed. However, that failure has been somewhat mitigated in certain areas through the operations of the international and domestic NGO communities.[30]

At the same time, the very existence of local NGOs, and the presence and operations of the growing numbers of international NGOs working or seeking to work in Myanmar, also legitimate the government. Aung San Suu Kyi has written, "Whether it is governments, United Nations agencies, or international NGOs, any help they give Burma should be conditional on progress toward democratization."[31] The question is whether the activities of international NGOs can assist in moving the country toward democratization, or whether their assistance should be contingent on prior movement. Insofar as the international NGOs that operate in-country and abroad are seen to support liberalization of the regime as well as the aspirations, if not the operations, of the opposition, this is used by the military regime as a means both to de-legitimate the NLD, for being the "axe-handles" (or tools of foreign interests), and to legitimate itself by appealing to the Myanmar people's strong sense of nationalism, which often borders on xenophobia. Local NGOs, now growing in numbers, can also provide a sense of legitimacy for the state, and indeed have been helpful in acting as go-betweens in some delicate negotiations between minority groups and the central government.

If one accepts as accurate the statements by the SLORC/SPDC that their goal is movement, at their own pace, toward "democracy" (whether "disciplined" as they have indicated, or otherwise), then fostering the growth of civil society will prove to be in their (as yet unrecognized) long-range interests, even if they are dubious about its shorter-range impact. Both indigenous and international NGOs, through their presence and their work, can eventually help to legitimate any government that comes to power.

It is also evident that the idea of allowing the populace to organize legal gatherings for any non-state approved purpose (even if the purposes are not anti-state) causes a degree of anguish in present government circles. Yet the development of pluralism, despite all the dangers that any authoritarian government would perceive, is something that would actually be in the interests of the state. Without a capacity for the legal, peaceful expression of diverse opinions, there is great potential for outbreaks of intense violence when significant elements of the populace consider that conditions are no longer tolerable, as has been witnessed in many societies and in Burma in 1988. A prescient state would be wise in its own interests to allow the development of pluralism that could mitigate potential chaos. If, as the SLORC/SPDC has charged, it was the chaos of 1988 that "forced" the military to take over (although there are many who question this justification), then prudent management would suggest that it would be wise to establish channels for the expression of popular opinion.[32]

The Role of Civil Society in National Reconciliation

It is highly unlikely that national reconciliation will take the form of a treaty-like single event. Rather, it is likely to be a gradual process that involves the building of trust, and it will probably have to be reinforced or renegotiated over time. To achieve successful national reconciliation, a complex situation of conflicting interests — of ideas, institutions, and attitudes — will have to be mediated. Areas of conflict that will have to be dealt with include not only the most obvious contention between the military and the National League for Democracy, but also conflict between the military and the minorities, amongst the minorities themselves, and conflict over the determination of the leadership within each minority. In addition, the protagonists will have to find some way of getting the outcome of the reconciliation process accepted by the international community.

One device that has been used in other countries and that could possibly be of use in such a process is a "truth commission", which would provide a mechanism for attempts to purge the tensions of the past. However, while truth commissions or the equivalent in Myanmar may be necessary or desirable, they are unlikely to satisfy many, and may lead to new forms of frustration. This is not to argue that they are inappropriate or unnecessary, but it is clear that everyone — people and government alike — must have realistic expectations about what they can and cannot achieve.[33] Such a commission would have to be distinguished from the issue of retribution against excesses by the military, either personally or institutionally.

This writer perceives seven cleavages or tensions within contemporary Myanmar that need to be mediated and reduced if national reconciliation is to take place. These are:

1. Conflict between Burman and minority nationalism — a critical variant of center-periphery relations;
2. Conflict between civil and military sectors of society;
3. Tension between the forces of globalization and nationalism;
4. Tension between tendencies towards centralization and towards pluralism;
5. Tension between orthodoxy and diversity of views;
6. Conflict among religious groups;
7. The international geopolitical rivalries that affect internal attitudes.[34]

Other, more abstract, tensions, that have to do with modes of behaviour, exist — between personalized and institutionalized decision-making, between transparency and secrecy, and between meritocratic advancement and personalized loyalty. These are intrinsic to the situation in Myanmar, and their modification will be fundamental to progress in any reconciliation process.

Some efforts towards mediation of these tensions — described below — have begun, but the very processes required have in most cases either stalled or have yet to be seriously attempted. Both international and indigenous elements of civil society have already indicated possible capacities and roles for their involvement in the reconciliation process. Even if the results are less than spectacular, the very precedent is important and the potential is evident. The Centre for Humanitarian Dialogue (Geneva, Switzerland, and Yangon) has acted as a link between United Nations Special Envoy Razali Ismail, the government, and Aung San Suu Kyi, and its involvement over several years of quiet dialogue provides one example of efforts to seek reconciliation. That the effort has not produced palpable results is not a criticism of that organization, but rather constitutes evidence that extraneous factors have caused the process effectively to dissolve. There may be other opportunities for international NGOs to contribute to this process.

Internal NGOs have had limited but significant successes and activities. The Shalom Foundation was an important intermediary in bridging the gap between the military and the Kachin Independence Organization (KIO) which facilitated the ceasefire that is still in effect. The Foundation has encouraged the KIO to participate in the National Convention, and seeks to promote the resolution of outstanding issues connected to the problems of the interaction between the Burman and Kachin communities, and between Buddhists and Christians. It encourages the employment of Kachin in various levels of government-sponsored institutions and other agencies to eliminate the hopelessness of youth so apparent in that community. It assists in leadership training as well.

The Metta Foundation has also been involved in leadership training for minorities, and it is perhaps this aspect of NGO activity — the building of capacities for both future public and private sector leadership — that is a critical contribution if national reconciliation is to have any hope for continuity. The revitalization of the education system, along with the growth of training to reflect the new requirements of modern government and non-governmental institutions, become critical elements for the reconciliation process.

Although the education and training of Burmese people must essentially be matters for internal resolution, external training in both newer disciplines and in analytical thinking, which in the past were discouraged and replaced by rote learning and the politicization of the educational process, is also necessary. From the perspective of Myanmar, the results of external training have been mixed, because many of those chosen for scholarships for external study have been reluctant to return to Myanmar. Not only does this jeopardize the state's willingness to allow students to study abroad, but it means those students contribute little to Myanmar society as a whole.

Before the coup of 1962, Burma was renowned as one of the few developing countries that had virtually no brain drain. Since that time, however, because of political repression and the lack of meaningful employment, the country has lost perhaps one per cent of its population, and those who emigrate are an educated potential elite. These estimates include neither the one million or so illegal workers in Thailand and in other bordering countries, nor the approximately 120,000 Karen and Mon refugees in camps across the Thai border. This is a loss that no country can afford to sustain. For any sort of effective development effort, major internal and external education and training programmes will be required.

Civil society, because it is close to the grass-roots, is able to anticipate and articulate the needs of local areas that the state often overlooks or to which the state is insensitive. Civil society has a vital function in helping any government to be responsive to local conditions and problems, and should therefore be viewed as necessary and supportive over the longer term, no matter how politically inconvenient it may appear at any one moment. Thus, rather than being perceived as a threat to any emerging political system, civil society should be considered as an early warning system (the proverbial canary in the coal mine) that could allow the state to make adjustments in the process of governance and development. The Burma Socialist Programme Party (BSPP) failed, as a very senior member of that government admitted, because the centralized system, although having a theoretical interest in reacting positively to local issues, was incapable of doing so because of subordinates' fears of displeasing those in higher authority in the hierarchical political system.[35] Civil society, simply because it lies outside the power structure, has a greater chance to affect positively the capacity of the state to serve the society and thus appear to be more efficacious; this could possibly extend any government's longevity and its legitimacy as well.

Although Track II diplomacy has not yet proven to be effective in the Myanmar context, this is no reason not continue the process with established players, such as the Centre for Humanitarian Dialogue, and other groups including think-tanks and research centres. There is no assurance of success, or even that positive effects will result, yet the process should not be abandoned; indeed, it should be expanded to bring as many as possible into the dialogue on all sides of the issues.[36] In January 2004, the Ministry of Foreign Affairs conducted a major seminar in Yangon to explain the situation in the country to Asia-wide members of Track II institutions and the diplomatic corps in the country. This writer has suggested that any future meeting be more open and collaborative.

Ashley South seems not very sanguine about the present role of civil society within the area of his purview, the New Mon State Party (NMSP), with which the Myanmar government has a ceasefire. He wrote, "Mon community networks within Burma have generally developed beyond the sway of the NMSP's political-cultural paradigms, which have tended to stifle the development of civil society in the party's 'liberated zones'".[37] Yet ceasefire groups may be able to "recreate" themselves as NGOs in the future if the constitutional process proceeds according to expectations. Their generally authoritarian structure may not allow for much grass-roots participation,[38] yet in some areas, such as the Kachin State, such local participation is encouraged.

In some ceasefire areas, the development of what might be termed civil society organizations may be slow. In some areas, such as the Kokang, Wa, Monghla, and Pao regions, the leadership does not give the impression of being willing to change its internal hierarchical organization (which seems to have been influenced by the Burma Communist Party authoritarian structure). In other areas, such as the Kachin region, there seems a genuine concern for grass-roots dialogue and participation. This means that among the minority groups will be found a mix of civil society organizations — some will be genuine, representative, grass-roots organizations, while others will mimic the state's authoritarian structure.

The need for civil society groups is especially important in border areas among minority groups. The International Crisis Group has noted that there is a long way to go:

> Nurturing the capacity of specific civil society organizations and networks is another important task. There is a relatively large and growing number of non-governmental development organizations (NGDOs) and particularly community-based organizations (CBOs) engaged in social welfare or development activities. There is also an intricate, insufficiently understood system of more informal social networks.[39]

One of the important roles for civil society organizations in any period of national reconciliation will be to rebuild the nation's human resource base, which has been eroded by the outflow of intellectual and economic, as well as political, émigrés. In the recent past, some international NGOs have been able to attract good Burmese staff to their employ and have sent some abroad for further training. This process is likely to be important in developing the competence of civil society groups and increasing their internal effectiveness. However, as has occurred in many public sector foreign assistance programmes of both bilateral and multilateral institutions, talented individuals are attractive as employees for international NGOs, and in turn are attracted to international NGOs, for the ability to serve, for educational opportunities, and for higher salaries. In the short term this can create a problem, because it depletes the pool of human resources available both to indigenous NGOs and to governments at varying levels should they at some stage be willing to employ such people. This danger should be recognized and efforts sought to mitigate the problem.

International NGOs have another important function. Their operations give foreigners an intimate exposure to societies in which they may, as a result, develop a continuing and professional interest, and on which they may become future specialists. Such specialists may go on to staff not only other international NGOs, but also governmental and public institutions, multilateral and bilateral, and they can bring to those positions sensitivities that are often lacking in official circles.

Civil society, as previously noted, is an attribute of, or helps create, social capital. It would be too sweeping a statement to say that there is little social capital in Myanmar. A recent study, based on a non-random sample of some five hundred people, indicated the complexity of the issue. Responses were varied, depending on the subject (institution or individual) and location. In response to the question of whether one trusts one fellow citizens, 20 per cent said yes, 23 per cent said no, and 45 per cent said it depends. But only 5 per cent indicated that they trusted the government, with 78 per cent saying no. At the same time, 33 per cent in villages believed that the SPDC cared about the individual, although 47 per cent said no. At the township level, only 9 per cent responded positively, and at the regional (state and division) level the positive figure was only 14 per cent. Trust in specific members of the SPDC varied widely, with General Khin Nyunt receiving the most favorable rating. Of the respondents, only about 10 per cent belonged to no civil organization, about 30 per cent to one, over 40 per cent to two, and about 18 per cent to three or more. The conclusions are that there is little social capital at the political level, but considerable on social issues. Since people cannot count on the state, they have to help each other.[40]

The Structure of Power in Myanmar and Civil Society

Since independence, there has been a discernable tendency for the government under any administration to attempt to centralize control. Even in the pre-independence period, this trend was evident in the writings of Aung San and his vision of a new Burmese state. In the civilian period under the AFPFL, authority was dispersed, mostly because the government was too weak to exert its imprimatur over the whole country, but the focus was on the center. As Geertz has written, "[the minorities] are catered to by a rather intricate and highly peculiar constitutional system that protects them in theory against the Burman domination that the party system tends to produce in fact."[41] The fictionalized union envisaged under the constitution of 1947 was dissolved following the coup of 1962, and has yet to be reinstituted in any form. When in 1969 a group of eminent Burmese leaders was asked by General Ne Win to recommend whether the state should be pluralistic or unitary, they opted for pluralism, but Ne Win implemented the reverse, with disastrous but predictable results. Whether the new constitution will make provision for some more decentralized approach at state or township level, or within the executive branch, or between the executive and legislative branches (let alone the judicial sector), in some manner deemed adequate or acceptable to the diverse minority groups, or even to the majority Burmans, is perhaps the most important question facing the state.

Yet the tendency to mobilize all elements of power within the hands of the government, and to institute orthodoxy, is one that should not be underestimated.[42] The government attempts to maintain orthodoxy through censorship and control of the distribution of information in any form, and by limiting the ability of people to gather together in public without government permission or surveillance. The reasons for such rigid control relate to the suspicions held by the regime, based on what has happened in the past, that the media will strongly criticize the administration, and that the private sector will go out of control and perhaps fall into foreign hands if not kept tightly constrained.

The regime is deeply concerned that personal interests will undermine wider interests, because it knows well that in Myanmar loyalties are personally based and are not oriented towards institutions, and that this has been the tendency throughout Burmese history.[43] When power and authority are conceived as having a personal orientation, it is predictable that factionalism will become a problem.[44] As power is focused on one person as a leader, an entourage develops; orthodoxy is expressed in terms of loyalty toward the leader, and toward his or her programme, and becomes a requirement. Of course, if that leader is purged, it can happen that a particular organization is decimated, as Military Intelligence was in 1982, and again, it seems apparent, in October 2004. In present-day Myanmar, attitudes of factionalized distrust permeate the political environment, and make national reconciliation extremely difficult to achieve.

These tendencies are coupled with a sense of hierarchy that is reinforced by a military command system (but which is pervasive even without that reinforcement), and this virtually makes it essential that advocacy groups which are a part of civil society (even though civil society has expanded under the SLORC/SPDC) will come under close scrutiny by the state.

Thus there is likely to be a strong sense that civil society should not threaten the unity of the state — which has been the cardinal priority of the military since independence — and that any divisiveness, whether ethnic or political or even programmatic, where the accomplishments, motives, or benevolence (*cetana*) of the state are questioned, is unlikely to be long tolerated.

The inclination towards orthodoxy has also been apparent within the National League for Democracy and among some of the dissident groups, both internal and expatriate; these groups have shown a tendency to splinter along personal grounds and will not tolerate dissent. Some members of the NLD were expelled for being "traitors" to the cause when they differed with NLD leaders on policy issues. There have been recent calls for the expansion of the NLD Central Executive Committee and for the inclusion of younger leaders to diversify power and bring in new ideas.[45] The student and expatriate opposition has split along both factional and ideological grounds. Some students in revolt have been executed by their comrades for supposedly being spies for the military. Frequently, opposition members living abroad as well as opposition supporters from academic circles, whose positions fall outside the established political parameters, are accused of being "spies" or in the pay of one side or another.

Some of the ceasefire groups have encouraged the same sorts of rigidities as did the military regime. South wrote:

> Rebel leaders tended to discourage the expression of diverse opinions, and socio-political initiatives beyond the direct control of the militarized insurgent hierarchies were generally suppressed. One consequence was the endemic factionalism of Burmese opposition politics, with most groups unable to accommodate socio-political (or personality) differences among their members; another was the suppression of pluralism in ethnic opposition circles, and the development of rigid political cultures in non-state controlled areas.[46]

As Christina Fink has written, "Even members of the pro-democracy movement find it difficult to develop the openness and tolerance required of a democratic culture... Rigid thinking, hierarchical power structures and a culture of mistrust have characterized not only the military regimes but, in many cases, the opposition groups as well".[47] She notes that constructive criticism is often viewed as a challenge rather than a contribution.

Any euphoria among observers that civil society organizations, as vital as they are to pluralism and the eventual formation of some sort of democratic structure in that state, will eschew these tendencies that pervade the society is to be avoided. If other countries are any indication, civil society organizations retain many of the same characteristics as those of the states in which they operate, albeit on a smaller scale. Such groups are often highly nationalistic, and insofar as they have even limited impact on policy, may move state policies and programmes away from more international involvement and influence.

The Burmese have exhibited considerable individualism, autonomy, and even independence in periods when the central authority has broken down, such as toward the close of the AFPFL period in 1958 and during the "Rangoon spring" of the summer of 1988 (not to mention the period shortly after independence when various Burman para-military groups went into revolt), but Burmese governments evidently fear such manifestations. This is evidenced by the civilian "invitation" to General Ne Win to form a Caretaker Government in 1958 in order to prevent civil war, and by the repeated statements from the military that the coup of 18 September 1988 was justified to prevent the chaos and anarchy (in their view) that had developed. The military regime has many fears: there is a constant dread of separatism among the minorities; fear that "federalism" would turn out to be the first stage of inevitable attempts by various groups to leave the Union; and fear that the private sector of the economy may fall into foreign hands (either based inside the country or external). All these mean that the pressures to maintain strong central or unitary control are indeed powerful. These attitudes are tragic, if understandable, within the Burmese context.

This is not to imply that these forces are fixed and cannot be eroded through good governance and an understanding external environment, but the pressures that they impose on the process of national reconciliation are massive. Any process toward political, social, ethnic, or any other form of reconciliation must take these issues into account if it is to succeed.

The October 2004 dismissal of Prime Minister Khin Nyunt has created a period of uncertainty concerning the operation of non-governmental organizations in Myanmar, since it has been believed that he was an advocate of their presence. At the time of writing this paper, it is too early to predict how such groups will fare under the reorganized SPDC regime.

Conclusions

The importance of civil society in the reconciliation progress, in the internal and external legitimacy equation, for the delivery of urgently needed goods and services, and for the development of pluralism and, eventually, some form of democratic governance, should not be underestimated. It is in the interests of all parties involved in contesting the legitimacy of the present government, and to the ordinary people (who suffer the most), that the state should encourage, rather than simply allow, the rebuilding of responsible national indigenous groups that can contribute to the building of the pluralist society that is so badly needed. As the state (which has never publicly denied that it cannot deliver basic services to its diverse peoples) continues to pursue economic and social policies that cause needed services to atrophy or decay, the role of civil society in all its forms becomes even more important.

Myanmar's government has believed that its emphasis on developing infrastructure has been of vital importance but has not been internationally appreciated. Whatever the eventual worth of such development, concentrating talent, organizational capacity, and funds on such projects in a society with limited resources cannot but continue to impoverish the people. Recognition of the obvious impoverishment should have provided an impetus for the state to encourage more civil society involvement to help fill immediate needs.[48]

There is evidence that since 1988 there has been a growth of civil society in terms of both community-based organizations and national organizations, while the number of international NGOs operating in the country has markedly increased. What does this mean? Does this mean a growth in social capital — that trust has increased in the society? At the national level? At the local level? Or does it mean that among the population there is an increasing sense of desperation because the government has not been able to provide needed goods and services, so the people must fend for themselves, and that this accounts for the spurt? Or is it an accepted means of indicating that the military in government has been inadequate, and thus it is a form of protest against the military administration? Or all of the above? We do not have the answer, but whatever it means, it is an opening toward a very limited and controlled elemental pluralism that should not be ignored, and indeed should be encouraged and expanded. Under any government, the potential contribution civil society could make to Myanmar/Burma is enormous, and all internal and external parties should contribute to its development.

National reconciliation, the immediate goal of ceasefires, dialogue, and the growth of civil society, seems still a distant hope, but one toward which every effort should be made. Compromise, an essential element of any such outcome, is an attitude that needs encouragement. The objective should be the quality of life of the people, for only with its improvement will the reputation of the military be salvaged, the struggle of the opposition be legitimated, and the position of the minority peoples be recognized.

Notes

1   For example, the debate in South Korea on the existence and origins of civil society in that country has gone on for some years in both the Korean and English academic environment.

2   The attempted suppression of Falun Gong in China is a case in point.

3   The country under discussion is often referred to as "Burma/Myanmar". In this paper, the author has used "Myanmar" to refer to the country in the period after 1988 (although the name change occurred in 1989), "Burma" to refer to the country before 1988, and both to indicate continuity. No political implications should be drawn from this usage.

4   For example, see Francis Fukuyama, *Trust: The Social Virtues and the Creation of Prosperity* (New York: Free Press, 1995). Also, Robert D. Putman, *Bowling Alone: The Collapse and Revival of American Community* (New York: Simon & Schuster, 2000). For an earlier study, see Gabriel Almond and Sidney Verba, *The Civic Culture. Political Attitudes and Democracy in Five Nations* (Princeton: Princeton University Press, 1963).

5   It is not inconsequential that many minority organizations in Myanmar are devoted to the pursuit of their minority's language and literature, both of which have generally been suppressed, and which embody some of the core values on which this identity is based.

6   See David I. Steinberg, *Burma: The State of Myanmar* (Washington, DC: 2001), p. 121, n. 3, for a personal communication from Michael Aung-Thwin on this point.

7   Such legislation includes the *Organization of Association Law* (1988); the *Partnership Act* (1932); the *Cooperative Society Law*, as amended (1992 from

1970); and the *Code of Civil Procedure* (1908). See Brian Heidel, "A Cubit a Day: Progressing Civil Society in Myanmar", Draft paper, p. 40.

8   In the Myanmar context, Myanmar Economic Holding Corporation Ltd and Myanmar Economic Corporation, both incorporated as private sector activities, are completely controlled and operated by the military, and thus for our purposes should be considered as state-sector institutions.

9   There are said to be 67,696 villages and urban wards in Myanmar. See Brian Heidel, "A Cubit a Day: Progressing Civil Society in Myanmar". Draft paper, also PowerPoint presentation, UNICEF, Yangon, April 2004, p. 9.

10 For a study of this phenomenon, see Kyaw Yin Hlaing, "Civil Society in Authoritarian Burma: Skirting the Regime's Rules", in *Civil Society and Political Change in Asia*, edited by Muthiah Alagappa (Palo Alto: Stanford University Press, 2004), pp. 389–418.

11 See, for example, International Crisis Group (ICG), *Myanmar: The Role of Civil Society*, Asia Report No. 27 (Brussels: International Crisis Group, 6 December 2001). The ICG report considers that there is little likelihood of civil society organizations engaging in "regime change" or overthrowing the government. A later report advocates development of civil society in border areas. See International Crisis Group, *Myanmar: Aid to the Border Areas*, Asia Report #82 (Yangon and Brussels: International Crisis Group, 9 September 2004). Ashley South is concerned about civil society in a transition; see Ashley South, "Ceasefires and Civil Society: The Case of the Mon", Draft paper, n.d. This essay is not concerned with revolution, but with reconciliation.

12 Although cooperatives in Western societies are considered part of civil society, in Burma/Myanmar they have been under the control of the state through the Ministry of Cooperatives, and cannot be considered part of civil society.

13 David Steinberg, "A Void in Myanmar: Civil Society in Burma", in *Strengthening Civil Society in Burma: Possibilities and Dilemmas for International NGOs*, edited by T. Kramer and P. Vervest for Burma Center Netherlands & Transnational Institute (BCN/TNI), (Chiengmai: Silkworm Books, 1999), p. 8. This sentence has been extensively quoted.

14 Heidel makes the point that even in the pre-colonial period, elements of "civil society" existed. See Heidel, "A Cubit a Day", and Steinberg, "A Void in Myanmar".

15 After 1988, the state limited the number of approved Buddhist sects and the curricula of Buddhist higher educational institutions.

16 In one of the very early village studies, the author found that villagers had little interest in banding together in civil society organizations except for religious functions, which were important. See Charles S. Brant, "Tadagale: A Burmese Village in 1950", Data Paper No. 13, Southeast Asia Programme, Cornell University, 1954.

[17] See, for example, Christina Fink, *Living Silence: Burma Under Military Rule* (Bangkok: White Lotus, 2001), pp. 56–58.

[18] Heidel, "A Cubit a Day". Of the religious groups surveyed, 43.2 per cent were Buddhist, 43.2 per cent Christian, 6.6 per cent Muslim, and 4.5 per cent Hindu. Although the Ministry of Information listed twenty-six indigenous NGOs, Heidel believes only five qualify in his system.

[19] See *Directory of Local Non-Governmental Organizations in Myanmar, March 2004* (Yangon, n.d.). This study also lists 205 NGOs nationwide by state and division, but a far larger figure at a township and ward level. The reasons for the discrepancy are unclear.

[20] Zunetta Liddell, "No Room to Move: Legal Constraints on Civil Society in Burma", in *Strengthening Civil Society in Burma: Possibilities and Dilemmas for International NGOs*, edited by T. Kramer and P. Vervest for Burma Center Netherlands & Transnational Institute (BCN/TNI), (Chiengmai: Silkworm Books, 1999), p. 67.

[21] Thirty-three are listed in: Burma UN Service Office (and The Burma Fund), *Humanitarian Assistance to Burma* (New York: March 2003). This is a pro-NLD publication. The number of such organizations is certainly higher. A study dated August 2004 lists forty-four such organizations plus two Red Cross groups. See *Directory of International Non-Government Organizations (INGOs) and Red Cross Movement Organizations Working in Myanmar*, compiled by International NGOs (Yangon: August 2004).

[22] For recommendations to the Japanese government and Japanese NGOs, see David I. Steinberg, "Myanmar's Minority Conundrum: Issues of Ethnicity and Authority", paper given to Japan Institute of International Affairs conference, "At the Front Lines of Conflict Prevention in Asia", held 6–7 July 2001, Tokyo.

[23] For a study of these external forces, including "computer-mediated communications", see Sandra Dudley, "'External' Aspects of Self-Determination Movements in Burma", QEH Working Paper No. 94, February 2003.

[24] Some members of the SLORC were in favor of the idea. It was explained that ceasefires with minority groups could only continue if the state provided the goods and services that had been promised. Where funding and capacity were lacking, the international NGOs could help fill the gap, and thus it was in the interests of the government and people to encourage more such activity. However, the government's fear of foreign involvement and separatism prevailed. Since then, this writer has brought the subject up repeatedly at high government levels, but without success. The list of such "challenges" to international NGOs is long. See Burma UN Service Office, *Humanitarian Assistance to Burma*, p. 17.

[25] One might remember that all the ceasefires with the various minority groups are verbal agreements, and to date none has been agreed in writing, although

the Karen National Union, now in process of negotiating a ceasefire, is reported to want a written agreement.

[26] For one such position, see Zarni and May Oo, "Common Problems, Shared Responsibilities: Citizens' Quest for National Reconciliation in Burma/ Myanmar", Report by a Citizen Exiles Group, The Free Burma Coalition, October 2004.

[27] In 1979, under the Carter administration, when human rights were supposedly being pursued by the United States government, this writer negotiated the reentry of the USAID programme into Burma. No mention, let alone consideration, of human rights was ever discussed at a substantive level within USAID or with the Burmese authorities.

[28] Ashley South, "Ceasefires and Civil Society: The Case of the Mon", Unpublished paper, n.d., p. 14.

[29] Muthiah Alagappa, *Political Legitimacy in Southeast Asia: The Moral Basis of Governance* (Palo Alto: Stanford University Press, 1997).

[30] The fact that the government has not delivered needed goods and services should not be equated with the expectation that the regime will collapse. Furthermore, differential access to state services and benefits keeps a substantial, if minority, portion of the population quiescent even if they are not satisfied.

[31] Reported at the FDL-AP Conference on "New NGO Strategy for Democratization of Burma", held in Seoul, 23–24 June 1999, p. 35.

[32] Over the last four decades, the various military governments have constantly emphasized the issue of chaos versus stability, claiming that only the military is able to ensure the latter.

[33] A commission has been proposed by the government in South Korea to investigate collaboration with the Japanese in the colonial period. Some have charged the administration with partisan designs against the opposition, but the first victim turned out to be the chairman of the government's own political party.

[34] See David I. Steinberg, "Military Rule and the Undermining of Civil Society", in *Social Cohesion and Conflict Prevention in Asia: Managing Diversity Through Development*, edited by Nat Colletta and others (Washington, DC: World Bank, 2001), pp. 269–70.

[35] Personal communication, Yangon, 1989.

[36] Although the government has said it has "written off" the official United States community, the U.S. Track II avenue could still be useful.

[37] South, "Ceasefires and Civil Society: The Case of the Mon", p. 1.

[38] When Philippine President Cory Aquino complained that her own government could not implement programmes and that NGOs were her favored groups, the wives of many Philippine officials formed their own "NGOs" in order to receive government largesse.

[39] International Crisis Group, *Myanmar: Aid to the Border Areas*.

[40] Kyaw Yin Hlaing, "Social Capital in Burma", Draft paper presented at the Burma Studies Conference, Northern Illinois University, October 2004.

[41] Clifford Geertz, ed., *Old Societies and New States. The Quest for Modernity in Asia and Africa* (London: The Free Press of Glencoe, 1962), p. 136.

[42] For an analysis, see David I. Steinberg, "Burma: The Roots of the Economic Malaise", in *Myanmar: Beyond Politics to Societal Imperatives*, edited by Robert Taylor, Kyaw Yin Hlaing, and Tin Maung Maung Than (Singapore: Institute of Southeast Asia Studies, 2005).

[43] See Michael Aung-Thwin, *Pagan: The Origins of Modern Burma* (Honolulu: University of Hawaii Press, 1985). There is anecdotal evidence that some of the problems of the administration are, at least in part, caused by the conflicting economic interests of the children of the leadership. Such conflict was widely rumored to be the reason for the supposed "coup" mounted by General Ne Win's son-in-law and grandchildren.

[44] Ironically, as power and authority are personalized in Burma/Myanmar, so too has U.S. policy towards Myanmar become personalized: it is focused on Aung San Suu Kyi, who in effect controls US policies.

[45] For example, Burmanet, 1 September 2004; Voice of America and Democratic Voice of Burma.

[46] South, "Ceasefires and Civil Society: The Case of the Mon", p. 20.

[47] Christina Fink, *Living Silence*, p. 253.

[48] Stress on infrastructure construction seems not only to have resulted in less funds being available for the social sector, but has also produced an increase in the money supply, and perhaps in the use of corvee labor. In some sense the regime has used its construction programme, which it feels is completely and inappropriately ignored abroad, as an important basis for its legitimacy.

References

Directory of Local Non-Governmental Organizations in Myanmar, March 2004. Yangon n.d.

Directory of International Non-Government Organizations (INGOs) and Red Cross Movement Organizations Working in Myanmar. Yangon: Compiled by International NGOs. August 2004.

Dudley, Sandra. "'External' Aspects of Self-Determination Movements in Burma". QEH Working Paper #94, February 2003.

FDL-AP Conference on "New NGO Strategy for Democratization of Burma". Seoul, 23–24 June 1999.

Fink, Christina. *Living Silence: Burma Under Military Rule*. Bangkok: White Lotus, 2001.

Heidel, Brian. "A Cubit a Day: Progressing Civil Society in Myanmar". Draft paper, also PowerPoint presentation. UNICEF, Yangon, April 2004.

International Crisis Group. *Myanmar: The Role of Civil Society.* Asia Report No. 27. Brussels, 6 December 2001.

International Crisis Group. *Myanmar: Aid to the Border Areas.* Asia Report No. 82. Yangon and Brussels, 9 September 2004.

Kramer T. and P. Vervest, eds, for Burma Center Netherlands & Transnational Institute (BCN/TNI). *Strengthening Civil Society in Burma.* Chiangmai: Silkworm Press, 1999.

Burma UN Service Office (and The Burma Fund). *Humanitarian Assistance to Burma.* New York: March 2003.

Kyaw Yin Hlaing. "Civil Society in Authoritarian Burma: Skirting the Regime's Rules". In *Civil Society and Political Change in Asia: Expanding and Contracting Democratic Space,* edited by Muthiah Alagappa. Palo Alto: Stanford University Press, 2004.

Kyaw Yin Hlaing, "Social Capital in Burma". Draft paper presented at the Burma Studies Conference, Northern Illinois University, October 2004.

Position Paper, adopted by the Third Congress of the Members of Parliament Union (MPU)-Burma. 24 March 2004. Washington, DC.

South, Ashley. "Ceasefires and Civil Society: The Case of the Mon". Draft paper, n.d.

South, Ashley. "Political Transition in Myanmar: A New Model for Democratization". *Contemporary Southeast Asia,* Vol. 26, Number 2, August 2004. pp. 233–55.

Steinberg, David I. *Burma: The State of Myanmar.* Washington, DC: Georgetown University Press, 2001.

Steinberg, David I. "Military Rule and the Undermining of Civil Society". In *Social Cohesion and Conflict Prevention in Asia. Managing Diversity Through Development,* edited by Nat Colletta and others. Washington, DC: The World Bank, 2001.

Steinberg, David I. "Myanmar's Minority Conundrum: Issues of Ethnicity and Authority". Paper presented at Japan Institute of International Affairs Conference, "At the Front Lines of Conflict Prevention in Asia". 6–7 July 2001, Tokyo.

9

Making a Responsible Corporate Contribution to Modern Diplomacy in Myanmar

Richard Jones

The non-financial responsibilities of organizations (environmental, social, economic and ethical responsibilities) have become increasingly scrutinized by stakeholders across the globe. Such obligations are felt especially keenly by international firms active in "difficult" countries like Myanmar. This paper will explain how even a small company like Premier Oil made a notable, and disproportionate, contribution.

In *The Millennium Poll on Corporate Social Responsibility*, which surveyed 25,000 consumers in twenty-three countries, nearly 50 per cent of respondents said that social responsibility is *the most* important factor influencing individual impressions of companies. The findings showed further that two in three citizens want companies to go beyond their historical role of making a profit, paying taxes, employing people, and obeying laws; they want companies to contribute to society.

Some areas of economic, social, ethical, and environmental responsibility require companies to comply with the law (for example, in relation to health and safety regulations, environmental protection, or corporate governance issues). Others are discretionary, such as commitments (and consequent activities) to maintain and demonstrate a positive economic, environmental, and social performance over time. In situations when the decision about what action to take is at the discretion of the particular company, how much or little it does, and what it chooses to do, all have a bearing upon the way it wishes to be perceived. In other words, the company's approach to its environmental and social responsibilities will help to define its corporate reputation.

Corporate social responsibility (CSR) is a concept which has both practical and ethical dimensions. It includes fundamental business concerns such as risk-avoidance and protecting reputation. But it can also mean "doing the right thing", investing in the community, or creating a place where people simply feel good about working for that organization or firm.

Companies at the forefront of implementing corporate social responsibility principles, which I will term "Leadership Companies", see corporate social responsibility as more than a collection of discrete practices, occasional gestures, or initiatives that are motivated by marketing, public relations, or other business benefits. Rather they view it as a comprehensive set of social, ethical, and environmental policies, practices, and programmes, including decision-making processes, that are integrated throughout a company's business operations, and which are supported and rewarded by top management.

Today, increasingly, the idea of corporate social responsibility focuses on a company's relationship with its stakeholders, those groups who affect, and/or are affected by, the organization and its activities. At the heart of this approach is a commitment to:

- an interactive dialogue with stakeholders in order to align business principles and practice with the reasonable expectations of the outside world;
- transparency and accountability, which mean saying exactly what the company believes in, what it has done, where it has done it, and then measuring performance by comparing results year on year, and striving for continuous improvement across the company's non-financial performance.

Global companies need, furthermore, to ensure that they promote a consistent approach to corporate social responsibility across all their member companies, with minimum standards that are applicable to all members, complemented by initiatives, programmes, and activities specifically tailored to local conditions and issues. This is manifestly a more pressing requirement in countries like Myanmar, where the overall operating environment for a foreign company is significantly complicated by the larger political problem, by allegations of widespread human rights abuses, and by the low level of development within the country.

Corporate Social Responsibility in Practice

For those like myself who labour at the coal-face of corporate social responsibility, it is good to have a chance such as this presentation to stand back from the daily commercial swirl and to think anew about the basic corporate social responsibility principles that are or should be guiding us, and about the potential benefits that could accrue to multinationals from consistent implementation of these principles.

On that basis, therefore, I would like to test three working propositions. In a sense they all hinge on the notion that the interplay between entrepreneurship, corporate social responsibility, and globalization is indeed dynamic and involves new interactions, inviting new definitions, requiring constant fresh analyses.

I want to pose three basic propositions about corporate social responsibility:

1. That the big challenge now for practitioners of corporate social responsibility — that is, for those advising leadership companies and others — is not only to convince corporate leaderships of the basic case for corporate social responsibility (for many, that phase of conversion has passed), but also to devise new ways of realizing and retaining the value of corporate social responsibility. This may sound simple and obvious, but it is in practice a very substantial intellectual and practical task;

2. That the goal for what I will call the corporate social responsibility community is to assist companies to engage in corporate social responsibility not at the point of minimum cost but at the point of maximum opportunity. This means not just converting the basic principles of corporate social responsibility into operational practices — though this will remain a crucial function — but also

realizing the value of what I will call "incremental stakeholder engagement": the inclination to navigate beyond formal commitments and to take advantage of other resources, such as the knowledge-banks and the supportive presence of NGOs or the different perspectives offered by varied shades of political opinion.

3.   That, in this new more sophisticated phase in the development of corporate social responsibility, the imperative remains: to build a stronger future focus into our thinking. It is the forecaster's cliché that the future is bound to be different. But, from all manner of empirical evidence, this is bound to be true for us. In its first phase, corporate social responsibility has clustered round simple principles and a limited number of issues. In that phase too, the relationship between NGOs, stakeholders, and companies has often been based on mutual suspicion, adversarial postures, jerky moments of strained cooperation. One has to wonder how many of these features will characterize the corporate social responsibility landscape in ten years' time. Of course, there is a very clear and present danger that too many companies will fail to put social responsibility programmes into operation, and will suffer as a result. We "corporate social responsibility doctors" still have our day jobs to do. But, as we run, we have to build into our work an active appreciation of how our issue, and the world around it, is changing. This proved especially the case in a country like Myanmar, where the corporate motives for engaging in corporate social responsibility are very transparent to sceptical outside observers.

The Intrinsic Value of Corporate Social Responsibility

Any high-impact company that is investigating development of a corporate social responsibility programme, perhaps in response to pressures from various stakeholders, will typically be confronted by the following questions: If we decide to invest in corporate social responsibility, will the company's share-value be affected? What is the real cost of not "doing" corporate social responsibility? What is the real value of doing it? How much is this social licence to operate going to cost us? Can we measure the benefits?

But the key question can be put another way: Does putting corporate social responsibility into practice offer cumulative, long-term protection to the company brand, protection strong enough to withstand even the most seismic media eruption? Does it provide a "stock-of-goodwill" that will stand the company in good stead?

It is my contention that as companies increasingly take actions in line with what they perceive to be their corporate social responsibility, there will be a corresponding demand for more sophisticated value-measurement devices. As time passes, more companies will be reflecting not on basic concepts of corporate social responsibility, but on which *model* of corporate social responsibility, which particular interventions and initiatives, and which *mix* of investments, will serve them best within their competitive landscape.

Once the commitment to corporate social responsibility actions is made, the issues that matter are those of delivery and measurement. Just how *good* a good thing is stakeholder dialogue? It is indeed fascinating to watch how inventive and sophisticated are some of the measurement models now being put in place by companies that are serious about corporate social responsibility, in order to try to capture the incremental value that accrues to the company name as a result of corporate social responsibility practices.

Multinationals and Constructive Engagement: Corporate Social Responsibility at the Point of Maximum Opportunity

I turn now to the question of corporate social responsibility and the "point of maximum opportunity" theory. How, in practical effect, can companies lead the corporate social responsibility debate, build new and special interactions with governments, NGOs, and supra-national companies, and do it so that the companies and these stakeholders, especially stakeholders in the developing world, come to see one another as a mutual resource?

Let me give you a practical example by referring to some areas of the work of Premier Oil in Myanmar.

I have argued above that corporate social responsibility is now firmly on the global public policy agenda. It is only natural that once we embrace corporate social responsibility, we like to see positive vectors. For Premier Oil, a company that I advise on corporate social responsibility issues and related matters, this reality was and is a key business driver. As with other major multi-national companies, Premier Oil's recognition of the complex nature of corporate social responsibility meant that the implementation of programmes to both predict and mitigate the impacts, social and environmental, of what the company was doing needed to be embedded within the core of its business. The board-level decision to proceed along this path was accelerated by the fact that, as the operator of a world-class gas project in Myanmar, the company needed to make a careful assessment of what its responsibilities were, what impact the company's operations would have in both Myanmar and at the home end, and of what expectations stakeholders had, if the potential for corrosion of the company's reputation was to be avoided.

But what exactly should companies be responsible for? Many have wrestled with this concept, and for some the debate has not yet been resolved. Premier Oil, however, decided to clarify its position. This decision was partly driven by the risk imperative — that is, *not* to take positive action in regard to its responsibilities might have meant that the company would be held responsible for "everything" that happened in Myanmar — and partly by the recognition that it is very attractive to have the company's values ("what we believe in") drive the development of clear policies ("what do we do about what we believe in"). These policies then became the DNA strands for Premier Oil's operational policies ("the way we work"), which set the boundaries within which Premier Oil's management and workers were expected to operate.

Premier Oil's top-level responsibilities are:

- Returning value to shareholders (that is, making money);
- Ensuring that the company and its workers act legally and lawfully, wherever they operate;
- Providing a safe and healthful working environment for all employees;
- Articulating the company's "rules of the road", those principles and policies that the company establishes to guide the behaviour of their employees;
- Understanding and testing (*and* then demonstrating through

monitoring and reporting) how the company continues to operate within those boundaries.

The next challenge that Premier Oil faced was to embed the ownership of these corporate social responsibility systems within the core of their businesses. This meant that the top-level policies, first principles, and best intentions had to be turned into a practicable business tool that identified risks, listed all stakeholders, and devised a strategy that would enable and sustain business operations. The development of practical rules and guidelines was especially important in a developing country such as Myanmar.

Premier Oil chose to embed the new competencies required to implement corporate social responsibility by introducing a Social Performance Management System (SPMS), which is not unlike the environmental management systems with which some people will be familiar. Such a system, supported by targeted training, can provide a framework for auditing and reporting on, and for managing, social performance, through the establishment of a defined set of indicators, of clearly delineated roles and responsibilities, and of practical "how-to-do-it" tools. This framework is what SPMS provided, and still provides, for Premier Oil.

As a recipe for acting in accordance with principles of corporate social responsibility, this would help to clarify why human rights and related issues became part of the company's operational landscape in Myanmar. Once the company had engaged with the various stakeholders in Myanmar, to do nothing was not an option. But how to proceed?

Constructively Engaging the Myanmar Government

Most commentators will agree that it not the business of business to take over the role that NGOs, individual governments, and supra-national organizations play in effecting lasting development and change in developing countries. However, the same commentators will also agree that the dividing line between these entities and business is not clearly marked. Some would argue further, that in the twenty-first century business has a *duty* both to acknowledge constructive engagement and to devote itself actively to constructive engagement. But the obvious question arises: how do we even *begin* to define this new role for business, so that it is a "comfortable" process rather than a collection of *ad hoc* initiatives?

Whilst Premier Oil did not seek to usurp the role that the Foreign and Commonwealth Office and individual countries play in effecting change in Myanmar, the company acknowledged, and actively engaged in, what we at Premier Oil term "modern diplomacy" on the company's behalf. This involved allying the control of clearly-stated areas of corporate responsibility with the wielding of influence within these areas, and in related spheres for which the company had no responsibility but might have the ability to influence, if the corporate will existed.

In light of that statement, I wholeheartedly believe that only a comprehensive understanding and ownership of corporate social responsibilities can form the basis for the kind of strength that enables companies to empower themselves to implement corporate social responsibility strategies and fully-grown constructive engagement. This is the route to the point of maximum opportunity.

The need to deliver on more than management systems

The framework for Premier Oil to begin to engage constructively with the Government of Myanmar, with NGOs, and with opposing groups both inside — and outside — Myanmar, in the area of human rights and related issues, rested on three basic points:

- first, the company's core belief ("what makes Premier tick?") that the operations of Premier Oil, in every country, should be a *net social and economic benefit* to the society concerned;
- second, clearly-defined responsibilities over which the organization has total control ("what are we going to do about our core belief?"). In this specific instance it was the company's responsibilities vis-à-vis human rights;
- third, the investigation of areas over which the company can exert influence because of its presence, and the relationships it has fostered, within its countries of operation. Premier Oil accepts that the company will also use its legitimate influence to promote human rights outside of its areas of operation.

Premier Oil's human-rights policy is based on the fundamental rights set out in the Universal Declaration of Human Rights and is guided by the rights enshrined in the core labour conventions of the International Labour Organization. Premier Oil accepts that these rights are to be protected and promoted throughout its business operations, and in its relations with both business and local community partners. The scope of Premier Oil's policy includes the rights of employees — their health and safety as well as their security arrangements and working conditions — and the development and human rights of external stakeholders, in particular local communities.

It was through the elaborate process of understanding and embedding the principles of corporate social responsibility that Premier Oil established a level of comfort and understanding necessary for company representatives to use their influence to engage constructively with the Government of Myanmar, with NGOs, the National League for Democracy (NLD), and other stakeholders. The company used this position to:

- encourage the Government of Myanmar to actively participate in human rights and humanitarian law training for a variety of officials;
- encourage the Government of Myanmar to participate in the establishment of a National Human Rights Committee;
- engage with the State Peace and Development Council in order to encourage cooperation with the International Labour Organization to begin the eradication of the use of forced labour in the country;
- implement a comprehensive programme of human rights monitoring in Premier Oil's areas of operation;
- write — and then actively promote — a proposal and framework for the Government of Myanmar to become a signatory of, and eventually to ratify, the International Convention on Economic, Social and Cultural Rights (ICESCR);
- hold dialogue with the Myanmar authorities in relation to the health and safety of political prisoners;
- hold constructive dialogue with the NLD (and groups and individuals in exile) in relation to the role of business in advancing transparency, governance, environmental protection, and human rights in Myanmar.

By any standard, this is not a thin, nor a casual agenda.

Central to the success of constructive engagement is the realization that there is a clear difference between responsibility on the one hand and *influence* on the other, and that to promote long-term change requires a proactive approach in both areas.

In my opinion, the clear outcome of adopting this policy of proactive constructive engagement was that it took Premier Oil out of the spotlight of media attention and turned it into a participant in a broader discussion of what should constitute responsible operation in the developing world. The outcome became one that could be *measured*; in business language, being able to measure progress is the final, important, element that sets constructive engagement apart from special pleading.

I believe that the need to establish links between embedded corporate social responsibility practices (areas of *responsibility*) and constructive engagement (areas of *influence*) will become clearer as companies become more confident in managing the social impacts of the company's operations. Some of the groups with which Premier Oil has already opened productive relationships may also feel more comfortable about publicly cooperating with the company.

This, I believe, is a fair inventory of gains from the initial investment made — and a great example of incremental stakeholder engagement in action in a highly troubled geo-political context.

Finally, the Need for a Focus on the Future

The corporate social responsibility agenda is finding traction in Asia. I believe that all companies in Myanmar, even in the light of US and new EU sanctions, must exercise themselves to become active in adopting corporate social responsibility. They must not allow themselves to become bogged down in the theory and detail of corporate social responsibility, and lose their grip on the subterranean trends that are changing shape of corporate social responsibility. These trends are causing multinationals to reassess the role that they can (and in my opinion *should*) play in addressing the impact of their operations while simultaneously fulfilling their corporate responsibilities for issues such as transparency, social justice in the workplace, good governance, and constructive engagement. All the more reason for a re-think all round.

I have a list of five corporate social responsibility wishes:

- For ever-more-sophisticated corporate social responsibility planning, modelling, execution, measurement;
- For less antagonistic relationships between companies and advocacy groups;

- For more *let's-not-wait-to-be-asked* initiative-taking by companies;
- For better research, especially among stakeholders;
- For more corporate leaderships that are committed to corporate social responsibility.

I hope these things come to pass.

Notes

1   *The Millennium Poll on Corporate Social Responsibility* for The Conference Board, published by Environics International Ltd, Toronto, September 1999.

2   For information about corporate social responsibility, see Corporate Social Responsibility Newswire Service, Brattleboro, VT, USA. Available at: http://www.csrwire.com. Accessed 25 June 2005.

3   For information about Premier Oil's actions, see Premier Oil, *Social Performance Report 2001* (London: Premier Oil, 2001). Available at: http://www.premier-oil.com/Asp/uploadedFiles/File/po-sp-final.pdf. Accessed 12 July 2005. Also, Premier Oil, *Sustainability Performance Report 2002* (London: Premier Oil, 2003). Available at: http://www.premier-oil.com/render.aspx?siteID=1&navIDs=19,27,32,113. Accessed 12 July 2005.

4   *Imp-Act* social performance management (SPM) network, "A Guide to Social Performance Management", Institute of Development Studies, University of Sussex, Brighton. Available at: http://www.ids.ac.uk/impact/msp/guide.html. Accessed June 2005.

5   For examples of negative media articles see, "Premier Oil Under Fire Over Burma", *Evening Standard*, 18 May 1999; and "Quit Myanmar, Premier Oil told", *This is Money*, 11 April 2000. For a more positive perspective, see Terry Slavin, "New Rules of Engagement: From Burma to Africa to London, Socially Responsible Investment Is Flexing Its Muscles and Getting Results", *The Observer*, 1 September 2002.

6   See Terry Macalister, "Premier Oil Admits Abuses in Burma: Executive Denials Crumble Under Pressure from Rights Groups and UK Government", *Guardian (UK)*, 16 May 2000.

10

Creating an Environment for Participation: International NGOs and the Growth of Civil Society in Burma/Myanmar

Karl Dorning

I have long wondered about an early experience that I had in Burma/ Myanmar shortly after I arrived in the country in January 1996. With family and some friends we had hired a small bus and driver and made our way to Pagan and Mandalay, and then back to Yangon. The travel, whilst somewhat exhausting due to the state of disrepair of the roads, was a fascinating introduction to the country in which we had chosen to live. It was on the final leg, and perhaps three or four hours south of Mandalay, in the middle of the countryside with not a village or town in sight, that we hit a very long line of traffic. The single-lane track (at least, that is how it seemed to us, having become used to driving on multiple-lane highways) upon which we were travelling was the main road between Yangon and Mandalay. It soon became obvious that the traffic was going no place fast, and while we tried to make the best use of our time by engaging passers-by on foot and bicycle in idle conversation (they, it must be said, were highly amused at the sight of a mini-bus full of foreigners, and were quite open in their efforts to communicate), I did start to wonder what could be holding us up for such a length of time in the middle of the country side. As the traffic inched forward, I noticed that the face of our driver remained calm and serene, and that no-one else appeared unduly concerned with the lack of progress (I recall how frustrated I had felt at the time). Finally, we inched up to the problem. It was not an accident, as I had feared, but in the middle of the road, parked at a 45-degree angle across the single Yangon-bound lane, was a small truck, of no more than two tonnes. Lying on the ground, sheltered by the truck from the sun and from the traffic approaching from the other direction, lay the body of, we assumed, the driver. He was not dead, nor injured. Simply fast asleep in the middle of the road (or at least pretending to be). Noticing that someone (presumably the recumbent driver) had hoisted the truck up on its wobbly jack, I assumed that he was now waiting for assistance from a colleague or friend that perhaps someone else had gone off to find and bring back, hopefully with a spare tyre and whatever else was required for the truck's repair. As we inched past the truck, I looked down at the face of the sleeping driver, who seemed to be in a genuinely deep slumber, and wondered about what had produced this situation.

Let us give our driver a hypothetical name, Naing Lin. Was the logic something like this? *"The roads are bad, that's not my fault"*, says Naing Lin to himself. *"If they were in better condition, my car would not have broken down. I am going to sleep in the middle of the road as a form of protest, and to hell with everyone else."*

Or perhaps it was more like this. *"I can't do anything until the owner of the car gets here from Mandalay, so I'll just leave it here and have a little rest. The only shade is here behind the car in the middle of the road. That'll do."*

Or perhaps Naing Lin was an inherently shy man and his response was a little more helpless. *"I don't know what to do. I can't fix this and I am a little too 'ah na de' to ask anyone else, so I'll contact my boss. No, not even that! Perhaps I'll just wait here on the roadside and have a little nap. He'll know something has happened when I don't turn up!"*

Of course, it is useless to speculate, as we will never really know the answer to the question, but more interesting, I think, was the fact that the lines of traffic kept inching past the sleeping driver, and I did not see one person stop to ask what the problem was and if there was anything that could be done to help.[1] Again, speculation could elicit a number of possibilities: people felt too mechanically incompetent to offer help; earlier drivers had tried to help but the driver wouldn't wake up, or perhaps did not care or couldn't be bothered. Whatever the reason though, for me, after spending some time contemplating the situation, the sleeping driver presents a metaphor for what is happening in Burma/Myanmar in relation to civil society, and that metaphor has relevance for the debate, thinking, and academic pondering over the growth of civil society in Myanmar.

First, our friend Naing Lin was solitary; there was no one to help, he had given up and was waiting for someone else to get him out of the spot. Many in Burma/Myanmar are like this, and one cannot blame them, they have little choice. Second, the passing parade was reluctant to help, unwilling to get involved; people were mostly concerned with getting to where they wanted to go and, once past the obstacle, did not really consider the plight of others. Third, take Naing Lin, the silent protester — a lone voice in the wilderness, "I am not going to take this any more". But then, what to do? — is lying on the road enough?

However one looks at this situation, the fact is that much of the debate on civil society in Burma has neglected or ignored the voices of the majority — those who do or will make up civil society — much as our friend Naing Lin was neglected by the passing parade of drivers. Instead, our thoughts and actions have been directed towards the major political players who, whilst undeniably important, do not in themselves constitute civil society. In order to understand the nature and role of civil society in Burma/Myanmar more clearly, therefore, this paper will:

1. Look at past thoughts and writing on civil society in Myanmar and come to some conclusion as to what civil society might mean in the Myanmar context. This will include some analysis of such terms as "participation: and "empowerment", which are often used in the discourse of development organizations presently in the country;

2. Give an update on some of the increasing number of local and international non-government organization programs in the country;

3. Analyse some specific examples of both local and international NGO (INGO) programs that could be regarded as an active part of

developing civil society, and argue that there is indeed a rich and potentially capable network of community-based groups and individuals who have begun to respond to issues both social and economic that impact on the lives of many of the poor and dispossessed in the country;

4. Make recommendations as to how both local and international organizations might work together more effectively to develop further space for the participation of "ordinary people" in the growth of civil society in the country.

Civil Society in the Myanmar Context: A Brief Review of Past Literature

"Civil society" is a term that covers a multitude of definitions, not all wholly applicable to the Burma/Myanmar context. James Manor, Mark Robinson and Gordon White suggest that:

> In normative terms, civil society has been widely seen as an increasingly crucial agent for limiting authoritarian government, strengthening popular empowerment, reducing the socially atomizing and unsettling effects of market forces, enforcing political accountability and improving the quality and inclusiveness of governance.[2]

This implies that civil society does not exist as a result of good governance or as a pre-condition to it. It is a separate entity, and a reflection of the needs — both social and political — of any given community or society. Whilst acknowledging the many inherent problems in providing a conclusive definition for the term, civil society can be seen as:

> An intermediate realm situated between state and household, populated by organized groups or associations which are separate from the state, enjoy some autonomy in relations with the state, and are formed voluntarily by members of society to protect or extend their interests, values or identities.[3]

Within this definition civil society can be seen as playing a number of roles:

1. Representation of the interests of specific groups in relation to government and to other sectors of society
2. Mobilization of social actors to increase their consciousness and impact

3. Regulation and monitoring of state performance and the behaviour and actions of public officials
4. Developmental or social action to improve the well-being of their own or other constituencies.

Thought and analysis about civil society in Burma/Myanmar is not new. A conference hosted by the Burma Centre Netherlands (BCN) and the Trans-National Institute (TNI) in December 1997 was titled, "Strengthening Civil Society in Burma: Possibilities and Dilemmas for International NGOs". Whilst it is some time ago that this conference was held, it is indeed interesting both to see if any progress has been made since then, and to use existing definitions as a starting point for analysis of the present situation.

David Steinberg noted in his conference paper that, in theory, civil society:

1. Is made up of institutions and groupings outside government;
2. Is a necessary part of democracy and an important element in democratic tradition;
3. Is an essential element of political pluralism — which enables the diffusion of power (away from the state) and is characteristic of modern democracies.[4]

Steinberg suggested, however, that civil society in Burma/Myanmar should be seen in a different light.

> [Civil society is] composed of those non-ephemeral organizations of individuals banded together for a common purpose or purposes to pursue those interests through group activities and by peaceful means. These are generally non-profit organizations, and may be local or national, advocacy or supportive, religious, cultural, social, professional, educational, or even organizations that, while not for profit, support the business sector, such as chambers of commerce, trade associations etc.[5]

This significantly broadens the understanding of what many may see as real civil society; given the realities of Burma/Myanmar, small, even individual, actions that contribute to social, economic, and political change can be seen to be manifestations of civil society in an embryonic stage.

Mark Duffield says of civil society that "At best it is an ill-defined space between the family and state in which plural civic institutions hold sway."[6] Martin Smith, himself a contributor to the TNI conference, suggests that there is a sense of ambiguity around the term, though it is clear that humanitarian organizations equate civil society with such things as the development of capacity, social mobilization, participatory planning, and empowerment. It should be acknowledged, too, that Smith argues that it is necessary to take into account the past decades of internal strife and ethnic conflict as a part of any discussion of civil society.[7] Whilst this is indeed a vital aspect of the overall picture, a thorough analysis of the ethnic issues relating to the growth of civil society is beyond the scope of this paper.

The third contributor to the publication, Zunetta Liddell defines civil society as: "Free associations of citizens joined together to work for common concerns or implement social, cultural, or political initiatives which complement, as well as compete with, the state".[8] However, she suggests that this presupposes citizens enjoying the "fundamental freedoms" of thought, opinion, expression, association, and movement, and that these freedoms are not respected by the present regime in Burma/Myanmar.

Marc Purcell, the final contributor, looks specifically at the role of international NGOs in building civil society, using the framework of David Korten that outlines four different "generations" or NGO strategies:

- First generation — direct delivery of services such as health, food, shelter;
- Second generation — development of the capacity of communities to meet their own needs — encouraging self-reliance;
- Third generation — focus on sustainable systems development to produce supportive environment (delivery systems) in which resources can get to where they are most needed. Response to HIV is used as an example;
- Fourth generation — facilitation of social movements which mobilize people for social change (such as the women's movement).

He makes the observation that many, if not all, international NGOs in Burma/Myanmar are focusing their efforts on the first and second generation stages, and that for civil society to grow, "It is crucial for INGOs to initiate development strategies which foster independent thinking, and democratic structures and management in the communities that they target, including their local staff."[9]

Whilst there is not total agreement between these writers about what constitutes civil society in Burma/Myanmar, there are areas of convergence that can be summarized as follows:

1. Civil society organizations require autonomy from the state in terms of decision-making structures and ability to implement their stated activities;

2. The meaning of the term "civil society" in the context of Burma/ Myanmar is not necessarily limited to mean the existence of well organized social and political lobby groups, but includes any organization or group that has as its central tenet the aim of bringing about social, economic, or political change for the "greater good";

3. Civil society groups include international actors (such as international NGOs) as well as local actors;

4. While civil society is a somewhat nebulous concept, it involves such elements as participation and empowerment.

Expectations of Civil Society in Myanmar

A report produced by the International Crisis Group (ICG) in 2001[10] detailed the development of civil society in Burma/Myanmar from the era before Ne Win's takeover of power, noting that a number of factors have inhibited its growth. These include the lack of the rule of law, severe restriction of access to communications technology, the stifling of independent organizations, and the corresponding growth regime-sponsored organizations (such as the Union Solidarity Development Association (USDA)), and limitations on educational and cultural development. The impact of all these factors is magnified in areas controlled by armed ethnic nationalist organizations.

Both this report and others[11] suggest that factions and the pursuit of power politics have been a key part of the Burmese political landscape from the very beginning, and that these have had a profound impact on the ability of people to organize and reach consensus through democratic means, as well as, therefore, on their ability to form any robust civil society movement. Rather, they suggest, the organizations that have developed have more often than not re-created the existing autocratic structures of power.

> Because Myanmar has been under military rule for so long, few people today understand the role that civil society is meant to play in a democracy or that a healthy democracy requires broadmindedness and a dispersion of power. Thus, even organizations outside the regime's direct control tend to replicate the hierarchical organizational structures and lack of tolerance for

dissent which characterize state-controlled organizations. Low levels of education and cultural factors mean many ordinary people in Myanmar lack confidence in their ability to effect change.[12]

If this is true, it would indicate that political reform will require much more than simply a change in government. The growth of civil society can and should become a tool through which processes of democratic decision-making and public accountability are engendered at every level of community life, a mechanism through which all people have the opportunity to participate on equal terms, despite their age, gender, ethnicity, or status. Ashley South suggests that:

> In general, opposition strategies have focused on elite-level politics, rather than grass-roots democratization. However, both approaches are necessary — while neither is sufficient in itself. Change at the national level is urgently needed, but sustained democratic transition can only be achieved if accompanied by local participation and 'development from below'.[13]

More recently, an ICG report published in 2004 suggested that capacity-building for institutions outside the military is necessary — for example, for the civil service as well as for political and civil society groups and the business sector.[14] The report concludes that decades of hierarchical decision-making have stifled initiative and creativity at the same time as corruption and absenteeism have grown due to poor wages and working conditions. The report makes a number of pertinent recommendations including the following:

1. That restrictions limiting funding to narrowly defined humanitarian projects should be relaxed, in order to allow institution of broader sustainable livelihood programs with a longer timeframe;
2. That NGOs and agencies of the United Nations (UN) should collaborate more effectively and use their comparative advantage to greater effect;
3. That human rights and development protection agencies should cooperate more;
4. That international agencies should not "crowd out" or impede the development of local networks.[15]

For these recommendations to be effective, it is essential that long-term development strategies be adopted and that investment in the capacities of both local groups and individuals through the delivery of more focused humanitarian assistance be promoted.

The earlier ICG report quotes Aung San Suu Kyi on linking development assistance to empowerment: "It is not enough merely to provide the poor with material assistance. They have to be sufficiently empowered to change their perception of themselves as helpless and ineffectual in an uncaring world." The report goes on to point out that in practice this requires introducing democratic organizational structures into community development work and encouraging creative and independent thinking.[16]

The notion that formal political change is a pre-requisite for all other change should be questioned. The case for "bottom-up" civil society growth is rapidly gaining credence. Paolo Freire reminds us that:

> This then is the humanistic and historical task of the oppressed: to liberate themselves and their oppressors as well. The oppressors, who oppress, exploit, and rape by virtue of their power, cannot find in their power the strength to liberate either the oppressed or themselves. Only power that springs from the weakness of the oppressed will be sufficiently strong enough to free both.[17]

Empowerment of all people, not simply reform of formal government structures, is necessary and whilst it would be naïve to suggest that civil society can grow unimpeded by formal government mechanisms of control, it will be shown quite clearly in the following section that distinct possibilities exist and that substantial steps have already been taken to that end.

NGOs in Burma/Myanmar — Who are They and What are They Capable of Doing?

Without going into a detailed typology of NGOs in Burma/Myanmar, some general distinctions can be made. There are, broadly speaking, four types of NGO:

- International NGOs;
- Government-sponsored NGOs (sometimes referred to as GONGOs), such as the Myanmar Maternal and Child Welfare Association and the more politically-oriented Union Solidarity Development Association. These should not be seen as civil society organizations;
- Local NGOs. Many of these have a religious affiliation, and there are also some that, although they have links with government departments (for example, the Myanmar Anti-Narcotics Association), do have more autonomy than the GONGOs;

- Small community-based organizations that cover a range of local functions such as organizing funerals and festivals, of which there are an amazing number in the country, about 214,000, according to David Steinberg.[18]

This paper will deal primarily with international NGOs and the more established local NGOs.

Local NGOs

There has been some debate about what constitutes a local NGO in Burma/Myanmar. A recent publication, *Directory of Local Non-Government Organizations in Myanmar, March 2004* listed sixty-two local NGOs.[19] In order to be included in the directory, these groups had to meet a certain number of criteria, including having an office in Yangon, being non-profit, voluntary, independent, self-governing, socially accountable, human-welfare oriented, acting as an intermediary, socially progressive and having clear leadership. Funding for the compilation of this directory was provided by Save the Children UK, Oxfam Great Britain, and the United Nations Children's Fund (UNICEF) Myanmar. Limitations of the funding meant that only NGOs with offices in Yangon could be surveyed, so this does not by any means represent the entirety of organizations in the country. Table 10.1 shows the numbers of local NGOs that work in various areas.

While most organizations are small, one or more are present in all states and divisions. Sixty-four work in Yangon, the greatest number,

TABLE 10.1
Local Non-Governmental Organizations — Areas of Work

• 31 work in education	• 25 work in health	• 20 are religion-based
• 20 have a social welfare focus	• 15 work in water and sanitation	• 14 work in HIV/AIDS prevention and care
• 11 work in agriculture	• 10 provide credit	• 8 provide emergency relief
• 8 focus on the environment	• 7 focus on nutrition	• 5 focus on capacity building
• 1 works on non-violence	• 8 work on other areas	

Compiled with information from *Directory of Local Non-Government Organizations in Myanmar, March 2004.*

whilst the smallest number of local NGOs in a State or Division is three, in Tanintharyi Division in the south. The majority have some religious affiliation, although groups such as the Myanmar Medical Association (MMA) and the Myanmar Literary Resource Centre are also represented. The goals of these organization cover a wide and varied ground, from providing drinking water for people at pagodas, monasteries, and other places to contributing to the "development of the Myanmar forest resources and natural environment, and entailing such statements as "transforming Myanmar into a learning society and develop human resources through non-formal education", and "bringing about a higher health standard for everyone through high-standard effective quality nursing". Some local NGOs are relatively small and cater for a specific number of beneficiaries, as, for example, some of the orphanage programs, while others, such as the MMA, have a country-wide affiliation with thousands of members. Table 10.2 shows the number of local NGOs established at different periods, and although a number date from before the 1950s, a marked growth has occurred over the past fourteen years.

TABLE 10.2
Establishment of Non-Governmental Organizations by Date

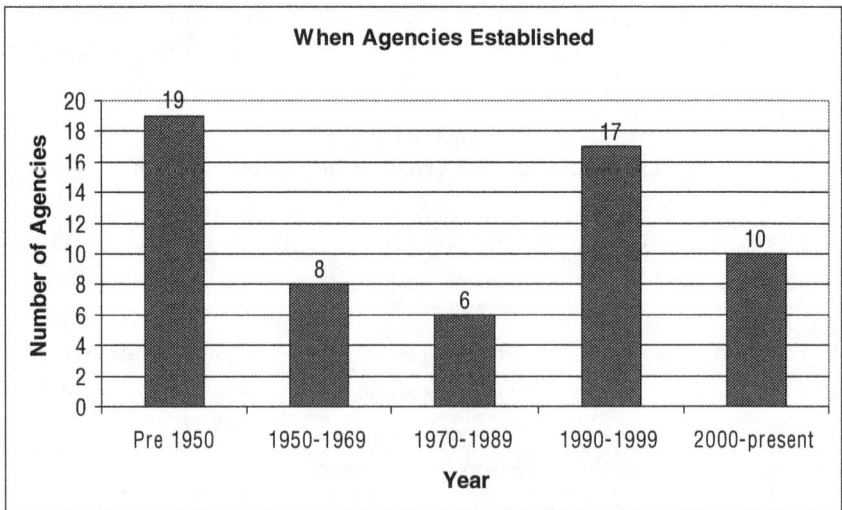

Compiled with information from *Directory of Local NGO Organizations in Myanmar, March 2004.*

International NGOs

Apart from the International Committee of the Red Cross, about forty international NGOs are working inside Burma/Myanmar.[20] Some have been operational for over ten years, while the majority have entered the country within the past five years (since the publication of the article by Marc Purcell mentioned above). Their focus, both in terms of sectoral as well as geographic area, is varied, ranging from the more specific health-related programs run by the Médecins Sans Frontières (MSF) alliance members to the broad-based community development approach followed by organizations such as World Vision. Whilst HIV/AIDS is a key component of many organizations' programs, most other development sectors are addressed: re-forestation, disaster relief, vocational training, street children and child rights, agricultural development, micro-credit, anti-trafficking, water and sanitation are just some of the ever-increasing areas covered.

International NGOs themselves can be seen to offer a number of concrete contributions to the development of civil society in Burma/Myanmar. While this paper will focus on two international NGOs only, it is important to identify some of the more common elements of international NGO programs. Though they relate primarily to the first and second generation of Korten's NGO strategies, they do, nonetheless, relate directly to civil society building.

1. First, most international NGOs have a community presence and rely on the commitment of volunteers to implement parts of their programs. These volunteers often form into well-established groups that play a primary role in the delivery of humanitarian aid. Often, they act as the interface between the international NGO and the community.

2. Second, international NGOs invest in the development of their national staff by fostering both technical and leadership skills. Although this training is insufficient to meet all the needs, a small but growing cadre of development professionals is being created. As a result, the work of international NGOs is increasingly being directed by national staff who are gaining increasing confidence in the identification, design, implementation, and evaluation of development projects. While only one international NGO is headed by a Myanmar national, all have nationals in senior management positions.

3. Third, community mobilization around specific issues, whether it be AIDS or water and sanitation or micro-credit, is a common strategy followed by international NGOs. This has brought about an understanding within communities of the importance of participatory democratic decision-making processes and lays the foundation for the greater involvement of civil society at a local level.

4. Fourth, working at a community level automatically puts international NGOs into close contact not only with local authorities but also with government-sanctioned NGOs such as the Myanmar Maternal and Child Welfare Association (MMCWA), USDA, and others. This kind of local-level interaction does have the potential to create meaningful dialogue around development issues. Another element in this interaction is that many international NGO programs work quite closely with government ministry officials at the local level, particularly with officials of the Ministry of Health in relation to work on HIV.

5. Fifth, advocacy before the United Nations is another valuable, though perhaps under-utilized, strength of international NGOs, since, except in a few instances, the United Nations does not work directly at community level. International NGOs have the ability to advocate with, and on behalf of, community groups and individuals when approaches on development and humanitarian issues are made to the UN. To a considerable extent UN agencies rely on international NGOs having this direct access to communities. In the absence of any consistent and structured means through which communities or NGOs can advocate to the government, advocating to the UN as an intermediary is at least a step in the right direction.

Some Examples of International NGO Programs and Civil Society Building

The following section will look at aspects of programs being implemented by a number of international NGOs, primarily World Vision Myanmar and the Burnet Institute. These two organizations have totally different responses to their role as development organizations in the country and therefore provide an interesting contrast to the broader analysis of the role of international NGOs in the building of civil society. The information in these sections is based on the author's personal experience in both organizations.

World Vision Myanmar

World Vision Myanmar has been operating in Burma/Myanmar since the early 1990s. Beginning with some very small health and HIV-related programs, it now has one of the largest international NGO programs in the country, with a budget of some US$5 million per year and a staff of over 230 people. World Vision Myanmar operates in most states and divisions, and covers a broad range of sectors, from relief to HIV prevention and care, micro-enterprise development, and work with street children. The mainstay of World Vision's presence in the country has become the Area Development Program (ADP) — broad-based community development programs that are funded primarily through the child sponsorship mechanism and that focus on a township area (generally a population of around 70,000 people). ADPs generally have a mix of activities, in sectors such as health, education, income generation and micro-credit schemes, water and sanitation, programs for the disabled, skills-training activities, anti-trafficking activities, HIV prevention and care, and social enhancement programs (with a focus on addressing domestic violence), and follow a long-term development plan that may cover up to fifteen years. Both ADPs and the more focused sectoral initiatives (such as street children) follow a participative approach in the development and implementation of interventions.[21]

While still evolving, this approach provides an example of how one international NGO is intentionally seeking to bring about growth of civil society. World Vision sees this as a process that begins with a situational analysis of a particular community (selected according to initial understanding of need and poverty level) followed by advocacy to local community leaders, both formal (to the local Peace and Development Committee (PDC)) and informal (to religious and traditional leaders), to inform them of the types and focus of World Vision programs. Once initial relationships have been formed, World Vision Myanmar staff spend some time in the community making a more thorough assessment of needs and potential responses to them. In the course of this assessment, community volunteers are identified (initially with the cooperation of the community leaders), and these, with a limited number of World Vision Myanmar staff, become the primary interface between the World Vision program and the broader community.

Establishing a credible and trusted presence in a community takes time, and it is generally a year before volunteers form into an identifiable group to become the conduit through which World Vision-funded initiatives can be delivered. During this initial phase, volunteers elect a community development committee, which (ideally) becomes the decision-making body for the project. Usually these committees and the other community volunteers undergo training in participatory and democratic decision-making as well as in the more development-oriented skills of conducting a situational analysis, developing targeted initiatives to address community problems, monitoring and evaluation of projects, and even in preparation of proposals. Their intended role then is to identify key development issues and to develop strategies and operational plans to respond to those needs. At the present time, committees operate with varying levels of autonomy. A recent evaluation of one program found that the committee (which consisted of a groups of volunteers aged between sixteen and sixty) was extremely well organized and active. They attended the evaluation with a complete plan for activities they wished to pursue over the coming year, a plan that included a budget and an outline of how they saw World Vision's role in the process.[22]

In some communities, a "community-based organization" (CBO) has been established with the encouragement of World Vision. These CBOs have been formed in the absence of longer-term child sponsorship funding in an effort to develop more sustainable interventions in a shorter space of time. They have been formed in a similar manner to the ADP committees, but from the beginning take far more responsibility for the development process and for the funding of initiatives. Whilst some funding is given by World Vision Myanmar, the community-based committees are also responsible for the development of income-generation activities that will provide ongoing financial support. In general, CBO activities focus on the quality of life of children in the community, with a particular emphasis on health and education. However, it is recognized that the well-being of children depends on the economic and social stability of their parents, and interventions of the CBOs take this into account. CBO committees represent villages or smaller urban communities and are elected by community members after a thorough orientation covering the aims and objectives of

World Vision as well as basic concepts of community development and empowerment. In turn, CBO committee members choose elected members to represent them on a township-wide committee. Each member is given training by World Vision staff in organizational management, conflict resolution, financial management, monitoring strategies, community mobilization, planning and implementing development projects, and technical aspects of projects.

Once established and trained, CBOs provide World Vision Myanmar with:

- A clearly articulated analysis of the problem that is being addressed and the strategies through which this will be done;
- A monitoring plan that is participative in nature — that is, which involves all stakeholders in understanding the impact of the project;
- A timeline illustrating a clear understanding of process;
- A sustainability plan that takes into account the reality of limited funding and seeks to attain financial sustainability within the given time frame;
- A reporting system that will enable both narrative and financial reports to be submitted in a timely fashion and with sufficient detail to illustrate that the project is moving towards achieving its goals.

The CBO approach has now been in operation in a number of communities for several years and is proving to be extremely successful.[23] There are obviously issues that need to be taken into account in developing such committees, and some would argue that it is simply too difficult to maintain independence from the government, which brings into question the extent to which such groups can actually be representative of civil society. However, World Vision experience has shown that these committees and CBOs can function in a democratic fashion and have led to substantial progress in the ability of communities to change their situation, even to develop a voice for advocacy, at least at a local level.

The Child Focussed Network

Another innovative program supported by World Vision Myanmar has been the Child Focussed Network (CFN). Initial funding from the Australian Government enabled World Vision Myanmar to encourage a group of local organizations dealing with disadvantaged children to come together with the purpose of providing mutual support and creating a network that would evolve on the basis of meeting shared needs. A series of meetings and discussions over the course of almost a year (during 2002) saw the involvement of adult and child representatives from each of the participating organizations as well as from a number of other international organizations (UNICEF, Save the Children UK, and Save the Children US) in deciding on a vision for the network and developing a proposal that was submitted to the Australian Government for funding. At the end of 2004, the network has been in operation for over two years and has taken on a distinct child-rights focus, because increasing understanding of rights was a key area identified by participants. The network has both child and adult representatives (this is a requirement of membership) and meets regularly to plan both training events (in areas such as HIV/AIDS, child rights, and children's participation) as well as more "fun-focused" activities, which have included sporting and art competitions and trips to places of interest. A major yearly event has been Child Protection Day, which has seen well over 2,000 children and adults from a wide variety of organizations come together in both Yangon and Mandalay for a day of celebration and activity based on the theme of child rights.

Although still in its infancy, the children's network is already fulfilling a valuable role in the promotion of civil society in the country through:

- Enabling isolated groups to come together around areas of shared need and concern;
- Providing impetus for the promotion of child rights in the increasing number of non-government organizations that are looking after disadvantaged children;
- Allowing children to be involved in decision-making around issues that affect their lives and thereby to develop skills and understanding of democratic processes;
- Having an increasing influence in a number of forums about children in country being organized by UNICEF and other international NGOs.

Figure 10.1 illustrates how the various partners of the CFN operate.

While the government has yet to officially recognize the CFN, the Deputy Director for Social Welfare has attended a number of functions that have been facilitated by the network and has encouraged the network to apply for registration. In addition, the coordinator of the network has

DIAGRAM 10.1
Partners of the Child Focussed Network

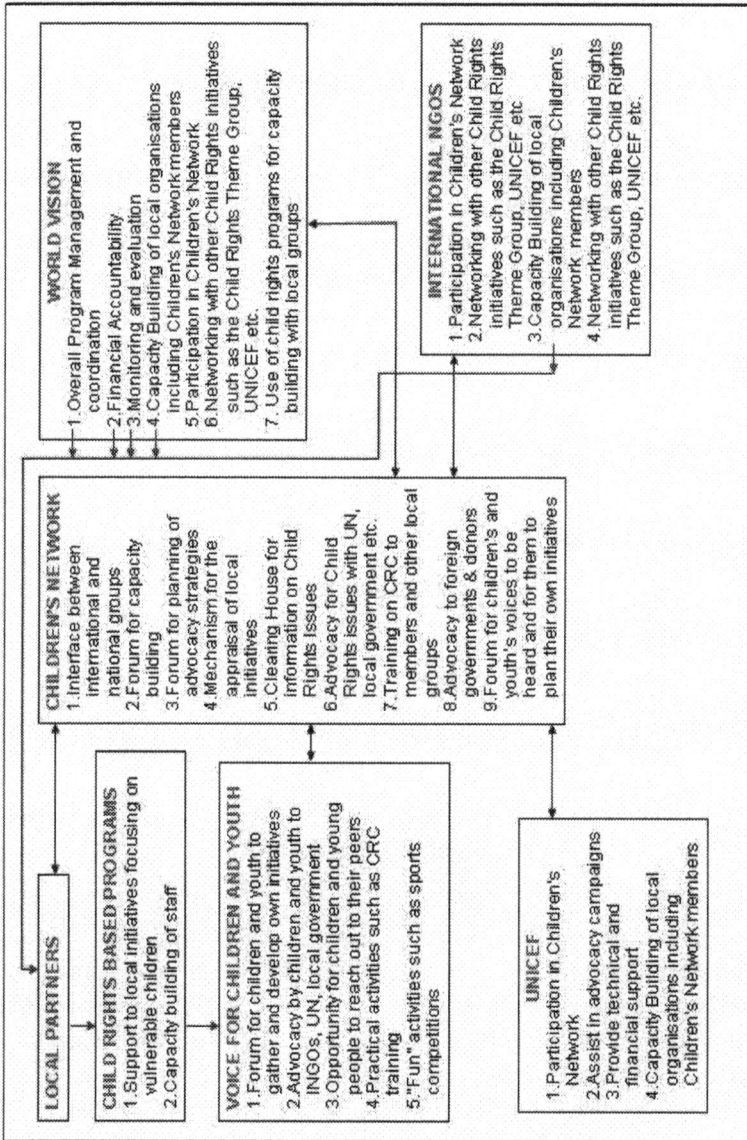

LOCAL PARTNERS

WORLD VISION
1. Overall Program Management and coordination
2. Financial Accountability
3. Monitoring and evaluation
4. Capacity Building of local organisations including Children's Network members
5. Participation in Children's Network
6. Networking with other Child Rights initiatives such as the Child Rights Theme Group, UNICEF etc.
7. Use of child rights programs for capacity building with local groups

INTERNATIONAL NGOS
1. Participation in Children's Network
2. Networking with other Child Rights initiatives such as the Child Rights Theme Group, UNICEF etc
3. Capacity Building of local organisations including Children's Network members
4. Networking with other Child Rights initiatives such as the Child Rights Theme Group, UNICEF etc.

CHILDREN'S NETWORK
1. Interface between international and national groups
2. Forum for capacity building
3. Forum for planning of advocacy strategies
4. Mechanism for the appraisal of local initiatives
5. Clearing House for information on Child Rights issues
6. Advocacy for Child Rights issues with UN, local government etc.
7. Training on CRC to members and other local groups
8. Advocacy to foreign governments & donors
9. Forum for children's and youth's voices to be heard and for them to plan their own initiatives

CHILD RIGHTS BASED PROGRAMS
1. Support to local initiatives focusing on vulnerable children
2. Capacity building of staff

VOICE FOR CHILDREN AND YOUTH
1. Forum for children and youth to gather and develop own initiatives
2. Advocacy by children and youth to INGOs, UN, local government
3. Opportunity for children and young people to reach out to their peers
4. Practical activities such as CRC training
5. "Fun" activities such as sports competitions

UNICEF
1. Participation in Children's Network
2. Assist in advocacy campaigns
3. Provide technical and financial support
4. Capacity Building of local organisations including Children's Network members

Note: CRC is the UN Child's Rights Convention

been invited to attended a number of UNICEF forums, including their annual review, at which a number of government ministries and departments have also been present.

The Myanmar NGO Consortium on HIV/AIDS

The Myanmar NGO Consortium on HIV/AIDS is a creative partnership of five non-governmental organizations — four international NGOs (CARE Myanmar, Marie Stopes International, Save the Children UK, World Vision Myanmar) and one local NGO (Myanmar Nurses Association). Established in 2002, the Consortium aims to implement a comprehensive response against HIV/AIDS by increasing knowledge and skills, improving access to quality services, and promoting a more enabling environment. Each consortium member contributes to the overall HIV/AIDS prevention and care program to deliver the following response:

1. Behaviour Change
   a. Young people living with HIV/AIDS
   b. High risk populations and their networks
2. Care and support
   a. Birth spacing
   b. Sexually transmitted infection treatment
   c. Voluntary counselling
   d. Community home-based care
3. Enabling Environment
   a. Condom distribution
   b. Advocacy
   c. Reducing stigma and discrimination
   d. Gender sensitivity.

The Consortium works in over sixty townships around Myanmar and has funding from a variety of donors, in particular from the Fund for HIV/AIDS in Myanmar (FHAM).[24] The Consortium is unique in that it brings together a number of international NGOs and a local NGO partner in a collaborative work environment that allows for exchange of ideas and technical expertise at both a practical implementation level as well as at the more conceptual level of project design, monitoring, and evaluation. It contributes to developing civil society through the implementation of programs with the help of community volunteers, as outlined above, and particularly through the partnership with the Myanmar Nurses Association. The Myanmar Nurses Association has benefited from its involvement with international NGOs, and has also contributed to development of the work of the International NGOs in the area of community home-based care for people living with AIDS.

Burnet Institute

The Macfarlane Burnet Institute for Medical Research and Public Health, located in Melbourne, has two international centres that focus on public health. Both have been working in Burma/Myanmar for some years now, initially through consultancies to the UN and international NGOs, and more recently (over the past two years) in programming related to HIV/AIDS.[25] Though involved in a range of HIV-prevention activities, Burnet Institute's approach has focused on the development of capacity of local groups to enable them to respond more effectively to the HIV epidemic. Over the course of the first year of the project, this capacity-building has included the following activities.

1. A group of six local NGOs and two international NGOs were selected according to a set of criteria that included having a focus on HIV and young people, the ability to operate programs in communities, and the availability of staff to attend an extended training program. All except one of the participating local NGOs are listed in the *Directory of Local Non-Government Organizations in Myanmar* referred to above, the exception being the Myanmar Red Cross Society. Organizations were approached to see if they were interested in the program, then key personnel were interviewed to ensure that they met the criteria for the program. Agreements between the Burnet Institute and each organization were then signed.

2. Candidates from participating organizations were chosen and attended a series of workshops which to date have included the following:

    a. An inception workshop (including an update on the HIV situation both around the world and in Burma/Myanmar, and an introduction to the program);

    b. A workshop on situation analysis and planning, that focused on skills in identifying underlying causes of HIV transmission (including both qualitative and quantitative research methods) and potential responses;

    c.   A workshop on proposal development, which taught participants how to develop proposals for submission to donors;

    d.   A workshop on monitoring and evaluation;

    e.   A workshop on project management.

3.   Between workshops, participants have been given tasks leading to the development of a project proposal for the Fund for HIV/AIDS in Myanmar.

4.   On-going technical follow-up has been provided by Burnet staff to each of the participating organizations to enable them to complete their between-workshops tasks and provide input into their respective programs.

An end-of-year-one review of the program found some encouraging results. All organizations indicated that their capacity had grown substantially as a result of the program. Although only one agency (the Myanmar Red Cross Society) was directly funded through the FHAM, the Burnet Institute, which also applied, was given additional resources in order to fund the remaining organizations, on the condition that on-going supervision and capacity-building was given to each organization. Burnet Institute has agreed to undertake this.

A second round of local NGOs has recently been accepted into the next intake of the program, and the Burnet Institute is just beginning to undertake a similar process with the Department of Railways. This approach, while focusing on HIV, enables participants to develop knowledge and skills that have far broader application. Research skills encourage local NGO staff to listen rather than to instruct; developing community-based responses to HIV means that community members become involved in decision-making about matters that affect them; monitoring plans encourages transparency and accountability, while management encourages participative processes.

These few examples, though limited in their reach, are a beginning. World Vision Myanmar now has over 1,500 active community volunteers, has trained many more, and has community committees in over twenty-five townships. After little more than a year, the Child Focussed Network as at mid-2004 has an influence over almost 5,000 children and their guardians. The organizations with which the Burnet Institute works interact with over fifteen townships. These results suggest that investment in community capacity is achievable, and that interaction with certain government departments is both necessary and possible. The following section of this paper will reflect on some of the lessons of these examples and suggest ways in which they could be further developed.

Does Civil Society have a Future in Myanmar?

As we have already seen, civil society is not an easy concept to define, and in the context of the intrigue within present-day Burma/Myanmar, every definition is made more complex. Civil society exists in many ways to fill the gap that government and state bureaucracies have been unable to.

> ... because governments and state bureaucracies have not been able to deal adequately with the needs and aspirations of large segments of the population in many societies, small and large, local and national organizations outside the framework of the state have risen in an attempt to address these unfulfilled and unaddressed needs.[26]

While this seems to have been the case in Burma/Myanmar in a substantial way (indeed, one wonders how people have been able to survive for so long without credible government support structures), civil society organizations, apart from having to undertake a government registration process that is essentially flawed, are subject to few controls and do not have to adhere by law to any particular standards or quality control measures (apart, of course, from those that are self-imposed). The programs mentioned above focus very strongly on the quality of local partners, but very few of the listed local NGOs in Burma/Myanmar have access to international NGO partners. The challenge, therefore, is the creation of what could be called an "enabling framework" for civil society which must include dealing with more esoteric concepts such as trust, transparency, openness, and accountability, as well as with the more practical, and obviously related, issues of standards and modes of operation. If this is not done, the exponential growth in local organizations will mean there is a distinct risk of these organizations recreating hierarchical power-structures that mirror the very official environment which civil society, by nature, seeks to confront. Developing this enabling framework, I would argue, should become a primary aim of international NGOs in Burma/Myanmar.

The recent history of international NGOs involvement in Burma/ Myanmar could be divided into three distinct phases. We have passed through the "Pioneer Stage", which saw a handful of international NGOs come to terms with the anti-engagement lobby and enter the country. Their activities were highly controversial at home, and among donor communities and, as a result, were generally localized and low-key. In many ways, their approach has been vindicated. While there are still political risks associated with working in Myanmar, in essence international NGOs have shown that they can deliver aid where it is needed, without using flawed or corrupt systems and services, and without inadvertently sanctioning the regime. This pioneering phase, however, saw some international NGOs creating more-or-less parallel systems of aid delivery that involved very little interaction with government counterparts and resulted in only limited development of the capacity of communities (apart from a handful of volunteers who saw themselves as volunteering for an international NGO project as distinct from being volunteers for their own community).

The second phase, which could be termed the "Establishment Phase", has been operational for at least five years, since late 1998–99, and this has been characterized by a number of factors including:

1. An increasing number and variety of international NGOs;
2. More clearly-defined areas of work, both by sector and by geographical location;
3. The creation of networks such as the NGO Consortium on AIDS;
4. Partnerships with the international community, as well as with national entities, around specific development issues, particularly HIV, which has resulted in the development of the Joint Program (involving the Ministry of Health, United Nations agencies, international NGOs and local NGOs), and the submission of a joint proposal to the Global Fund for HIV, TB and Malaria;
5. The increasing interest of international donors and their recognition of the humanitarian urgency within the country.

In addition to the increase in number of international NGOs working inside Burma/Myanmar, a corresponding increase in local organizations that seek to meet local needs has occurred. Although there has been relatively little communication between these two groups, there is great potential, and arguably an increasing urgency, for this to happen. However, these local NGOs are facing their own problems.

1. First, local NGOs are often seen primarily as religious groups, and the authorities are suspicious of all religious groups to some extent — Christian groups are seen to be proselytizers; Buddhist monks are sometimes too involved in domestic politics; Islamic groups are seen as fundamentalists; and so on.

2. A second problem relates to the inherent risk, mentioned previously, of replicating in the organization the hierarchical structures that people are most used to (that is, top-down autonomous rule that lacks transparency and accountability); even the most progressive of groups (including international NGOs!) seem to suffer from this dilemma.

3. Third, there is a particular and significant lack of capacity among many, if not all, local NGOs in terms of human resources, both in terms of numbers as well as of skills and education.

4. A fourth problem facing local NGOs is the difficulty of obtaining official registration with the authorities. Without registration the local NGOs risk not being able to operate freely, or at all. This has been particularly difficult for some religious-based NGOs, though the problem is by no means confined to them.

5. A fifth issue relates to the nature of government interaction. While some local NGOs seem to maintain a low profile and deal with government in a low-key manner, others are like the Myanmar Women's Entrepreneurs Association, which was essentially co-opted by the government not long after it began in 1995.

6. A sixth issue relates to the lack of accountability mechanisms. Many local NGOs revolve around the charisma and leadership of a particular person or group. While this pattern is not very different from what happens in many countries, it does seem to engender a form of decision-making that defies consensus and lacks transparency.

7. Most local NGOs have only limited operational ability. Many of them lack capital resources and therefore lack the ability to develop more than merely local responses. While there exist some country-wide local NGOs, such as the Myanmar Nurses Association, they too lack the financial and technical resources to enable them to

give effective support to their members and to develop sustainable programs.

8. Finally, there is a lack of inter-agency support. Local NGOs could benefit from interaction with each other, but for a myriad of reasons this does not happen in a structured or coordinated manner.

These issues were the same issues that concerned Aung San Suu Kyi when she spoke to a number of international NGOs in Yangon during 2002–03. Most of the international NGOs experienced in working in Myanmar indicated at that time that they endeavoured to take these factors into account in determining their working arrangements with local NGOs, while maintaining the integrity of their programs. But the issues do, nevertheless, pose ongoing problems for effective activities in Myanmar.

In addition, alarm bells are beginning to ring in relation to another matter. International NGOs require well-trained staff. Initially, during the pioneer phase, the expectation was that resources needed to be invested in developing the capacity of locally-engaged staff. Now, however, with the increasing number of international NGOs and the increasing demands to meet targets and deadlines that are placed on them by donors and mechanisms such as the Fund For HIV in Myanmar, the focus has moved away from this kind of capacity-building. Employment with international NGOs that pay good salaries in US dollars is seen as being both lucrative and of high-status, so the few available staff who have some of the skills that the international NGOs are looking for are drawn away from lower-paying local groups. In turn, staff from international NGOs, once trained, are drawn to positions with UN agencies.

The result is that a vacuum is being created at the community project management level. Added to this is the exponential growth of donor funding, particularly following the sudden impact that HIV has had on the country. The large budgets of international NGOs create certain needs which are becoming increasingly difficult to meet. This in turn brings about situations that may indeed work against the development of local capacity and begin to undermine the progress in community development that has already been achieved. For example, it was recently reported to me that in some areas villagers are managing to have themselves certified as HIV-positive, in order to enable them to take advantage of the comparatively lucrative benefits (school fees for children, food, and income assistance) that are provided by international NGO programs for HIV-positive people.

With the increasing number of international NGOs, their increased funding, and the related difficulty of absorption of this funding, the development community in Burma/Myanmar faces an interesting dilemma — it could be argued that there is too much money available (at least, in certain areas) but insufficient capacity for implementation to use it effectively. If more international NGOs were to come into the country, the problems would become clearly evident.

On the other hand, given the mounting number of local NGOs and community-based organizations, there is increasing potential for international organizations to begin to engage more seriously with local counterparts. This could be seen as the third phase of international NGO involvement — let us call it the "Consolidation Stage". In a sense this is a mixture of the third and fourth-generation NGO strategies outlined by Korten and related in Marc Purcell's paper on international NGOs and civil society building mentioned previously.[27] This would significantly enhance the capacity of international NGOs collectively to influence the policy responses of both the Myanmar authorities and the UN agencies.

In order for this to happen, though, a number of specific steps need to be taken.

1. First, it is important to recognize that the raw material is there. The *Directory of Local Non-Governmental Organizations in Myanmar* listed only groups with offices in Yangon, but many more are functioning around the country. However, as most of these groups (apart from some of the more established religious organizations) have grown up around a charismatic leader, they are not beholden to registration standards or public accountability. The Myanmar authorities need to articulate standards and develop systems of registration that are not overly bureaucratic and that provide some form of support, to enable groups to understand why such requirements are made and how they might be implemented. As an example, a recent initiative of the Child Focussed Network is that organizations wishing to join the network must agree to attend a child rights training program and maintain certain rights-based standards in their operations, and must accept that these will be audited. Ideally, this kind of registration process would be undertaken by the

government, and indeed the government does have its own system of registration for local associations. However, it would not stop the formation of local associations such as the CFN that require further standards to be enforced; rather, it both provides support for this to happen as well as accountability mechanisms that are necessary criteria for membership. These mechanisms must be transparent and seek to build democratic decision-making processes within organizations. This takes time and commitment.

2. Second, international NGOs need to invest more in developing the capacity of their own staff. There is a shortage of middle management — people with the skills to manage and deliver aid and with the ability to pass on such skills to local organizations. Again, the raw material is there, but few organizations have the time or the money to undertake the necessary training. This outcome is largely a result of the nature of donor funding, which is currently very much related to HIV/AIDS and, increasingly, to "hot issues" such as people trafficking, and which is very short-term in focus. International NGOs such as World Vision Myanmar are fortunate in that they have the base funding now to develop longer-term strategies. Most international NGOs do not have that luxury. Donors need to identify capacity-building for the local staff of international NGOs as a key priority.

3. Third, international NGO programs must begin to focus more and more on building the capacity of their local partners, rather than their own institutional capabilities. World Vision Myanmar now has a local staff of well over 250 people, and while it and other larger international NGOs deliver good services to communities, there is a danger that staff will become more concerned with the propagation of their own programs rather than with investment in grass-roots community capacity for sustainable development. With over 214,000 community-based organizations and local NGOs in the country, there is great need for such investment. Where there are no existing local groups it is possible to create CBOs and provide them with ongoing support, as World Vision has done. This can and should be done with the full knowledge and sanction of the authorities. Such a process, however, would also require a departure from the present donor priorities and a move towards

investing in longer-term mechanisms that seek to develop local capacities and grass-roots democratic decision-making processes.

Finally, it is vital to accept the limitations of this approach — that action must start in a small way, and that it will not be possible for civil society groups to challenge the government openly or to hold the Myanmar authorities accountable for the rule of law.

In the words of Seng Raw from the Metta Foundation, one of the more established local NGOs: "There is currently a window of opportunity to help build capacity and work directly with local communities. Let us start to make our own decisions about development."

Conclusion

The people of Myanmar, who join so positively in international NGO programs, are clearly looking to international NGOs to help them develop the capacities to deal with the many serious problems they face, problems that cannot be solved by Myanmar Government efforts alone. The Myanmar authorities themselves, more than at any time in their past, seem prepared to acknowledge that international NGOs have a substantive role to play in Myanmar. Without such programs and capacity-building, the essential characteristics of civil society that must form a key element in the democratic Myanmar of the future cannot be built.

Notes

[1]   I must point out here that this experience contradicted what I observed generally happened in such a case; usually people would appear from nowhere and happily offer their assistance.

[2]   J. Manor, M. Robinson and G. White, *Civil Society and Governance: A Concept Paper* (Brighton: Institute of Development Studies, University of Sussex, 1999), p. 1.

[3]   Ibid., pp. 4, 5.

[4]   David Steinberg, "A Void in Myanmar: Civil Society in Burma", in *Strengthening Civil Society in Burma: Possibilities and Dilemmas for International NGOs*, edited by T. Kramer and P. Vervest for Burma Center Netherlands & Transnational Institute (BCN/TNI) (Chiengmai: Silkworm Books, 1999), p. 2. See also David Steinberg, "Approaching Burma/Myanmar: Foreign Policy Dilemmas", Lecture Transcript, Monash University, Melbourne, 1999.

5   Steinberg, "A Void in Myanmar: Civil Society in Burma", p. 3.
6   Mark Duffield, quoted in M. Smith, "Ethnic Conflict and the Challenge of Civil Society in Burma", in *Strengthening Civil Society in Burma: Possibilities and Dilemmas for International NGOs*, edited by T. Kramer and P. Vervest for Burma Center Netherlands & Transnational Institute (BCN/TNI), (Chiengmai: Silkworm Books, 1999), p. 21.
7   Martin Smith, "Ethnic Conflict and the Challenge of Civil Society in Burma", in *Strengthening Civil Society in Burma: Possibilities and Dilemmas for International NGOs*, edited by T. Kramer and P. Vervest for Burma Center Netherlands & Transnational Institute (BCN/TNI), (Chiengmai: Silkworm Books, 1999), pp. 15–53.
8   Zunetta Liddell, "No Room to Move: Legal Constraints on Civil Society in Burma", in *Strengthening Civil Society in Burma: Possibilities and Dilemmas for International NGOs*, edited by T. Kramer and P. Vervest for Burma Center Netherlands & Transnational Institute (BCN/TNI), (Chiengmai: Silkworm Books, 1999), p. 54.
9   M. Purcell, "Axe-Handles or Willing Minions? International NGOs in Burma", in *Strengthening Civil Society in Burma: Possibilities and Dilemmas for International NGOs*, edited by T. Kramer and P. Vervest for Burma Center Netherlands & Transnational Institute (BCN/TNI), (Chiengmai: Silkworm Books, 1999), p. 124.
10 International Crisis Group, *Myanmar: The Role of Civil Society*, Asia Report No. 27 (Bangkok/Brussels: International Crisis Group, 6 December 2001).
11 See, for example, Steinberg, "A Void in Myanmar: Civil Society in Burma".
12 International Crisis Group, *Myanmar: The Role of Civil Society*, p. ii.
13 Ashley South, "Roadmaps and Political Transition in Burma: The Need for Two-Way Traffic", 2003, p. 1. Available at: http://www.ibiblio.org/obl/docs/Ashley-South_Political_Transition.htm. Accessed 17 May 2005.
14 International Crisis Group, *Myanmar: Aid To The Border Areas*, Asia Report No. 82 (Yangon/Brussels: International Crisis Group, 9 September 2004).
15 Ibid., p. ii.
16 International Crisis Group, *Myanmar: The Role of Civil Society*, p. 21.
17 Paulo Freire, *Pedagogy of the Oppressed* (Harmondsworth: Penguin, 1972), p. 25.
18 According to David Steinberg's presentation at the Burma Update conference held in Canberra in November 2004 (see Chapter 8).
19 *Directory of Local Non-Governmental Organizations in Myanmar, March 2004* (Yangon, n.d.). A companion compilation is the *Directory of International Non-Government Organizations (international NGOs) and Red Cross Movement Organizations Working in Myanmar*, compiled by International NGOs, Yangon, August 2004.

20   Not all international NGOs in the country are registered, so this figure is necessarily vague. By comparison, however, there are over 200 international NGOs working in Cambodia.
21   As reported in "World Vision Myanmar Annual Report, 2003".
22   As observed by the author, who conducted the final evaluation for the program.
23   For example, as reported in the end of project evaluation of the Kawthaung HIV/AIDS Prevention and Care Project in 1999, funded by the Australian Government.
24   A body administered by UNAIDS that receives funding from of a range donors, including a number of government aid agencies from member-states of the European Union.
25   The AusAID-funded Burma Youth HIV/AIDS Training and Support Facility began in January 2003, and Burnet's FHAM funded initiatives began in October 2004.
26   J. Vichit-Vadakarn, "Civil Society: Diverse Forms and Multiple Constituencies", 2003. Available at: www.ids.ac.uk/ids/civsoc/PolicyBriefs/policy.html. Accessed 17 May 2005.
27   Purcell, "Axe-Handles or Willing Minions?

11

More Than Saving Lives: The Role of International Development Agencies in Supporting Change Processes in Burma/Myanmar

David Tegenfeldt

In an April 2003 editorial on how to support the establishment of a liberal, constitutional democracy in Iraq, David Plotz asserts that "there's a tendency in democracy-building to mistake elections for a stable democratic government".[1] Plotz states that, prior to the holding of national elections, the hard work of building integrity and trust in the rule of law, establishing checks and balances through the diffusion of power to independent commissions, and the development of associations and civil society, needs to be undertaken. Indeed, transforming situations of repression and protracted conflict into situations where diversity and difference is productively managed, is the challenge to peace-builders everywhere. In our increasingly diverse and complex world, the need to be able to deal constructively with our differences is of paramount importance. In few places is this challenge greater and more complex than what is faced in present-day Myanmar.

After six decades of armed conflict — starting from the Japanese invasion of British colonial Burma in 1942 and continuing through insurgency and counter-insurgency up until the present time — and after four decades of relative isolation from and by the international community, Myanmar finds itself significantly lagging behind its neighbours on most socio-economic indices. Poverty, health, and education indicators show significant suffering by the population, with ethnic minority populations experiencing the most dire situations — particularly as a result of the decades of armed conflict in their regions.

During the Ne Win era, from the early 1960s until the beginning of the 1990s, civil society organizations were dismantled and any organizational activity outside the sphere of government was tightly constrained. From the early 1990s, in a departure from the policy of the Ne Win era, Myanmar's military government has gradually opened up space for international and domestic humanitarian development agencies to provide assistance to improve the plight of the people. Over the past dozen years, the number of international development agencies operating in Myanmar has grown to number around fifty, and the number of informal and registered domestic organizations has increased as well. Though the scope of work being undertaken by these humanitarian development agencies continues to widen, the need far surpasses the available resources.

One legacy of the decades of armed conflict, isolation, and repression is the limited presence of social capital in society. Trust between individuals and groups at many levels of society is lacking, and, of particular note, trust *within* many identity groups is also lacking. Rigid adherence to hierarchy and patronage systems — a common feature of Myanmar society — leaves little room for genuine dialogue and leads to feelings of threat and exclusion, often resulting in marginalization and fragmentation. It is critical to understand the systemic dynamics which contribute to fragmentation of Myanmar society, and not attribute it too easily and singularly to the "divide and rule" policy of those in power. These dynamics permeate many levels and spheres within Myanmar society. Only when one understands these dynamics and accepts responsibility for the spheres where one has influence or control, can actions be taken to counter destructive practices and to begin to build social capital.

Instructive Examples of Changes Through
Civil Action in Other Countries

Although Myanmar is unique and has its own set of complex dynamics, it may be instructive to consider three situations of protracted, destructive conflict where dramatic changes have been realized.

In light of the positive relationship between France and Germany today, it may be easy to forget that this relationship has a history of being very contentious and destructive. But as students of European history know all too well, this positive relationship cannot be taken for granted. The transformation of the Franco-German relationship was accomplished through a very deliberate and comprehensive effort on the part of leaders and private citizens of the two countries as well as by strong support from other interested parties in Europe and the United States.

In describing the peace-building process in postwar Europe, Alice Ackerman describes three fundamental processes which have achieved a transformed and peaceful relationship between France and Germany:

1. The humanizing of relationships among leaders and their respective constituents and societies;
2. The creation of a domestic environment conducive to peace through promotion of people-to-people contact, mainly with official sponsorship but with some private sponsorship also;
3. The creation of cooperative linkages that provide incentives, institutional support, and continuity to the political and psychological processes.[2]

German leaders saw reconciliation between France and Germany as the only way to guarantee peace and security for their two countries and for the rest of Europe. As a result, numerous informal contacts were made by French and German politicians and private citizens in the immediate postwar years. Through the building of these relationships, destructive stereotypes were broken down and "the other" was humanized.

In order to establish an environment conducive to peace, German political leaders made many public statements aimed at dismantling any psychological and cultural barriers that acted as stumbling blocks. The two countries entered into a joint process of reviewing and rewriting the way in which their respective histories were written. The practice of "twin-towning" was established, in which relationships and regular exchanges between respective towns were set up. Over the years, student exchanges and cooperative relationships between universities were promoted, as were technological exchanges and vocational training programmes. A focus on encouraging participation by the youth of the respective countries was a specific strategy of the reconciliation process.

Marked by the Franco-German Treaty of 1963, institutionalization of the reconciliation process began in earnest. The Treaty called for regular consultation between government counterparts, including the obligation for consultations prior to all decisions on questions of vital foreign policy interests and on other issues of common interests. This has led not only to a strong relationship between the two countries but, as we have seen in more recent years, also to the formation of the European Union. The effect is that the extensive linkages between the countries would now make it too costly for conflict to be carried out by violent means. Conflict between these two countries, and within the European Union, must now be resolved through the political processes of bargaining and compromise.

In a complementary finding which looks at peace and conflict between identity groups within a country, Varshney, in his book titled *Ethnic Conflict and Civic Life* studied the factors which contribute to the prevention of communal violence between Hindu and Muslim communities in India.[3] He found that *associational ties* — developed through ethnically integrated organizations, including business associations, trade unions, professional groups, political parties, and sports clubs — stand out as the most effective ways of preventing communal violence. While informal interactions between ethnic/identity groups are helpful in promoting harmony, he found that these informal interactions are not sufficient to prevent violence. Instead, Varshney argues, formal associations of mixed membership are required to prevent violence. According to Varshney, a relatively greater focus needs to be placed on building an integrated civil society if we are to be effective in reducing violence between ethnic/identity groups.

Associational ties, where relationships are established in areas of shared interest, are a way to institutionalize relationships between diverse and opposing groups. Rather than choosing to dwell on the issues that divide their communities, individuals have chosen to enter into relationship with "the other" on issues where they have shared interests. The power of *associational ties* is that these relationships, rather than being merely informal, are institutionalized through formal associations. It appears, as in the Franco-German example, that two dynamics are at work in the institutionalization of these respective relationships: mechanisms have been established through which differences can be negotiated; and the relative impact on the overall community of destructive violence has become more costly.

Turning to our third example, one of the strongest themes that comes out of the South African experience is the role played by relationships that were built between persons in opposing political camps. It is quite astounding to learn how former enemies, who feared and hated each other, took the risk to develop relationships with each other. In some situations, individuals took significant personal risks to reach out to the other side to begin to forge relationships that eventually allowed negotiations to be conducted in a more conducive atmosphere. Though he was clearly not the only individual who took these risks, Mandela's leadership and example in pursuing relationships and negotiation with apartheid leaders is a testament to what is possible even in the most repressive and violent situations. Allister Sparks' book, *Tomorrow is Another Country*,[4] describes how many of these unlikely relationships began and then were built upon. They became the foundation of trust from which the negotiations for a new South Africa evolved. In quite a number of instances, these relationships were instrumental in salvaging negotiations and clarifying misunderstandings between and within groups as the negotiation process ran into difficulties. Regarding early secret meetings between the African National Congress (ANC) and Afrikaner leaders Sparks writes:

> On the Afrikaner side they dissolved the demonized image of the ANC that had been built up by years of propaganda, while on the ANC side they sensitized black liberators to white anxieties, particularly Afrikaner fears about their survival prospects under black rule.[5]

Only because they had built a basis of relationship were the respective parties able to enter into genuine dialogue — a process by which one risks being changed by genuinely listening to "the other".

In each of these three examples, we can see the key role that encounter and engagement played in transforming a situation of protracted and deep conflict into one where the respective parties could begin to forge relationships of mutual trust, cooperation, and interdependence. An approach of encounter and engagement contrasts significantly with the isolationism which has tended to dominate the international community's policies towards Myanmar. Furthermore, particularly in the Franco-German and South African examples, we also see that a comprehensive, multi-faceted approach is critical to facilitating and creating positive change in situations of protracted conflict.

An Approach that can be Effective in Myanmar

What implications can we draw from these examples regarding the type of approach to be considered in situations of protracted and deep conflict? I can think of at least three implications, though I am sure there are more that will need to be considered.

First, the approach needs to be "relationship-oriented" and "change-oriented", rather than "solution and agreement" driven. Too often the focus has been on protecting the interests of each party through the finding of solutions and making agreements. In the case of Myanmar, an approach involving encounter and engagement will require the focus to be as much on building relationships and developing a longer-term perspective towards "change-orientation" as is usually placed on the issues in contention.

Second, there needs to be as much focus on the process of initiatives as on the content or outcomes. In other words, the questions of *who* is involved and *how* decisions are made and communicated are of equal importance with *what* is being decided. In many situations, there is little understanding and appreciation for how important the process is. Often, in order to achieve the desired outcome and in an attempt to avoid conflict, certain individuals and groups are excluded from the decision-making process or, if physically included, are not afforded the opportunity to truly express diverse views. In Myanmar, where critical thinking and analysis skills have not been encouraged, the need to develop and support this process-oriented capacity is particularly acute.

Third, protracted and deep conflicts require multi-faceted and complementary processes of change that involve broad groups of people who are willing to adopt innovative and constructive initiatives. There are multiple and complex dynamics at work in these types of situations. A singular focus and independent initiatives are less likely to be effective in creating and sustaining constructive change than multi-faceted and complementary approaches. We can ill afford to continue on the separate journeys of "first track" and "second track" thinking. Instead, we need to consider how various initiatives impact on each other and how initiatives in one sphere have the potential to complement initiatives in other spheres.

In his book, *Building Peace: Sustainable Reconciliation in Divided Societies*, international peace-building expert John Paul Lederach describes a model which empowers resources within a society and maximizes contributions from the international community.[6] We would do well to consider Lederach's model and move beyond the unproductive debate of "isolation or engagement" and "top-level diplomacy or grass-roots mobilization". Framing the questions in this type of "either/or" dualistic thinking, limits the options. Instead, a more holistic approach which appreciates the need for creative and multi-faceted complementary approaches is needed. Further, in terms of the time-frame for achieving progress, the focus needs to move away from short-term objectives to the longer-term time horizons that are needed for these types of change processes.

Over the past dozen years, during which humanitarian assistance to Myanmar has increased, there has been a gradual enhancement in the understanding by the Myanmar authorities of the role of international and domestic humanitarian assistance agencies. There has also been a gradual increase in the geographic and sectoral space within which these organizations operate. The operating environment, though still somewhat constrained, is a more constructive environment than in years past.

As has been documented recently by Save the Children–UK, there are many local, small, informal community organizations in Myanmar.[7] Apart from these small community organizations, there are a number of regional and national religious and community organizations that engage in humanitarian activities and which are part of a larger network of organizations dedicated to responding to the needs of the vulnerable. Most of these organizations are either not officially registered or they operate under the auspices of a religious organization umbrella.

The past five years have witnessed the establishment of a few officially-registered domestic humanitarian assistance agencies. Two of the better-known of these are the Metta Development Foundation, which focuses on providing assistance in post-conflict regions of Kachin, Shan, and Kayah States, and the Shalom Foundation, which focuses on providing training in peace-building for ethnic minority communities.[8] It is an encouraging sign that these organizations have been able to initiate and establish activities across regions and across identity groups, and have been able to consult and facilitate dialogue across existing divides. Both of these organizations have worked on developing transparency in their relationships with central government authorities and regional commanders, as well as on cultivating positive relationships with the leaders of armed political groups which have entered into ceasefire arrangements. Though both the Metta and Shalom Foundations are in their infancy, and as yet have limited capacities, these and other organizations have demonstrated the possibility that domestic organizations can address humanitarian needs and work in ways that cross existing divides and attempt to build understanding between various groups.

Financial support for these domestic regional and national organizations has come from a number of private international donor agencies, many of which receive funding from European governments. Technical assistance is provided by visiting consultants and some locally-based international agencies. However, what is significantly lacking in the current context is more regular and intensive support for enhancing their organizational capacity and effectiveness.[9] With enhanced capacities to be more oriented towards relationships and change, and with a greater sensitivity to and awareness of process issues, these local organizations will more effectively facilitate the constructive change processes which are needed to address the issues of local and national reconciliation.

The Role of International Development Agencies

International and domestic relief and development agencies are having an increasingly positive impact on sustaining and improving the lives of Myanmar's poor. Following from the discussion above, I want to suggest, however, that these development agencies could more effectively contribute to positive social change by more fully incorporating a change-oriented approach when they design development initiatives. Specifically, international development agencies should consider incorporating the following tactics as part of their approach.

1.   Intentionally design projects and initiatives to create engagement and encounter between individuals and groups that are *not* like-

minded, with the goal of facilitating the building of relationships and trust. The agencies should ask themselves how projects and initiatives can build social capital at the same time as they address sectoral and content issues, and should design measures for fostering these aims in the programme. For example, when a training workshop is conducted, does the international agency specifically invite a diverse group of participants and use the training workshop as an opportunity to build relationships as much as an opportunity to build knowledge and skills? Are the training sessions only one-off, or is there a series of training sessions offered, with follow-up opportunities? Another possibility is for the international agency to become a partner with two or more communities or organizations in designing and implementing a particular project, with the specific intention of building relationships and developing civil society.

2. Explore partnerships with domestic organizations and groups that enhance the capacities of local organizations. At present the capacities of local organizations are relatively weak. International agencies should commit themselves to strengthening local capacities through cooperating in analysis of the local context, training, joint planning and implementation, and through consultations and mentoring of partner staff. Further, international agencies should encourage local organizations to use principles of inclusive processes in the design and implementation of initiatives, and to link with others in ways which cross established boundaries (such as ethnic and religious boundaries).

3. Use the activities and conduct of the international agency, and its relationships with other agencies, to provide a model of sensitivity to principles of good process. Ask the questions — In its daily working, does the agency demonstrate dialogue and inclusive processes? Does it encourage and appreciate diversity? How does it address issues of destructive rigid hierarchy and client-patronage systems? And so on.

In-country programmes of international agencies are often driven by the pressures of their home offices and by requirements outlined in project agreements with donors. A change in approach as suggested here will require country representatives to negotiate these issues with their home office and with donors. Additionally, home offices need to support policy approaches that will incorporate capacity-building for local change processes at the same time as focusing on sectoral improvements.

The Role of International Donors

In addition to what implementing agencies can do in the design and implementation of their humanitarian assistance initiatives, the international donor community can have a significant influence in supporting the approach suggested above by setting their policy approaches and funding criteria to reflect this type of approach. Unfortunately, because of the fears of many donors — largely unfounded — that humanitarian assistance prolongs military rule in Myanmar, development assistance remains very small compared to what is needed.

The international donor community has an opportunity to encourage and support constructive social change in Myanmar. For some donor agencies, this will require a change in policy from only funding "basic humanitarian assistance" to funding support for longer-term social-change processes. In general, this type of policy change requires a greater investment and longer-term commitment than most donors have been willing to commit to up to now. The following is an initial list of possibilities that could be considered by international donors.

1. Support initiatives that build the capacity of local individuals and groups, particularly through the use of international partner agencies based in Myanmar which can support intensive capacity-building efforts. At present there are a number of international agencies doing only direct implementation of projects, without contributing to the strengthening of civil society. On the other hand, there are numerous agencies that provide funding and occasional training sessions directly to local agencies although they have no on-going presence inside the country nor do they do any coordination with on-site international agencies.

2. Most domestic organizations are in their infancy in terms of organizational development and in terms of their capacities to analyze, plan, and implement initiatives. Closer and more intense

partnerships are required to build the capacities of domestic organizations. International donors should require these types of partnerships as part of their funding criteria.

3. Encourage international development agencies to support existing platforms of initiative in innovative ways that build social capital and develop greater capacities. In particular, look for opportunities that can involve young people and provide non-formal educational opportunities. For example, various local organizations have undertaken initiatives to train young high-school graduates as volunteer teachers for remote communities. Small amounts of private funding have supported these initiatives. If additional funding were available, these initiatives could be expanded and could add additional components which build significantly greater individual, organizational, and community capacities.

4. Create greater opportunities for exposure, training, and education to be provided inside the country, as well as opportunities for students to travel abroad for higher education. Up to now, most major donors have only supported international educational opportunities for individuals who have fled Myanmar and have little chance of returning and contributing to positive changes in the country. This policy approach is very short-sighted. Instead, what is needed is support for significant increases in training and education — specifically focused on individuals who can make a difference inside the country — that will build capacity for civil society development and the strengthening of domestic institutions.

International funding for humanitarian assistance in Myanmar has shown a gradual increase in recent years. It appears that the international assistance community in Myanmar has been an effective advocate for the idea that the "humanitarian emergency" is worsening, with particular concern about a growing HIV/AIDS problem. While there can be no doubt that there is a humanitarian emergency in Myanmar, an equally strong case must be made for the need to resource greater capacities to facilitate constructive social change processes. If this is not done, the effort to address the "humanitarian emergency" will continue to require a larger and larger financial bandage, with no prospects for changing the underlying dynamics that contribute to it.

In Conclusion

In recent years many pleas have been made for support to address a number of worrying humanitarian needs in Myanmar. Among these needs are such problems as the plight of former subsistence opium farmers who have had their crops eradicated; continuing health needs, including high malaria mortality, high malnutrition rates, alcohol abuse, and growing concerns regarding the spread of TB and HIV; poor education access and declining educational performance; high unemployment and under-employment; human trafficking; destructive logging practices, depletion of soil fertility and environmental degradation; and many others. While there is an urgent need to address these issues, the need for the international community to engage in supporting positive processes of change that encourage and support diverse groups in Myanmar to enter into genuine dialogue to address the issues dividing them is equally urgent. Working together on issues of humanitarian development provides opportunities for encounter and engagement between individuals and groups who would not normally come together. Dialogue is not a separate process from humanitarian assistance. Neither is dialogue a process reserved for relatively high-level political discussions. Instead, relationship-building and dialogue needs to be part and parcel of the humanitarian assistance enterprise in Myanmar. While supporting initiatives which save lives, the international community can also be contributing to the process of reconciliation.

Notes

[1] David Plotz, "Democracy — Faster, Better, Smarter", *Slate Magazine*, 25 April 2003, p. 2.

[2] Alice Ackermann, "Reconciliation as a Peace-building Process in Postwar Europe: The Franco-German Case", *Peace and Change*, Vol. 19, No. 3 (1994), p. 232.

[3] Ashutosh Varshney, *Ethnic Conflict and Civic Life* (New Delhi: Oxford University Press, 2002).

[4] Allister Sparks, *Tomorrow is Another Country: The Inside Story of South Africa's Road to Change* (Chicago: University of Chicago Press, 1995).

5   Ibid., p. 81.

6   John Paul Lederach, *Building Peace: Sustainable Reconciliation in Divided Societies* (Washington, D.C.: United States Institute of Peace Press, 1997).

7   Whether these small community organizations contribute significantly to the building of civil society and social capital, however, remains a question.

8   Another recently registered domestic organization is the Lawkahta Sariya Foundation.

9   For the past two years Hope International Development Agency has been based in Myanmar, focusing on enhancing the organizational effectiveness of domestic organizations that are committed to facilitating understanding and constructive change processes. A few other international agencies devote some limited resources to this endeavour, but the international community has yet to embrace this need and to make the necessary commitment to addressing it.

12

Exit, Voice and Loyalty in Burma: The Role of Overseas Burmese in Democratizing Their Homeland

Zaw Oo

During the prolonged rule of successive military regimes in Burma for the last fifty years, waves of people have left the country in protest against unjust authority. The largest wave of such exodus happened in 1988, when several thousand young Burmese students fled to the Thai-Burma border following a violent crackdown on popular uprisings they had peacefully organized. For good reason, the students dreamed of fighting back against the regime from the border areas, where resources and sanctuary for such a project were readily available. The existence in the neighbouring countries of exile groups who had left Burma in earlier struggles influenced the large exodus and attracted more to leave. The majority ended up staying in the Burmese border areas and took up arms to wage a guerrilla war against the State Law and Order Restoration Council (SLORC). The SLORC, the name the military regime assumed when it took power in 1988, quickly became synonymous with brutal campaigns waged by the regime against the pro-democracy movement. Repression against the students (who at that time arguably represented the voice of the people) in the form of arrests, torture, and long closures of the universities, was harsh and continuous. The chance of persecution exceeded by far the available civic space for organizing resistance inside the country. As a result, in the years following 1988 many more students joined the flight.

The students who arrived at the Thai-Burma border at the end of 1988 were highly loyal to the mission which they presumed they would accomplish in a relatively short time. However, their adventurous engagement in armed resistance under the banner of the All Burma Student Democratic Front collapsed within a few years in the face of the sheer military capability of the SLORC. Many students gave up being guerrillas and searched for an alternative means to change the authoritarian regime in Burma. Some settled in the United States, Canada, Australia, or Europe, and were able to continue their education there.

This group of dissident students was quickly drawn into the exciting culture of "globalization" and the "information revolution" of the early 1990s; a number got "wired" and launched a global awareness campaign on Burma. A new battleground had emerged: the Internet became another medium for the Burmese exiles to continue their fight against the regime from outside. Within a few years, information networks connected thousands of people in the Burmese diaspora, who were gradually empowered by the Internet to leverage democratic changes in Burma. Today, the most effective weapons against military rule in Burma are not the bands of revolutionary guerrillas.[1] The opponents most feared by the regime are the hundreds and thousands of "netters" who organize numerous boycott campaigns, influence their host governments' strategies and willingness to put pressure on the regime, and raise funds for the democrats and refugees.

This chapter has three central objectives. The first is to analyse the evolution of the political struggle of the Burmese exile community by borrowing and modifying Albert Hirschman's popular construct of the "exit-voice-loyalty" model.[2] The model provides a useful path for following the waves of exodus from Burma since its independence in 1948 and for examining the qualitative progress of the "voice" against the regime and the prospects for eventual return.

The second is to examine how dispersed and small actors among Burmese exiles in the vast arena of international politics overcome the obstacles to transnational collective actions. Theories of social network predict that "any social movement in the absence of activists whose ties cross national boundaries on a regular basis and exhibit mutual trust and reciprocity" will find it very hard to link themselves in a network, let alone accomplish any intended goals.[3] In fact, the Burmese exiles defied this conventional wisdom by building their diaspora network of activists with the purposeful goal of changing the political system of their home country. To most of the exiles, the changing of the political system in Burma is an absolute pre-requisite for their return to their homeland, and many believe that they will be able to achieve this only through a collective struggle.

Last but not least, this chapter also attempts to analyse one particular mechanism that the Burmese diaspora has used to overcome obstacles to accomplishing their goals: namely, drawing help from others. One political opportunity given to the Burmese diaspora is to enlist the power of their host countries, often powerful Western democracies, to support the democratic cause in Burma.[4] However, given the small size of Burmese communities — even in countries where Burmese exiles have settled in large numbers — most political opportunity theorists would not predict that Burmese exiles would have much chance of gaining entrance to the foreign-policy-making process of the host governments.[5] This article attempts to explain how a relatively marginal political force of Burmese exiles living in the Western democracies has championed its democratic cause by pushing a relatively little-known Burma agenda to the top of foreign policy considerations.

Exit: Historical Waves

Popular leader and Nobel Peace laureate Daw Aung San Suu Kyi sees Burma as having experienced two important struggles for independence. The first struggle was spearheaded by General Aung San, a leader of the anti-colonial movement, who organized armed resistance movements against the British and the Japanese, and who was instrumental in Burma being given national independence in 1948, although he himself was assassinated in 1947. The second was led by thousands of young students in 1988, when they protested and brought down the dictatorial rule of General Ne Win. Daw Aung San Suu Kyi, daughter of General Aung San, became the leader of the second struggle for independence as the military continued to rule the country and denied freedom to its population.[6]

The struggle that General Aung San led to achieve independence in 1948 has certain features of "exit-voice-return" evolution. It is true that successive generations of Burmese people had resisted British colonial rule since Great Britain first occupied the lower half of Burma in 1824. However, it was the student and *Thakin* movement led by young leaders such as Aung San, Nu, and Kyaw Nyein from Rangoon University from 1935 onward that was the catalyst for national independence in the next decade. At the height of the struggle, the exit of General Aung San and his thirty comrades to seek foreign assistance and possible military training, first from the Communist Party of China and then from the fascist Japanese, fundamentally changed the nature of the liberation movement in Burma. The voice of the Thirty Comrades, expressed in their first declaration in Bangkok in 1944, had sent thunderous waves of patriotism across the country, as the thirty comrades marched across Thailand into Burma while recruiting able-bodied Burmese males into the new independence army. To many historians, the larger events of international politics and the movements of geo-strategic forces were key explanations for the relatively quick attainment of national independence by Burma after the Second World War. To millions of Burmese, it was General Aung San, with his masterful leadership of the Burmese Independence Army, subsequent mobilization of grand-coalition strategy through the Anti-Fascist People's Freedom League, and tactical alliance with ethnic nationalities, who brought independence to Burma.

The myth of the Thirty Comrades — a story of successful resistance through "exit and return" — had a profound impact on the Burmese body politic for many years. The act of "exit" had become an acceptable mode of dissent, particularly when the institutions of governance were still nascent. Immediately following independence in 1948, several of the former Thirty Comrades joined the communist insurrections, whereas many units from the Burmese army defected to the revolt initiated by the Karen National Defense Organization.[7] Since then, the examples of *taw-kho* (going into armed insurrections) and *pyi-pyay* (going into exile) have inspired several political groups and personalities to follow the route of exit and exile in their political struggle against the dominant powers in Burma.

Such precedents of "revolution from outside" continued throughout the fourteen years of the parliamentary democracy period between 1948 and 1962. The trend was unfortunate, given a relatively strong growth of civic associations and political freedom during that time. However, the fault seemed to lie within the dominant political party system that failed to accommodate "dissenting point of views" and channel elite competitions into "loyal opposition".[8] By 1958, elite conflicts at the apex of power structure had devastated the Anti-Fascist People's Freedom League, the single political party that had dominated the liberation movement and post-independence multiparty system. It broke into two factions: the "clean" faction led by Prime Minister U Nu, and the "stable" faction, led by Deputy Prime Ministers U Kyaw Nyein and U Ba Swe. The split brought down military intervention, and an end to the democratic era in Burma.

The political divisions were further complicated by the ethnic diversity of the population. Several ethnic groups demanded greater autonomy from the central government. The country's independent constitution tried to accommodate such demands under a quasi-federal structure, with some attempts to recruit elites from the nationality groups into central administration as cabinet ministers. However, from the perspectives of many ethnic nationalities, these measures were insufficient and largely ineffectual, with the result that a number of ethnic groups defected and organized anti-government insurrections along the border areas of Burma. According to Martin Smith, from the time of independence there were at least two dozen ethnic nationality groups fighting against the central government. Mainstream opposition groups, centred mainly on the Communist Party of Burma and the right-leaning Parliamentary Democracy Party, made up another dozen anti-government insurgent groups throughout the post-independence era.

Popular unrest, the result of multiple causes for dissent accumulated since 1962 under the oppressive dictatorship of Ne Win and the socialist policies of the Burma Socialist Programme Party, exploded in 1988 when hundreds of students protesting against police brutality drew thousands more people to come out and stage demonstrations on the streets throughout the country. Several months of prolonged demonstrations brought down the socialist government and changed three presidents, but without any resolution over the form and pace of post-socialist reform. The military, who had intervened violently on behalf of the socialist government in the months of March, July, and August, made a final assault against the pro-democracy movement in September 1988, when it declared martial law and established the jurisdiction of state authority under the State Law and Order Restoration Council.[9] Violent suppression of pro-democracy activists and the subsequent crackdown that followed the military takeover triggered a mass exodus, mostly of students, to the Thai-Burma border and other border regions.

In the remaining months of 1988, after the military coup, as many as 10,000 students arrived at the Thai-Burma border, while the areas bordering China, India, and Bangladesh received a few thousands. These student activists, who had witnessed the brutalities of the military on the streets of Burma's major urban centres, felt that armed struggle was their only alternative. In spite of their relatively high social status in the urban communities where they originated, these students chose to form an umbrella front called the All Burma Student Democratic Front (ABSDF), with well-intentioned goals of mobilizing armed resistance movement inside Burma. They were inspired by revolutionaries such as Che Guevara, but their most vivid role model was their own local hero, General Aung San, who formed the Burma Independence Army in Bangkok and successfully invaded the country in 1943. Not surprisingly, the first Congress of the ABSDF celebrated a symbolic gesture of "blood comradeship", the same ritual the Thirty Comrades had observed forty years earlier before they launched their invasion against the British colonial regime.

In the next fifteen years, several thousand more students, activists, and refugees fled from Burma. However, the impact of this exodus on the stability of the regime was negligible. In terms of numbers, the size of each exodus represented only a fraction of the total population of fifty million Burmese. On the one hand, the emigration rate, in the form of voluntary exit, was low compared to the size of population, and would remain so as long as the military regime strictly controlled the emigration process. On the other hand, the existence of alternative forms of internal resistance made the exodus of political activists from Burma largely ineffectual. Until the recent detentions of Aung San Suu Kyi under house arrest, the majority of democracy movement activists preferred to stay inside Burma under the leadership of the National League for Democracy (NLD). Ironically, the departure of the most active segments of the activist groups also helped the regime to control domestic political space more effectively. Last, but not least, the lack of political opportunities in neighbouring countries, and the relatively harsh conditions for sanctuary there, inhibited a sustained outflow of political activists from Burma.

Voice: From Inside-out to Outside-in

The 1990 elections provided the most legitimate voice in support of democratic changes in Burma. Many observers have also suggested that the resounding victory of the National League for Democracy, the most vocal critic of the ruling military regime, also represented a referendum-like disapproval of military rule. The voice against the military regime was loud and clear; however, this voice has not yet shaken military rule. According to Freedom House and other human-rights institutions, Burma has remained one of the most repressive police states on earth. It is exceedingly dangerous to express in public one's opinion about the state of the union inside the country, let alone criticize the military regime in power.

According to Freedom House, "Burma continues to be ruled by one of the world's most repressive regimes. The junta rules by decree, controls the judiciary, suppresses nearly all basic rights, and commits human rights abuses with impunity."[10] As such, Burma has fallen into a deep crisis of "fear", manifesting fear as twin phenomena: public fear against the regime's persecution, and the regime's fear against possible loss of power. Although it is not rare to find individual heroes who have come out in public to make their voice heard against the regime, it has been almost unthinkable for the rest of the crowd to join the hero, given the evident readiness of the regime to suppress such dissent. It is also unthinkable for the regime to tolerate open dissent, since it has seen, in 1988, how quickly a political dynasty can fall apart. With mutually-felt fear as a basic characteristic of the relationship between the regime and the public, there seems to be no room for an effective voice for change in the country.

The military regime continued to commit serious crimes and errors that needed to be criticized, and it required a long journey for the voice for change to reach the constituency. In this process, the underground networks inside Burma would compile the evidence of oppression inside the country, then deliver it outside the country to foreign media and broadcasting stations, from whence the information could be relayed back to the mass population inside the country. In this "inside-out" and "outside-in" channeling of voices for democracy, the role of exiles in interpreting and articulating the original voice of dissidence became very critical. The role of exiles in articulating domestic dissidence was particularly important in the instances when the leading personalities of the domestic democracy movement were either in jail or under house arrest. However, such flow of information is not automatic in either direction. The actual contribution of those in exile in processing an effective voice for change in Burma can be understood only when the entire chain of activities employed by the Burmese exiles is thoroughly examined.

The Role of Exiles in Democracy Promotion: Some Comparisons

The role of diasporas in the perpetuation and resolution of their homeland conflicts is well recognized. For instance, the Jewish and Armenian diasporas are acknowledged to be the most effective of such groups in advocating their priorities within the US political system. Several possible factors come into play in determining the effectiveness of diaspora activism in influencing international opinion and the policies of foreign governments toward the diaspora home countries. First, the size of diaspora population in any particular country is an important factor. The Jewish diaspora in the US, which numbers about six million persons, can certainly influence US policy towards Israel and its involvement in the Middle East conflict.[11] Second, the economic strength of the diaspora community and its control of monetary flows (remittances) into the home country can also be an important factor. For instance, the twenty million Indians who live and work overseas have a combined income of US$160 billion, which is equal to 35 per cent of their motherland's gross domestic product. With that in mind, the Indian Government in 2003 rolled out the red carpet for its diaspora, hosting a lavish three-day conference in New Delhi.[12] The Burmese diaspora, in contrast, lacks both the numbers and the financial resources to influence governments in either host countries or the home country to this extent. How, then, did this diaspora community come to influence the foreign policies of major Western powers towards Burma?

In order to answer this question, the definition of "diaspora", particularly in the context of the international promotion of Burmese democracy, needs to be explained. According to Faist, a diaspora is a "transnational community" with the characteristic of "mobilization of collective representations within (abstract) symbolic ties: religion, nationality, ethnicity". Faist added another factor as being characteristic of the diaspora — many of its members are people who have undergone traumatic experiences and yearn to return to their lost homeland.[13] Likewise, Tambiah found two different causes for the origin of diaspora communities. First, a diaspora could arise as the result of the voluntary migration of groups of peoples, mostly with useful occupational skills, searching for better economic opportunities and a higher standard of living elsewhere. Second, a diaspora could also arise as the result of the involuntary displacement of people fleeing from political turmoil and wars, or seeking refuge from natural disaster in their country.[14]

The exodus of the Burmese diaspora began when the military took power in 1962 and introduced an extreme form of socialism to the country. The Revolutionary Council under General Ne Win cut back Burma's external ties; for instance, for the first seven years of this regime, the longest visa available for entry into Burma was for seventy-two hours.[15] The result of this severe isolationist policy was a steady outflow of Burmese intellectuals and academics to Western countries, where many of them had been sent as scholarship students by the civilian government of U Nu in the late 1950s. Those who left Burma in the 1970s and early 1980s were permitted only a one-way departure from the country, and the Burmese socialist government refused to issue visas to returning émigrés.

A second wave of exodus resulted when the Burmese military regime adopted a policy of mounting a war of attrition against the ethnic resistance groups. As serious armed conflicts raged in the regions controlled by the Kachin, Shan, Karen, Karenni and Mon ethnic groups, thousands of refugees fled to neighbouring countries, from where they were able to resettle in third countries, mainly in the United States, countries of the European Union, and Australia.[16] Another large wave of Burmese fled the country following the brutal suppression of popular uprisings in 1988. The majority of this group was young students who spearheaded the non-violent movement, and they fled with the dream of continuing their struggle from the border areas. This group continued to be the most politically active; the majority of them lived in exile in Thailand, although some resettled in the West. However, the lucky ones who were able to secure a final refuge in Western countries are indeed small in number. For instance, the total number of Burmese refugees and asylum-seekers granted lawful permanent resident status by the United States in the last fifty years is only 1,344. Compare this with the figures for smaller Laos, with 202,813 nationals resettled in the US.[17] The United States is by far the preferred destination for most Burmese émigrés and refugees, and its Burmese population is estimated to be around 50,000.[18] Therefore, the total number of the Burmese diaspora living in all Western countries is estimated to be not more than a few hundred thousand.

With their small numbers, Burmese diaspora communities were not able to form and organize the necessary political interest groups to exert influence on their host countries to push for changes in Burma. Until the 1990s, there was no coordination of activities between communities even within countries such as the United States, the United Kingdom, or Australia, let alone the organization of trans-national campaigns for Burma. In short, political opportunity structures through which members of the Burmese diaspora could organize effective campaigns on behalf of their brethren at home simply did not exist.

The information revolution changed this inherently weak political opportunity structure of the Burmese diaspora into one of the most vibrant transnational movements.

Struggle for Return: The Evolution of the Burmese Diaspora

The process of evolution — from a passive and marginal diaspora community into an active and influential movement that was able to build a transnational Burmese exile network — involved several phases. Unlike the situation in some countries where the exit of groups going into exile was of itself a major factor for regime change in the home country, the number of Burmese who left the country had only a marginal impact on the military regime in Burma. In addition, the geo-strategic interests of Burma's neighbours also acted as a major inhibitory factor against the exiles, effectively forming a sanctuary against spring-boarding anti-Rangoon activities from the border areas. As a result, many exiles had no choice but to resettle in third countries in order to survive the harsh conditions endured in their transit. Due to the strict requirements of destination countries, only a few thousands out of approximately 200,000 refugees were able to settle in countries such as the United States, the

European Union countries, Australia, and Canada. In that process, several groups of political exiles were dispersed among a number of countries, which left the exiles no option but to regroup and continue their struggle against the military regime at home. It was a huge challenge for the Burmese exiles just to maintain their network, let alone try to have an impact on promoting democratic changes at home.

In spite of these challenges, Burmese exiles seem to have overcome several obstacles and were able to maintain a few networks that mobilized international campaigns synergistically with emerging transnational movements focused on human rights and corporate responsibility. It began with the development of basic information infrastructure for the networks, and involved the gradual building of policy constituencies in the Western democracies.

Phase 1: The "Boomerang" of Promoting Information Flow, Awareness, and Transnational Networking

The role that modern information technology plays through the various mass-communication channels of satellite television, free radio, and other media, in helping pro-democracy movements around the world — the "CNN effect" — is widely recognized. When one's neighbours and the world are able to watch, the cost of repression for authoritarian regimes goes up.[19] Many Burmese observers agreed that the year-long brutality of the 1988 crackdown on the pro-democracy movement might have been mitigated if the international media had been able to cover the protests.[20] Without accurate and timely information, the worst kinds of human rights violations in Burma have gone unnoticed and without effective action in response from human rights organizations and international human rights mechanisms. For instance, Amnesty International published its first full report on Burma only in 1990, two years after the mass killings.[21] The extent of what really happened in Burma was not fully known by the Burmese diaspora. At that time, only foreign broadcasting stations such as the British Broadcasting Corporation (BBC) and Voice of America (VOA), together with a few Thai newspapers, carried news about Burma regularly. However, many members of the Burmese diaspora living in Western countries were unable to tune into these radio stations or obtain newspapers from Bangkok.

Gathering credible data on human-rights violations in Burma as evidence to raise the level of international concern and to garner support for action to pressure the military regime to end its abuses was not only difficult but also time-consuming. This gap was in essence filled when a group of Burmese students, aided by Douglas Steele, an American volunteer who made his mark on the Internet with his pen name *Strider*, established BurmaNet in 1994 to post news and reports from Thailand and the border areas to some seven hundred subscribers across the world.[22] It was Steele who perused an on-line usenet newsgroup called *soc.culture.thai* and realized that the Bangkok dailies' in-depth news coverage of events and stories from Burma could be a goldmine for thousands of Burmese exiles and expatriates cut off completely from their homeland.[23]

BurmaNet was an instant hit for thousands of Burmese and friends who wanted to help Burma. Working with a team of Burmese student exiles in Thailand, Steele facilitated the collection of first-hand reports and information about the situation in Burma and disseminated them faster and more cheaply than any method that had previously been used by the Burmese exiles. BurmaNet also fostered links between Burmese activists and international human rights groups, who established transnational networks to work for the promotion of human rights in Burma. It allowed the Burmese activists to bypass the traditional filters of the news media and international NGOs and to disseminate daily reports of events and stories in Burma rather than awaiting sporadic coverage by regional and mainstream media. Indeed, several foreign broadcasting stations such as BBC, VOA, Radio Free Asia, and the Democratic Voice of Burma (that had been set up by the Burmese exile government) picked up BurmaNet news items and redirected them through their Burmese programmes to millions of listeners in Burma. Therefore, it also helped break the news blackout imposed by the military regime inside the country.

Before the advent of the Internet, foreign radio stations like the BBC and VOA had played an important role in getting news to people inside Burma.[24] The military regime controlled all internal news media, whether TV, radio, or print, and used them for propaganda. Only foreign broadcasts provided "real" news about Burma — information that was absent from the state-regulated media.[25] In this context, the Internet boosted the resourcefulness of old technology in two significant ways. First, BurmaNet was able to multiply vastly the number of stories being "published", and rapidly gained credibility as a unique source of Burmese news. It helped to certify other "unpublished" news that was directly fed to it by Burmese activists, and this news was in turn rebroadcast by the foreign radio stations. Second, the introduction of web-based multimedia radio instantly transformed the role of foreign radio broadcasts from mere short-wave broadcasts that could not be picked up easily outside Asia into a truly global medium that found another important audience outside Burma — thousands of the diaspora living outside the region. In this way the combination of Internet and radio connects homeland and diaspora, and nowadays people can interactively be aware of what is going on in relation to Burmese people and communities all around the globe.

Scholars of international politics such as Keck and Sikkink have long noted the importance of "transnational networks" that emerge at times when aggrieved domestic societal actors are denied access to the political process at home.[26] When the local actors have by-passed recalcitrant local states and have reached foreign and international NGOs, foreign governments, and international organizations, they may be able to enlist a transnational effort to bring international pressure upon the regime in power — in other words, to "boomerang" back on local authority. Only when BurmaNet established its services in 1995 could this crucial boomerang effect, working through transnational advocacy networks, be applied against Burma. The boomerang effect also has an important domestic component: various isolated local groups inside Burma can learn at greater speed than before, through BurmaNet and the various foreign radio stations, about the experiences of local groups in different parts of the country or about events within the country, all accounts of which are systematically suppressed by the military regime.

The cost and speed of email, its ease of use, and the access it provides are well suited to the needs of Burmese dissidents. With a relatively short period of training and some seed money, the under-funded Burmese activist organizations are able to make good use of what email offers, especially since email connections can be made with a minimum amount of time on-line and even in areas with unreliable telephone lines.[27] Many local human rights organizations were set up in remote parts of the Thai-Burma border by taking advantage of available Internet connectivity up to the border areas inside Thailand. Groups such as the Association for Assisting Political Prisoners (AAPP), the Human Rights Education Institute of Burma (HREIB), and the Human Rights Documentation Unit (HRDU) all used emails to feed regular reports on political prisoners, forced labour situations, and other pressing human rights conditions in the country to international organizations and United Nations (UN) bodies that monitor the situation in Burma.

Phase 2: Cyber-Activism — Global Campaigns and Local Actions

Energized and angered by the tragic news of repression and human-rights violations in Burma, a group of Burmese students and concerned Americans began to organize a network of activists who were willing to mobilize collective action in support of freedom in Burma. The first activities were somewhat similar to actions Burmese themselves had tried inside the country when they staged non-violent protests against the Socialist regime during the 1988 pro-democracy uprisings. It was Zarni, a Burmese PhD student from the University of Wisconsin at Madison, who initially wanted to organize an indefinite hunger strike to protest the human rights situation in Burma, but who later, with a group of concerned American students, used the Internet to launch, instead, a national protest against Northwestern University officials with various ties to American corporations doing business in Burma.[28] He gathered support for a National Day of Action, an idea he borrowed from fellow "spiders" outside the United States, and many students in seventy-five campuses around the world joined the action on 27 October 1995. Email-based networking transformed the National Day of Action into the "International Day of Action", and within seven weeks of starting preparations this lone activist in Madison inspired a truly global action against the military regime in Burma.[29]

Amazed by such an impressive response from cyber-networking, in November 1995 Zarni set up a Free Burma email list server through the University of Wisconsin. Burmese students who previously had only had experience of organizing street-level activism benefited greatly from the efficient and quick diffusion of ideas about protest and tactics across national borders through the Free Burma list server. Several protest ideas on petitions, demonstrations, and consumer boycotts were being discussed on the Net before a more effective action plan was drawn up to maximize the impact on the regime. From 1995 to 1998, when the activism of the Free Burma adherents reached its peak level, Zarni and his fellow activists launched several successful campaigns that were planned entirely through the Internet. The most successful of these included the Pepsi Boycott Campaign and the facilitation of the passage of Selective Purchasing Laws. The campaigns culminated in 1996 in the historic adoption by the State of Massachusetts of the "Burma Law", which event had a deep impact not only on Burma but also on the constitutional discourse of American federalism.

The impact of international boycott campaigns on the military regime is tremendous. By 1997, twelve American cities, including New York, had passed Free Burma selective purchasing laws that banned city governments from concluding contracts with any companies doing business in Burma. The Internet was a very effective tool, not only for connecting different communities across the United States that from a variety of perspectives had some interest in Burma, but also in setting a "rights" agenda for action. Without the campaigns, these communities could have acted differently on Burma, and the disparate actions might have lost momentum as time passed.

Instead, the Internet allowed different groups to brainstorm, debate, and choose tactics that would have the most effect in their anti-SPDC campaigns. Veteran campaigners who had prior experience mobilizing campaigns for South Africa knew exactly how a crescendo of local actions would finally influence the US Congress to take a stand on Burma, but there was no strong support base — no Burma constituency — in the United States to mobilize such a course of action. Under these circumstances, the Internet-based networks amplified local actions to affect sentiment at the national level.

In the case of the Harvard students' boycott campaign against Pepsi, an important campaign for Burma, only a handful of students interested in Burma was available to organize the action. The aim was to influence the powerful student government body to reverse a decision to sign a contract with PepsiCo, which had a growing business in Burma. Emails could be used to multiply the numbers, and they became an effective lobbying tool for promoting awareness and identifying sympathetic key individuals. Not only did Harvard's student government drop the contract with Pepsi, their actions inspired a shareholder resolution at the Pepsi board meeting. News about the boycott was picked up by the mainstream media, which spread the campaign all over the world.[30]

The success of the Free Burma Coalition in America inspired many other Burma "spiders" around the world to stage similarly successful campaigns in their localities. "Think globally, act locally" was a predominant strategy of the emerging transnational movement for Free Burma, and the Internet was the key that connected every local group to a global movement for planning, prioritizing, and targeting the best attainable goals. As a result, two popular European beer-makers, Heineken and Carlsberg, were forced by local Dutch and Danish activists groups to withdraw their investments from Burma.[31] A year after the beer companies' withdrawal, another European giant, the Ericsson company, decided to withdraw its bid for mobile phone operations in Burma.[32] In 2002, the joint actions taken by many Europe-based Burma groups forced Zurich-based lingerie giant Triumph International to close down its manufacturing factories in Burma.[33] Under the slogan "Support Breasts — Not Dictators", cyber-activists in the United Kingdom and other countries urged European consumers to boycott the firm until its Rangoon factory was closed.[34]

In the meantime, more traditional political organizations such as the National Coalition Government of the Union of Burma (NCGUB), the exile government constituted by elected parliamentarians, began to recognize the power of the Internet as an organizational tool. On one occasion, it mounted an Internet campaign to reach out to thousands of fellow parliamentarians to support the convening of parliament in Burma.[35] The appeal, carried out by local friends of Burma, was aided by a web-based kiosk that served as both an information resource and a motivational source for the campaign. As a result, the Global Parliamentary Solidarity Campaign received over two thousand signatures from parliamentarians around the world in support of elected MPs from Burma and their call for democratic changes in the country.[36]

Although the majority of Free Burma campaigns have affected political developments in Burma only indirectly, through actions against the regime's business partners, some have had a more direct effect on the regime. One such campaign was the boycott of "Visit Myanmar Year" in 1996, a much celebrated tourism promotion launched by the regime. The direct impact of cyber campaigns discouraged many Western tourists from visiting Burma, and the promotion, which had targeted one million tourist entries for that year, was an abysmal failure, with actual tourist arrivals being only a fraction of the desired number. The campaign had a measurable, and some believe lasting, impact. Burma never became the popular tourist destination the generals had hoped for. Barely 200,000 tourists visited in 2000, far short of the 500,000–1 million target that had been set by the generals during "Visit Myanmar Year" in 1996. Since 2000, arrivals have trickled in at about the same glacial pace.[37] It was a big slap in the face for some top generals who had personally promoted the campaign. Perhaps this campaign sent a strong signal to the regime, which itself then turned to the Internet for launching counter-campaigns against the exile movement and opposition groups. To some extent, the regime's reaction to the Free Burma campaigns has demonstrated the impact these activities have had. Significantly, the campaigns deprived the regime of critical income from outside investors. They also provided a broad platform for sustaining international policies on Burma, some of which had an important deterrent effect in preventing further abuses by the regime and protecting domestic populations.

Phase 3: Creating a Credible Alternative

The Internet has proved a powerful instrument for exiled Burmese activists: while it has altered the dynamics of cyber-activism and transformed the impact of democracy promotion in Burma, the target of these campaigns was primarily criticism of the military regime itself and its international friends (that is, multinational corporations, business firms, and apologist authoritarian governments). Another benefit of the Internet cannot be underestimated: it has lowered the transaction and organizational costs for the exiled activists and their trans-national networks. Not only has this enabled them to deliver a formidable protest campaign against the military regime in power, but it has also facilitated a learning process that has allowed the development of communication and networking among many groups within the Burmese diaspora, some of which had previously been passively quiet on the democratic cause in Burma.

In the beginning, cyber-activism was mostly organized and staged by politically active exiles and refugees who represented, in a sense, personified consequences of their violent and tragic flight from Burma following the 1988 political uprisings and their subsequent years of opposition to rule by the current military regime. These late-arriving additions to the Burmese diaspora tend to view themselves as "kidnap victims", and have an inherent and direct interest in the process of democratization in Burma. Their perspectives have often provoked them to respond strongly to other Burmese who had arrived in Western countries much earlier (sometimes as much as thirty years earlier) and who were better integrated into these societies and relatively insulated in their lives, and thus generally not as keenly interested in the current politics of Burma.

The present regime in Burma recognized this split within the Burmese diaspora and began to exploit it, trying to drive a wedge between the different generations of exiles. It reversed its thirty-year-old policy of outright visa-bans against foreign citizens of Burmese origin. This policy had been a very effective tool to manipulate people who had been separated from their kin for many years so they would acquiesce and keep silent about the regime's policies in order to be able to return for family reunions. The regime even went so far as to invite a select number of prominent Burmese expatriates to visit Burma and treated them as honoured guests, as a way of trying to enhance the regime's legitimacy at home and abroad.[38]

The Internet has enabled the activist groups to re-energize and inform these less vocal groups from the Burmese diaspora so they become more aware of the real situation in Burma and of the manipulative tactics of the regime. It has enabled members of the Burmese diaspora to create an enduring common identity around many diverse groups, in spite of different degrees of detachment and attachment to the social movement and to the home country, and in spite of the varied reasons for their departure from Burma and their different experiences.

As the use of the Internet among the Burmese diaspora grows to maturity, the agenda of their Internet-based participatory politics has moved away from a focus on protest movement toward building a credible alternative to the military regime. As a result, the target of their Internet-based politics has become both external and internal, the external target being the military regime and the internal target being the pro-democracy opposition itself. Here, the role of the Internet lies in fostering new opportunities for civic engagement and contributing to governance processes within the pro-democracy opposition. Since basic freedoms and democratic rights have for several decades been denied to Burmese living in Burma, the Burmese pro-democracy opposition needs to build democratic political culture within its own movement. Although political parties had been established prior to the elections in 1990, all previous efforts to conduct representative politics had been undermined by severe repression and harsh restrictions imposed by successive regimes. The "stolen election" of 1990 did produce 485 elected representatives, of which

National League for Democracy candidates won 80 per cent. Since then, however, the military regime has closed virtually all channels of communication and meaningful advocacy between citizens and such representatives. Although the 1990 election results confirmed a strong national consensus that the military regime must go, consensus regarding how such transition could occur was less certain. Under these circumstances, the Internet provides an alternative channel for involvement in the opposition movement, at least for the Burmese exiles who have access to cyberspace.

To large extent, the Internet has transformed the mode of political participation for Burmese democrats in exile. Although many of their representative bodies, including the government in exile, have retained traditional hierarchical organizations, their one-dimensional ladder of participation has been effectively transformed into a more participatory and "poly-vocal" model through Internet-based civic engagement. Nye and Keohane have noted that the "opening of a public space for deliberation which interfaces with the actual decision-making process in the broadest way possible can significantly enhance input legitimacy".[39] Many representative bodies within the Burmese pro-democracy movement have stepped up their consultative processes inside the Burmese diaspora, and this enhances not only good governance within the pro-democracy opposition but also the building of a credible alternative to the regime, which can effectively influence international opinion toward supporting regime transformation in Burma, from tyranny to a participatory and pluralist democracy.

Within a brief period of time, since about 1995 when Burmese exiles and opposition groups were introduced to it, the Internet has become the mainstay of the information infrastructure for the Burmese exile movement. The Burmese government in exile, constituted by the elected members of parliament in exile, has set up a website (www.ncgub.net) in order to provide accurate information about Burma as well as about its policies and procedures for promoting democratization in the country. The use of the Internet by the government in exile has enormously improved the transparency and openness of its activities promoting democratization in Burma and has fostered its link with the grassroots of the movement.

The changing role of the Internet is also evident in the way that politically oriented messages are posted to the Usenet newsgroups such as soc.culture.burma. In the early years, the Usenet newsgroup's messages were mostly likely to express opposition to the SPDC, but in later years there has been an increasing number of messages targeted at strategies aimed by the pro-democracy opposition toward the SPDC, as well as allegations of power abuses.[40] Although some exiled Burmese political leaders are allergic to open criticism,[41] most opposition groups and their leaders are responsive to such messages, clarifying their positions and improving transparency and openness in the conduct of their activities. By 2002, as many as a dozen Burmese e-groups had been set up with the aid of freely-available list serve services, which conduct discussions aimed at waging cyber-activism against the military regime as well as at promoting internal democracy within the opposition movement.

Moderating forces have shaped the political role in exile of Burma's ethnic minorities, whose members have migrated over many years to different parts of the world, due to repressive discrimination at home. Members of these groups have impressive and substantial achievements. Several different ethnic groups have attempted to create a virtual community that supposedly eliminates the distances that separate them in the real world. Dispersion from their homelands to countries all over the world has threatened efforts to retain cultural heritage and keep in touch with ancestral roots in Burma. Nowadays disparate members of ethnic groups can interact and develop strategy in Internet "chat rooms", and the outcomes of these interactions seem to have mobilized greater sympathy and support around the world than the struggle of their predecessors fighting in the Burmese jungles. A dozen or so ethnic groups in Burma have set up discussion groups or forums focusing on a range of issues from cultural preservation to provision of humanitarian assistance to their kin back home. A few have set up websites that contain both information and organizational messages. Most focus on the role of ethnic nationalities in the process of democratization in Burma.[42] In some circumstances the Internet can act to amplify an existing predisposition and radicalize the ethno-nationalistic claims of long-disenfranchised groups,[43] but the cybernauts of Burmese ethnic groups have been moderate and very realistic in their consistent demand for a federal union in Burma.

The impact of all these efforts on the international stage is easily visible. The Burma agenda has moved higher up the foreign policy priorities of many Western democratic governments, thanks to a series of United Nations General Assembly resolutions and UN Human Rights Commission hearings on Burma. The governments of the United States and the European

Union have imposed sanctions regimes on the military junta since the late 1990s, and have increased the pressure of these mechanisms recently. The Association of South East Asian Nations (ASEAN) has been mobilized to push for changes within Burma before Burma assumes the chairmanship of ASEAN in 2006. Emergency relief operations undertaken inside the country are now subject to strict standards of accountability, transparency, and fair delivery — essential steps towards linking relief to democratization. Most important of all, when the voice of domestic opposition has been effectively silenced by the regime, it is the leaders of the exile movement who provide an alternative vision and focus of authority for the desperate populations inside the country.

Phase 4: Preparing for Transition Through Virtual Knowledge-sharing

Among many legacies of military rule in Burma, the enormous damage inflicted on human capital over more than three decades poses the greatest challenge for any successful transition to democracy. During the Ne Win socialist era, discrimination against educated people and intellectuals was thorough-going: the main official motto of the Burma Socialist Programme Party was "*Lu-gaung Lu-Taw*" or "Preference for the loyal man over the efficient man". Nepotism and favoritism continued under the new leadership of the military government that came to power in 1988, and the depletion of human capital continued unabated, as thousands of students, teachers, intellectuals, and professionals left Burma for neighbouring countries or Western nations in search of freedom from both poverty and fear. Worse still, those who stayed behind suffered further when the military regime closed down all institutions of higher education for many years in order to prevent students from organizing anti-regime protests.[44]

At the time of writing, the destruction of civil society, the liquidation of all participatory institutions, and the economic crisis have combined to make Burma's problems extremely intractable and enormously difficult to resolve. While the political leaders, particularly Daw Aung San Suu Kyi and the National League for Democracy, may be able to consider sensible options for resolving the problems inside the country, their initiatives, however sound and sensible, still lack well-informed research on which to base their recommendations. Outside Burma there is no dearth of scholars who do high-quality research on Burma, but very few of these apply their work to the demands articulated within the society. As a result, the link between "knowledge" and "power" is missing — a link that permits the transmission of policy-relevant information from a variety of sources to the ears and eyes of public leaders — and this hinders the capacity for advancing changes within the society. The growing popularity of the Internet among expatriate Burmese experts, who were originally drawn to it by political mobilization for cyber-activism, provides a bridge for connecting intellectuals and activists. Their joint efforts to prepare a number of policy-oriented studies on Burma's myriad of challenges provide an instant intellectual platform for the pro-democracy movement to present alternative visions for Burma.

The importance of learning from others for the process of Burmese democratization reached its highest point in 1998 when Tun Myint, a Burmese PhD student at Indiana University, launched the *Maykha* list server, to promote educational and academic exchange between Burmese students studying abroad. He added another list server in 2001 for the Technical Advisory Network for Burma (TAN), a group of progressive scholars who volunteered to create a "virtual think-tank" for generating policy-relevant information and research critical to the democratic transition in Burma.[45] These list servers undoubtedly enhanced the sharing of policy knowledge among Burmese experts who were dispersed around many academic campuses and international organizations, allowing them to build consensus on important policy issues and to present a collective input to the political leadership of the pro-democracy movement. Having more than just a behind-the-scenes role, these activists-cum-scholars have greater freedom to test new ideas and to engage in politically sensitive initiatives than the leadership of the pro-democracy movement, who cannot afford to undertake such essays before the terms of debate have been tested by comments from scholars and the diaspora.

The Internet provides flexibility and autonomy for scholars to address policy problems in a timely fashion as they arise. For instance, when Burma was hit with a banking crisis in early March 2003, a group of economists was able to exchange views and issue analyses within the days of initial news.[46] In particular, the Internet enables the pro-democracy movement to tap a wide range of intellectual resources around the world regarding questions on particular problems and issues. Not only do Burmese scholars provide a distinctive service in raising the standard of debate and broadening the agenda, but they can present alternative views, advocating new paths and policy shifts. Internet-based mass surveys and opinion polls have helped build consensus and public support on certain policy options and measures. In 2002, the British Broadcasting Corporation ran an opinion survey about sanctions against the military regime in Burma; an overwhelming number of respondents supported tougher sanctions despite the many anti-sanction arguments available to the audience.[47]

Looking Forward: The Future Role of Burmese Exiles

For the time being, the role of exiles in promoting democracy in Burma is limited to what can be achieved through the channel of the international community to exert pressure on the military regime. The Internet has equipped the Burmese diaspora to unite and organize in order to influence the policies of the international community towards Burma. However, it is still not possible for Burmese exiles to have a direct impact on creating a civic space or political liberalization inside the country, since the regime maintains strict control within Burma. Opportunities for direct action inside the country could emerge, as Burma's military rulers are forced to integrate the economy with the ASEAN region that is now openly embracing free trade, visa-free travel, and e-commerce. Meanwhile, the Burmese diaspora has moved on from cyber-activism to knowledge-sharing. It is to be presumed that Burmese exiles will play a major role in the country when the authoritarian regime finally opens up. On one hand, returned exiles can provide an effective resource for restoring the gaps in human capital during the process of reconstruction. On the other, active participation by exiles who have wide experience of the procedural mechanisms and functions of mature democracies will enhance good governance and accountability during the transition, and this in turn will help to consolidate the fragile process of democratization.

Notes

[1]   This evolutionary process is best described in the personal story of U Htun Aung Kyaw, the leader of the All Burma Student Democratic Front, who resettled at Cornell University and continued his fight against the military regime. See Michael Ryan, "He Fights Dictators with the Internet", *Parade*, 23 August 1998.

[2]   I wish to thank Shu-Yun Ma of the Chinese University of Hong Kong, who modified and applied the model to analyse the case of Chinese exiles, for his generous guidance in applying it to Burma. For his excellent application of the model to the Chinese case, see Shu-Yun Ma, "Exit, Voice, and Struggle to Return of the Chinese Political Exiles", *Pacific Affairs*, Vol. 66, No. 3 (1993). For the original concepts of exit-voice-loyalty, see Albert O. Hirschman, *Exit, Voice and Loyalty: Responses to Decline in Firms, Organizations and States* (Cambridge, MA: Harvard University Press, 1970).

[3]   Charles Tilly, *From Mobilization to Revolution* (Reading, MA: Addison-Wesley Publishing Co., 1978).

[4]   Margaret Keck and Kathryn Sikkink, *Activists Beyond Borders. Advocacy Networks in International Politics* (Ithaca: Cornell University Press, 1998).

[5]   Peter Eisinger, "The Conditions of Protest Behavior in American Cities", *American Political Science Review*, Vol. 67 (1973), pp. 11–28; Donald R. Culverson, "The Politics of the Anti-Apartheid Movement in the United States, 1969–1986", *Political Science Quarterly*, Vol. 111, No. 1 (Spring 1996), pp. 127–49.

[6]   For a more comprehensive account of national struggles for independence and subsequent developments, see Josef Silverstein, *Burma: Military Rule and the Politics of Stagnation* (Ithaca: Cornell University Press, 1977); David I. Steinberg, *Burma's Road Toward Development: Growth and Ideology under Military Rule* (Boulder: Westview Press, 1981); and Mya Maung, *Totalitarianism in Burma: Prospects for Economic Development* (New York: Paragon Press, 1992), p. 19.

[7]   Mary P. Callahan, "Democracy in Burma: Lessons from History", in "Political Legacies and Prospects for Democratic Development", *NBR Analysis*, Vol. 9, No. 3 (May 1998), pp. 5–26.

[8]   Ibid. The destructive form of power struggles at the apex of the dominant power system continued well into the socialist era of General Ne Win. See also, Kyaw Yin Hlaing, "Reconsidering the Failure of the Burma Socialist Programme Party Government to Eradicate Internal Economic Impediments", *Southeast Asia Research*, Vol. 11, No. 1 (2003), pp. 5–58.

[9]   An excellent account of popular uprisings in 1988 can be found in Bertil Lintner, *Outrage: Burma's Struggle for Democracy* (Bangkok: White Lotus Press, 1990).

[10] Freedom House, "Burma", in *Freedom in the World 2003* (Washington, D.C.: Freedom House, 2004).

[11] Yossi Shain, "The Role of Diasporas in Conflict Perpetuation or Resolution", *SAIS Review*, Vol. 22, No. 2 (Summer–Fall 2002), pp. 115–44.

[12] Amol Sharma, "Come Home, We Need You", *Far Eastern Economic Review*, 23 January 2003.

13 T. Faist, "Transnationalization in International Migration: Implications for the Study of Citizenship and Culture", *Ethnic and Racial Studies*, Vol. 23, No. 2 (March 2000), pp. 189–222.

14 S. Tambiah, "Transnational Movements, Diaspora, and Multiple Modernities: Transnational Movements of People and Their Implications", *Daedalus*, Vol. 129, No. 1 (Winter 2000), pp. 163–94.

15 Timothy Syrota, *Welcome to Burma and Enjoy the Totalitarian Experience* (Bangkok: Orchid Press, 2001).

16 There is an estimate that two million Burmese refugees and illegal immigrants are living and working in the neighboring countries of Thailand, India, and China.

17 Office of Immigration Statistics, *2002 Yearbook of Immigration Statistics* (Washington D.C.: Office of Immigration Statistics, 2002). However, the numbers do not include those who could have entered the United States under normal immigration procedures. The individuals under asylum-seeker and refugee categories represent a segment of the diaspora population that is traumatized but may be more politically active than those in other categories.

18 Author's estimate, counting those who continue to associate with and participate in Burmese traditional events and festivals organized by the diaspora communities around the United States.

19 Philippe C. Schmitter, "The Influence of the International Context upon the Choice of National Institutions and Policies in Neo-Democracies", in *The International Dimensions of Democratization: Europe and the Americas*, edited by Laurence Whitehead (New York: Oxford University Press, 1996). There was no foreign television coverage of the popular uprisings in Burma in 1988. The killings in Burma that year were much more brutal and sustained than those that occurred a year later in Tiananmen Square in China. However, international awareness of Burma's uprisings was low in comparison with knowledge about the Tiananmen Square "massacre", which was widely covered by CNN and other foreign broadcasting stations.

20 Roger Matthew, "A Beaten, Tortured People", *Financial Times*, 19 May 1990. Likewise, a long-time Burmese observer, Professor Josef Silverstein of Rutgers University, wrote in the *New York Times* on 15 September 1989, "[T]he world was thrilled and then horrified by events in Tiananmen Square, but forgot or did not know that more people took part in peaceful demonstrations for democracy in the Burmese capital between Aug. 8 and Sept. 18; that more students were murdered by the military in Myanmar than were killed in China."

21 Amnesty International, "Myanmar: Prisoners of Conscience, Torture, and Extrajudicial Executions", *Amnesty International Country Report: Burma*

(*Myanmar*) (London: Amnesty International, 1990). Human Rights Watch and other human rights organizations followed suit in succeeding years.

22   "Myanmar: Arachnophilia," *Economist*, 10 August 1996.

23   A. Lin Neumann, "The Resistance Network," *Wired*, Vol. 4, No. 1 (January 1996).

24   Josef Silverstein, "Burma's Uneven Struggle", *Journal of Democracy*, Vol. 7, No. 4 (October 1996), pp. 88–102.

25   Chris Tenove, "Radio Free Burma", *Thunderbird* (University of British Columbia Journalism Review), Vol. 2, No. 4 (March 2000).

26   Keck and Sikkink, *Activists Beyond Borders*.

27   The Open Society Institute (OSI) of the Soros Foundation funded the BurmaNet project and other information and Internet-related activities. In the initial years of emerging connectivity among Burmese organizations, the Burma Project of the OSI used at minimum 25 per cent of their project funding (on average about $400,000) on information and ICT activities during 1994 and 1996. See, Open Society Institute-New York, "Burma Project Report 1994–1996". Available at: http://www.soros.org/burma. Accessed 27 July 2005.

28   See Zarni's "Foreword" in Free Burma Coalition, *The Free Burma Coalition Manual: How You Can Help Burma's Struggle for Freedom* (Madison, WI: Free Burma Coalition, 1997).

29   Ann Scott Tyson, "Political Activism on Campus Takes on a Cyberspace Twist", *Christian Science Monitor*, 31 October 1995.

30   A very good account of campaign dynamics and the importance of the Internet in cyber-activism on Burma are covered in Tiffany Daniz and Warren P. Strobel, *Networking Dissent: Cyber Activists Use the Internet to Promote Democracy in Burma*, Virtual Diplomacy Series No. 3 (February 2000), United States Institute of Peace (Washington D.C.: United States Institute of Peace, 2000).

31   "Heineken NV: Brewer Decides To Pull Out of Its Business in Burma", *Wall Street Journal*, 12 July 1996.

32   In fact, Ericsson headquarters cited US boycotts for its concerns and eventual decision to suspend business in Burma. See Ericsson official announcement at: http://www.ericsson.com/press/archive/1998Q3/19980901-0023.html. Accessed 17 May 2003.

33   BBC News "Bra company pulls out of Burma", 28 January 2002.

34   BBC News, "Barbed-wire bra protest over Burma investment", 10 December 2001.

35   International Parliamentary Union (IPU), a body that represents over a hundred national parliaments around the world, in its 166th conference adopted a resolution calling for all its members to sign the solidarity resolution. See http://www.ipu.org/hr-e/166/myn01.htm. Accessed 17 May 2003.

[36]   The government-in-exile's website, www.ncgub.net, served as a campaign headquarters that contained frequently asked questions (FAQs) about the campaign, as well as a list of signatories, updated frequently to show the growth of support on a daily and weekly basis.

[37]   Mark Lander, "On the Road to Mandalay: An Ethical Predicament", *New York Times*, 1 January 2002.

[38]   For instance, the internationally-renowned meditation teacher, S.N. Goenka, was invited as a state guest, and the title of *Maha Saddhamma Joti Dhaja*, the highest title awarded to any layman in Burma, was bestowed on him.

[39]   Robert O. Keohane and Joseph S. Nye, Jr., "Power and Interdependence in the Information Age," *Foreign Affairs* (September/October 1998), 105.

[40]   In an interesting comparative study done by Kevin A. Hill and John E. Hughes, during the week of 26 October 1996, 40 per cent of messages on the usenet newsgroup, soc.culture.burma, were politically oriented and 24 per cent were anti-government. This author finds that the website soc.culture.burma remains highly political. However, it has begun to include a number of messages highly critical of the opposition leadership along with anti-military messages. See Kevin A. Hill and John E. Hughes, "Is the Internet an Instrument of Global Democratization", in *Cyberpolitics: Citizen Activism in the Age of the Internet*, by Kevin A. Hill and John E. Hughes (Lanham, MD: Rowman and Littlefield, 1998).

[41]   An independent Thailand-based Burmese reporter commented that "[W]e have to be afraid of the Thai authorities, the Burmese authorities and the rebel authorities." Cited in A. Lin Neumann, "Burma Under Pressure: How Burmese Journalism Survives in One of the World's Most Repressive Regimes", Press Freedom Reports from Around the World, for the Committee to Protect Journalists, 2002. Available at: http://www.cpj.org/Briefings/2002/Burma_feb02/Burma_feb02.html. Accessed 27 July 2005.

[42]   From 1996 onward, successive United Nations General Assemblies have passed a unanimous resolution on Burma, calling for a "tri-partite dialogue" process involving the military, the NLD, and ethnic nationalities, to resolve the political stalemate in Burma. The Internet has encouraged several ethnic nationality groups in exile to re-assemble their representational positions toward this goal.

[43]   Steven R. David, "Internal War: Causes and Cures," Review Article, *World Politics*, Vol. 49, No. 4 (1997), pp. 552–76.

[44]   Mya Maung, *Burmese Way to Capitalism* (New York: Praeger, 1998).

[45]   The list servers are hosted by the Indiana University at Bloomington; messages can be sent to maykha-l@indiana.edu, and tan-l@indiana.edu.

[46]   Sean Turnell and Alison Vicary, "Burma's Banking Crisis: A Commentary,"

Burma Economic Watch, Macquarie University, Sydney, Australia, 6 March 2003.
See http://www.burmalibrary.org/search.php?t=k&sstr=banking&c=0&q=
all&o=d&f0=1&a0=1&v=1. Accessed 27 July 2005.

[47] The BBC has also put up commentaries for and against the use of sanctions in
Burma. See www.bbc.co.uk, accessed on 1 March 2003.

References

Allott, Anna J. *Censorship in Burma — Inked Over, Ripped Out: Burmese Storytellers and the Censors.* Chiang Mai: Silkworm Press, 1994.

Ashton, William. "Burma Receives Advances from its Silent Suitors in Singapore". *Jane's Intelligence Review,* Vol. 10, No. 3 (1 March 1998).

Associated Press. "Myanmar Issues Tough Restrictions Even Before it Allows the Internet". 21 January 2000.

Eccarius-Kelly, Vera. "Political Movements and Leverage Points: Kurdish Activism in the European Diaspora". *Journal of Muslim Minority Affairs* Vol. 22, No. 1 (2002).

Everett, Margaret. "Latin America On-line: The Internet, Development, and Democratization". *Human Organization* (Winter 1998).

Hachigian, Nina. "The Internet and Power in One-Party East Asian States", *Washington Quarterly,* Vol. 25, No. 3 (Summer 2002), pp. 41–58.

Iyer, Venkat. "Acts of Oppression: Censorship and the Law in Burma". Article 19, London, March 1999. Available at: http://www.ibiblio.org/obl/docs3/Acts%20of%20Oppression,%20Art19.htm. Accessed 31 July 2005.

Kalathil, Shanthi and Taylor C. Boas. "The Internet and State Control in Authoritarian Regimes: China, Cuba, and the Counterrevolution". Working Paper, Global Policy Programme, Carnegie Endowment for International Peace. Washington D.C.: Carnegie Endowment for International Peace, July 2001.

Keck, Margaret and Kathryn Sikkink. *Activists Beyond Borders. Advocacy Networks in International Politics.* Ithaca: Cornell University Press, 1998.

Krebs, Viola. "The Impact of the Internet on Myanmar". *First Monday,* Peer Reviewed Journal on the Internet. Available at: http://www.firstmonday.org/issues/issue6_5/krebs/. Accessed 27 July 2005.

Metzl, Jamie F. "Information Technology and Human Rights," *Human Rights Quarterly,* Vol. 18, No. 4 (November 1996), pp. 705–46.

Naim, Moises. "The New Diaspora," *Foreign Policy,* No. 131 (July–August 2002), pp. 96–99.

Nonini, Donald M. "Transnational Migrants, Globalization Processes, and Regimes of Power and Knowledge". *Critical Asian Studies,* Vol. 34, No. 1 (1 March 2002), pp. 3–17.

Norris, Pippa. *Digital Divide: Civic Engagement, Information Poverty and the Internet in Democratic Societies*. New York: Cambridge University Press, 2001.

_____. *Democratic Phoenix: Reinventing Political Activism*. New York: Cambridge University Press, 2002.

Tarrow, Sidney. "Beyond Globalization: Why Creating Transnational Social Movements Is So Hard and When It Is Most Likely To Happen". Departments of Government and Sociology, Cornell University. Unpublished memo.

Teferra, Damtew. "Revisiting the Doctrine of Human Capital Mobility in the Information Age". International Conference on Brain Drain and Capacity Building in Africa, Addis Ababa, Ethiopia, 22–24 February 2000.

Wahlbeck, Östen. "The Concept of Diaspora as an Analytical Tool in the Study of Refugee Communities". *Journal of Ethnic and Migration Studies*, Vol. 28, No. 2 (April 2002).

Strobel, Warren P., Richard J. Newman, and David E. Kaplan. "A Glimpse of Cyberwarfare". *U.S. News & World Report*, Vol. 128, No. 10 (March 2000).

Zinnbauer, Dieter. "Internet, Civil Society and Global Governance: The Neglected Political Dimension of the Digital Divide". *Information & Security*, Special Edition on Internet and International Relations, Vol. 7 (2001), pp. 45–64.

IV

Charting the Way Ahead

13

Foreign Aid: A Myanmar Perspective

U Myint

This chapter comments on some of the pre-requisites for foreign assistance to flow to Myanmar, but seeks to do this from a Myanmar perspective. It identifies ways in which international assistance might be designed to enhance maximum long-term benefits for the people of Myanmar in the particular circumstances they face.

The Issue of Self-Reliance

In thinking about foreign aid, one issue that arises in the Myanmar context is the high importance the country attaches to self-reliance. This is a useful attitude to have, as no country has ever developed without relying on its own efforts. In Myanmar, however, from the early 1960s until the present day "self-reliance" has been taken to mean that the country must do things in its own way, by its own efforts, relying on its own resources, which are believed to be ample to ensure a favorable outcome. The fact that the outside world offers markets for Myanmar products, and opportunities to secure investment funds, technology, and development finance, and that it possesses vast experience with respect to alternative ways of doing things and solving problems, has somehow not been given sufficient attention in Myanmar over all these years.

It will, however, be useful to keep matters in proper perspective. This is because in the present increasingly interdependent world economy, there are things that a country can do by itself and things that are not necessary for it to do by itself. For instance, Myanmar can grow rice and beans and undertake public works without help from anyone because it has been doing these things since the days of the Burmese kings. But if it wants a national electrical grid system that is reliable and a telephone system that works, doing things on its own is no longer a viable option. It is easier and more cost-effective to acquire the equipment and the technology from an outside source that has the capability and expertize in these areas.

Just as it is not possible to build a modern army based on traditional Burmese weapons and traditional concepts of warfare, it is not possible to build a modern economy by relying on traditional commodities such as rice and beans and on traditional approaches to development such as building public works. To modernize the economy, Myanmar, recognized as one of the least developed countries in the world, must avail itself of the opportunities that best suit its capacities and must have adequate and fair access to the technology, knowledge, expertise, and resources that are available in the rest of the world. At present there is a major deficiency on this score.

The Paucity of ODA Flows

According to UNCTAD's *Least Developed Countries Reports*, over the period from 1982 to 1988 Myanmar received an average of US$342 million[1] per year as official development assistance (ODA) from the Development Assistance Committee (DAC) member countries and the multilateral agencies. During the period 1989 to 1995, ODA flows to Myanmar fell by 56 per cent to an average of $150 million per year. There was a further decline to an average of $115 million in the years 2000 to 2002. During the same period in the new millennium, ODA flows to Laos averaged $267 million, while for Cambodia the average came to $427 million. In per capita terms, ODA receipts of Myanmar in 2000 to 2002 amounted only to $2.40, far below the $50 per head received by Laos, $32 per head received by Cambodia, and $21 per head average that all least developed countries received over the same period.[2] In fact, Myanmar's per capita ODA figure is the lowest among the forty-nine least developed countries given in the UNCTAD reports, and hence probably the lowest in the world. Recently, Myanmar, North Korea and Iran were designated as donor-constrained countries.

Myanmar's experience with external assistance over half a century since gaining independence has not been a happy one. There were long periods during the Burma Socialist Programme Party (BSPP) era when the country unilaterally renounced assistance from USAID, the World Bank, and the IMF. There was also a long self-imposed delay in joining the Asian Development Bank. Perhaps there are useful lessons and insights to be drawn from this historical experience. Our historians will be able to tell us more about this.

But coming to the present and thinking about the future, those with goodwill towards the country will agree that external assistance to Myanmar should be revived and enhanced once the political impasse is overcome. However, it is important to bear in mind that resumption of ODA flows, even if it were to come in substantial amounts, might not by itself help to improve the welfare of the ordinary people of Myanmar, and especially the welfare of the large majority of the poorest people at the bottom of the income scale. A World Bank policy research report entitled *Assessing Aid: What Works, What Doesn't, and Why*[3] in reviewing the organization's fifty years' experience with development assistance, observed that foreign aid performance at different times and different places has ranged from highly effective to totally ineffective and everything in between.

Road Racing as an Option for Moving Forward

Keeping the above in mind, let us now consider the conditions that will need to be satisfied for aid to contribute to Myanmar's aim of becoming a modern, developed nation, assuming that the precondition that Myanmar make concrete progress on national reconciliation is met in order for ODA to be resumed by the major donor nations and international development agencies.

A useful way to consider how external aid could assist Myanmar's economic and social development is to think in terms of road racing. To win a road race three things are required: a powerful engine, a smooth track, and a skillful driver. In the case of an economy, sound policies provide the powerful engine. Good infrastructure with good economic and social institutions constitute the smooth track. The skillful driver is a person who inspires confidence, is blessed with sound judgment, and has the managerial capabilities to run the economy in an efficient and effective manner. Thus foreign aid can help a country if it does these things: assists in formulating and implementing good policies; provides technical assistance and finance to help build infrastructure and institutions; and imparts training to improve human capacities to perform tasks in a more productive and efficient way.

For Myanmar and other least developed countries, it may be desirable to bear in mind two other factors. These have to do with figuring out where we are at present in the race, and the nature and state of the car we are driving. Let us consider these in turn.

Ford Popular Sedan, 1950 model

Let us begin with the car. At the start of the race in Myanmar, fifty years ago, we were driving the state-of-the-art and top-of-the-line Ford Popular Sedan, 1950 model. Our flashy car was envied by many, both near and far. We were tipped as the most likely country to reach the finish line and successfully industrialize well ahead of others in the region.

In the course of the race over the past half-century, our neighbours became able to afford better cars, through good ideas, diligence, and hard work on their part. They switched models, and, from about a decade and a half ago, began zooming around in Pajeros. But we prefer to do things our way and opted to stick to our Ford Popular 1950 model. Obviously, after fifty years on the road, obsolescence has set in and there has been considerable wear and tear. However, we repainted the car several times, so it retained its sleek and shiny good looks. In addition, a pair of new halogen head lights and mag wheels were installed. These did nothing to improve the car's performance, but it did make us feel good and contributed to our sense of satisfaction and well-being.

Rough Ride

In recent years, the going has become rough, and the ride in the Ford Popular, to put it kindly, has not been comfortable. The passengers in the back seat are often dazed and bruised by constant buffeting and being bounced around in their seats. Not much imagination is needed to figure out the problem, and any taxi driver will confirm for us, that this problem has to do with the shock-absorbers which, due to overuse, abuse, and neglect over all these years, have ceased to function. In addition, the whole suspension assembly has fallen apart, as it has outlived its useful economic life by several decades. A cursory glance through the window reveals that the road is full of pot-holes and strewn with boulders. Besides, we are running out of gas. While we are making the best of a bad situation and suffering in silence, we are told that the ride, in fact, is as smooth as silk. This is self-deception. It is clear that while this delusion is being imposed on us, no amount of foreign assistance, or anything else, will help to overcome the ills that most people believe are afflicting the nation.

Sins of Omission

Our unease heightened when Dr Maung Maung, the last president of the country under the previous regime, in assessing the outcome of Burma Socialist Programme Party's stewardship of the nation and the economic consequences of the *Burmese Way to Socialism*, made the following observations:

> As I have written earlier, we were all to blame. We failed. We had our opportunity to make Myanmar into a land of peace and plenty, but we made a mess of that opportunity. But much of the failure was in omission — in pretending everything was alright, in making false reports and saying sweet words, knowing full well all the time that things were going wrong.
>
> One of our failures lies in the Myanmar habit of *arnade*, a word that seems to have no equivalent in other languages: feeling bad about hurting or embarrassing people, shyness or backwardness, resulting in reticence. To a degree it is a good habit, for it makes for consideration for others and civility for which the Myanmar people are deservedly famous. However, in its name many sins of omission are also committed. What should be said goes unsaid; what should be done is left undone. Lack of moral courage can be disguised under its cloak.
>
> A feeling of fatalism, or karma, of whatever will be will be can also be added to *arnade*, which is probably a typical Myanmar trait. ... Thus, feelings are pent up — irritations, frustrations, anger. Over the years they gather into a storm.[4]

Many Burmese would probably have reservations with regard to Dr Maung Maung's interpretation and analysis of the circumstances leading to, and the events that took place, in the 1988 upheaval in Myanmar. However, his remarks about the sins of omission and his suggestion that we were all to be blamed for the mess and the failure to make Myanmar into a land of peace and plenty should be given further thought and consideration by the people of Myanmar, although with a qualification. The qualification has to do with the fact that Dr Maung Maung might also have mentioned that the regime, with which he had long been associated, does not take kindly to expression of views at variance with its own. The airing of opinions that diverge from the official line is looked upon as unpatriotic and traitorous, or worse, and as deserving of punishment appropriate for such seditious behaviour. This factor, in combination with Burmese feelings of *arnade* and the preoccupation with karma, has contributed to the reluctance of the people of Myanmar to act in accord with the dictates of their conscience and to express views in a free and frank manner, even though they also knew full well, all the time, that things were going wrong and the situation was just the opposite of what the official rhetoric expected them to believe. They see little alternative other than to let Dr Maung Maung pretend that, as in the well-known fable of our childhood days, the emperor's new clothes were of the finest material and the top of fashion in the realm. The era, of course, had its dissenting voices, but these were few and far between, voices in the wilderness, which were harshly silenced — until 1988 when the storm broke.

Dr Maung Maung's comment about "what should be said goes unsaid; what should be done is left undone" is a matter that has bothered me over the years. I believe that members of the economic profession, to which I belong, have greater responsibility than others to draw attention to misconceived ideas and flawed policies that in the past have led the country down the road to ruin, so that future generations do not think too unkindly of us. The predicament is far worse for those members of the profession who act as advisors to governments. For example, the economist Ashok V. Desai, on reflecting upon his short stint as advisor to the Government of India, noted that:

> ... an economic advisor's job is to tell it as it is and advise as he sees right. But the basic instinct of the government is political survival. To tell it as it is would be treason if the facts give ammunition to the opposition, and to advise what the government should but cannot do would point to its impotence.[5]

The Burmese people, like people all over the world, believe things can be better. But it has to be realized that no society can get something for nothing. Bringing about change for the better involves costs and sacrifices. Thinking unpleasant thoughts, and saying and doing things that may not please everybody, form an element of this cost. But it should not be an unbearable cost, or a binding constraint. Because the alternative course of action — to say nothing, do nothing, and to put on one's best face and pretend with the powers that be, that everything is fine, although burning with anger and frustration inside — has high costs and will lead to disastrous consequences, as is elaborated in Dr Maung Maung's book.

I make no pretence at having any special insight into the Burmese national character, culture, or traditions. However, Myanmar is primarily a Buddhist country, and as far as I am aware, humility, compassion, understanding, tolerance, forgiveness, gentleness, compromise, conciliation, moderation, and pursuit of truth and reason are virtues that a Buddhist is expected to hold dear. Regretfully, not much of these are in evidence these days. I believe we would gain a lot of domestic as well as international prestige and recognition if the fundamental precepts of our religion were more appropriately reflected in the conduct of our national affairs, and not confined to the performance of rituals and merit-making deeds that are steeped in our customs and beliefs. I also believe that the people of Myanmar must try harder to be more forthcoming and to put forward independent thoughts and ideas, not in anger or frustration or to criticize or to blame, but as good Buddhists in the pursuit of truth and reason, in moderation, and in an objective and tolerant way, so that better results can be achieved in the efforts currently under way to establish a modern developed nation.

Living in a Fantasy World

A Buddhist monk from Myanmar is said to have observed:

> [T]he truth is, those pro-democracy people abroad and the Western governments have their own fantasy as to what things should be like in Myanmar. They probably even have a fantasy as to what things are like in Myanmar now. Thus, when they look at Myanmar, it is always from their perspective. They don't pay attention to what we really want and how we want things to be. We have become the victims of their fantasies.[6]

A very perceptive monk. He will probably agree that pro-democracy people abroad and Western governments are not the only ones fantasizing about the Burmese condition. The powers that be in the country also have their own fantasies about Myanmar. Such fantasies cover not only what things are like in the country now, but also how things have been in the past and how things will be in the future. So, in addition to becoming victims of foreign fantasies, there is the more worrisome prospect of Burmese becoming victims of their own fantasies.

A Dose of Honesty and Self-analysis

It would be nice if foreign assistance could provide us with a new car — not necessarily with a Pajero 2004 model; we would be quite content to receive a good second-hand and properly reconditioned Toyota Mark II 1994 model, preferably with air-conditioning, to ease our current discomfort. Unfortunately, this is unlikely to happen. I suspect that there is nothing particularly appealing about the condition of our roads and our driving ability for donors to entrust us with a new car, especially if one also considers the outcry from their constituencies that such a move would probably generate. So, for the foreseeable future, we are stuck with our Ford Popular.

For foreign assistance to help us, and for that matter, for us to help ourselves, we must be honest with ourselves. And the first thing that is required for greater honesty will be to make a frank and objective assessment of where we are at present in the road race, as well as to make a thorough inspection of the car to ensure its roadworthiness to convey us to the promised land. A good start in this regard could be made by a formal official admission and public declaration of a fact that everyone in the country knows, and the whole world knows: namely, that the economy of Myanmar is not in good shape and that it needs to be fixed.

This is not asking for the moon. Singapore, for example, is saying that for it to survive in the twenty-first century, it will have to reinvent itself. Japan recognizes that its economy has been in a mess, and the present prime minister came to power on the strength of a promise to get the country out of the mess by undertaking the necessary economic and political reforms. Even the prime minister of China noted that despite the country's impressive economic achievements, sixty million people in the rural areas of the country still "live in extreme poverty with insufficient food and clothing", and he further recommended that "leading officials must go to the grass roots, among the peasants and workers and understand what the masses are thinking, their concerns, their difficulties and what problems they want solved."[7]

Incompetence, mismanagement, corruption, poor governance, and lack of transparency and accountability that have proved disastrous for other economies have also become a cause for serious concern among many of Myanmar's neighbours. After the shock of the 1997 Asian financial and economic crisis, a lot of soul-searching has been going on in these countries concerning why things went wrong and how they might be put right in the years ahead. Hence, it is an opportune time for Myanmar to "let it all hang out", get over its "emperor's new clothes" syndrome and other hang-ups, and declare to its people and to the world: "Like others in the region, our economy is also in a mess and it needs to be fixed."

Mandate and Assurances: A Two-Way Bargain

Once an official admission and declaration is made on the need to fix the economy, the next step will be to come forward with some workable ideas and proposals with respect to what exactly are the things that need fixing and how to go about fixing them. For present day Myanmar, this should not be too difficult. But before we embark on such a task three conditions are essential and must be fulfilled:

- First, there must be a clearly expressed desire and mandate from the powers that be that they would like to have a frank and objective review and analysis of what ails the economy, and that they would welcome practical recommendations and proposals for what can and should be done to address the difficulties;
- Second, the authorities must give assurance that they will give serious consideration to the recommended proposals, measures, and courses of action;
- Third, after careful review of the proposals, the authorities must agree to take concrete action and must guarantee that they will marshal the required political will and commitment to implement the recommended measures, to the extent that resources and capacities in the country permit.

The Likely Response from the People

The Burmese people, both within the country and abroad, can be counted on to respond favourably to such an approach. If the authorities were to grant them the mandate and give them the sort of assurances mentioned above, they would almost certainly come forward with many proposals and ideas of their own. Many people in the country have lived with the Ford Popular most of their lives, they are familiar with it, and are thus well placed to point out its shortcomings and to recommend remedial action. This is something they have been doing all the time anyway, in their private thoughts and conversations.

It may be desirable to begin by fixing the dials, gauges, and meters on the instrument panel that are not functioning properly. The speedometer looks particularly suspicious. We know from experience that a car of this vintage cannot be speeding along at the rate the speedometer seems to be showing. If it does, there is danger of the engine overheating. Unfortunately, the thermostat has broken down, so there is no device to warn us of this danger. In the meantime, someone has covered up the fuel gauge with a piece of paper. Maybe it would prove embarrassing if passengers in the back seat notice that the gas tank is empty and the car is running on its emergency fuel reserves. To add to our woes, the mileage indicator got stuck several years ago. So, although we are aware the car is in motion,[8] we are unsure of the direction it is heading, have no clear idea of the distance that has been covered, and are mostly in the dark as regards the miles we have to go and the years we must put up with to reach the finish line. This is not a good situation for any participant in a race to be in. Hence, fixing the dials and gauges and improving the quality and availability of our statistical indicators, data, and information seems like one area that deserves priority attention at the present time. It also appears to be an area that holds high promise for foreign aid, and technical assistance in particular, to have a significant impact.

Areas of Concern for Urgent Policy Action

Mr Lee Kuan Yew, the former prime minister of Singapore, has observed that whenever he is faced with a problem he usually finds that some country has already faced the same problem and has dealt with it, and that useful lessons and insights can be drawn from that country's experience.[9]

What is more important, the people in that country will gladly give all the information needed, if someone just takes the trouble to ask them. They will tell you both the good and the bad — the success stories to emulate, as well as the failures, disasters, and pitfalls to avoid.

It is not difficult to think of areas of current concern for Myanmar where a dose of foreign aid and some sound advice from neighbours could be expected to do a lot of good. The following come readily to mind:

1. Establishment of a stabilization fund to restore macroeconomic balance and stability in the country;
2. Addressing the demand-pull, cost-push, and structural factors that contribute to rapid inflation;
3. Unification of the exchange rate;
4. Reform of the monetary, financial, and fiscal sectors;
5. Civil service reforms, including addressing the adequacy of public sector salaries, and taking measures to change the mindset of bureaucrats so they act less like regulators and more like facilitators of business;
6. Assistance in establishing the legal and institutional underpinnings necessary for a well-functioning market economy;
7. Privatization of, and improving the performance of, public enterprises;
8. Fighting corruption;
9. Reform of agriculture and other sectoral reforms;
10. Facilitating the transfer, acquisition, adaptation, and assimilation of technology, including a critical re-examination of policy regarding the Internet and information technology;
11. Reform of the education sector, with special attention being given to what the students, teachers, parents, and education ministry staff are telling us (in private);
12. Consideration of what to do about the energy problem;
13. Trade liberalization and improving the balance of payments;
14. Improving access to health facilities and promoting more efficient delivery of public services;
15. Bringing underground economic activities into the legal fold;
16. Ensuring that safety nets are in place to take care of special needs that will arise for those that are likely to be left behind in establishing a market-oriented economic system, such as the poor, women,

    youth, aged, ethnic minorities, physically handicapped, and the
    geographically disadvantaged;

17. Environmental protection.

I can go on adding to the above *dhobi* or laundry list. But what has already
been listed will keep us busy for the next fifteen years, so we can stop here
for the moment.

The Bottom Line

Through their enquiry into what works and what doesn't with development
assistance, the World Bank policy research group found out that aid works
when the following conditions are satisfied:

- First, the timing of aid is important. If donors come forward with
  aid at a time when a recipient is making a genuine and determined
  effort at economic reforms, then good results are achieved;
- Second, although money is important, giving only money is not
  good. Giving aid as a mix of money and ideas or know-how is
  more effective;
- Third, the recipient country must demonstrate that it has the
  capability to manage its affairs and that it can make effective use
  of aid.

In light of the above, the ball is in our court to revive and revitalize ODA
flows into the country. To achieve this, we will have to do the following:

- First, we will have to convince the donor community that we are not
  suffering from any self-delusion. On the contrary, we must show
  that we are realistic, practical, and hard-nosed, and that we want aid
  to be needs-driven rather than donor-driven. Hence, we will come
  forward with concrete proposals concerning our needs, give
  justification for the desirability of donor support for them, and will
  also provide convincing arguments why we believe they will
  contribute to our economic reform and restructuring process;
- Second, we will inform the donor community that, in the half-
  century since we gained independence, it has not been lack of
  resources, but rather misconceived ideas and flawed policies that
  have been our undoing. Hence, although money is important, at
  this stage we are also interested in getting from them relevant ideas,

expertize and knowledge about better and more efficient ways of doing things that will help improve the well-being of all our people. We want not only ideas but also support that will enable us to translate these ideas into concrete action;

- Third, we will also have to convince the donor community that we have got rid of the constraints, hang-ups, confused ideas, and misdirected policies that in the past have made us incompetent and ineffective, and that we are ready to demonstrate to them that we can put our house in order, manage our affairs, and deliver the goods.

If the above three conditions can be satisfactorily met — and this is a big IF — then foreign aid will come to Myanmar. And it will be effective.

Notes

1   All amounts are given in US dollars.
2   UNCTAD, *The Least Developed Countries Report 1997* (New York: United Nations, 1997), Table 26, p. 180. Also, *Least Developed Countries Report 2004* (New York: United Nations, 2004), Table 27, p. 347.
3   World Bank, *Assessing Aid: What Works, What Doesn't, and Why* (New York: Oxford University Press, 1998).
4   Dr Maung Maung, *The 1988 Uprising in Burma* (New Haven: Yale University Southeast Asia Studies, 1999), p. 134.
5   Quoted by Deena Khatkhate in a review of Ashok V. Desai's book, *My Economic Affair* (New Delhi: Wiley Eastern Limited, 1993). The book review appeared in IMF/World Bank, *Finance and Development*, March 1995, Vol. 32, No. 1.
6   Kyaw Yin Hlaing, "Will Western Sanctions Bring down the House?", in *Reconciling Burma/Myanmar: Essays on U.S. Relations with Burma*, edited by John H. Badgley, NBR Analysis, Vol. 15, No. 1 (Seattle, Washington: The National Bureau of Asian Research, March 2004), pp. 73–85.
7   *New Light of Myanmar*, 1 December 1996, p. 10.
8   Some say there is a sensation of motion because the car is rolling downhill.
9   Lee Kuan Yew, *From Third World to First, The Singapore Story: 1965–2000* (Singapore: The Straits Times Press, 2000).

14

A Comprehensive International Approach to Political and Economic Development in Burma/Myanmar

Morten B. Pedersen

Recent developments in Burma/Myanmar underline the failure and counter-productivity of the "democracy paradigm" that has guided Western policy on the country since 1988, a paradigm that was based on misleading models from South Africa and Eastern Europe. The removal in late 2004 of Prime Minister Khin Nyunt and ministers loyal to him, together with a sweeping purge of military intelligence and related agencies, has significantly weakened the capacity of the military to manage the state and seen the government withdraw further into its shell. A resumption of armed conflict, rising crime rates, and a further fragmentation of the state, although perhaps not imminent, cannot be ruled out. These developments strongly suggest that there is a need to refocus current international efforts to effect change in Burma/Myanmar by working towards a more gradual and stable transition that maintains, and indeed strengthens, the capacity of the state and society to deal with the country's broader development needs.

The Fallacies of Current Western Policy Thinking

The core strategy of Western countries, which involves the use of censure and sanctions to isolate the military regime and force it to transfer power to a civilian, elected government, was developed in the late 1980s and early 1990s, when Burma/Myanmar seemed to many outside observers to have moved into a "democratic transition zone". This strategy, however, is based on a number of fallacies or misleading notions about the situation both inside and outside the country that have become increasingly exposed over time.

The Military Perspective

The policies of the military regime, contrary to frequent claims by pro-democracy groups, are not based on pure opportunism. Many of the military leaders genuinely believe that the armed forces are the only institution that can keep the centrifugal forces in check and that democratic government would be bad for the country. When adding the obvious corporate and personal interests that they have in maintaining power, this mindset leaves very little room for negotiating political reform — at least, not in any form that might undermine the military's ultimate control of the government. The regime does have a national agenda, however, and has taken some important — though insufficient — steps towards the goal of building a "modern, developed nation", primarily in the form of ceasefires with more than a dozen armed groups, embryonic market-oriented economic reforms, and an unprecedented, nationwide infrastructure-development programme. Generally speaking, its failures in these regards are not due to ill will, but rather to fear, limited understanding of development processes, and the poverty of the state. There may, therefore, be more space for cooperation on a social and economic development agenda than is commonly acknowledged by both the opposition and Western governments alike.

International censure and sanctions may have helped induce some limited cooperation on the part of the government in relation to sensitive human rights issues. However, the potential benefits of this cooperation remain untapped due to the rigid policies of Western governments, which have consistently refused to reward, or even fully recognize, any positive steps made by the military regime. It is clear that since early

2003, if not before, the generals running the government of Burma/ Myanmar have decided simply to ignore the West and to rely on their growing links with countries in the region. Meanwhile, Western sanctions and overt Western support for Aung San Suu Kyi have only reinforced the military's siege mentality and deepened the regime's hostility to the pro-democracy opposition. They may also have contributed to the government's abandonment since the mid-1990s of most of its original market-oriented, open-door economic reform agenda, which would have left the regime more vulnerable to foreign influences. Certainly, it was counter-productive to deny the government international technical and financial assistance to help implement and improve reforms that would not only have had significant social benefits but could also have led to greater pluralism.

The Balance of Power

Western governments are also guilty of greatly underestimating the strength of the military regime and overestimating the strength of the opposition. The conventional wisdom that the regime is brittle and close to collapsing under intense popular pressure for democracy is wishful thinking, and has created highly unrealistic expectations about how change is going to come about. The military apparatus controls almost every lever of power in the country and is therefore virtually undefeatable unless segments of the armed forces turn against each other, something which has not happened since the earliest days of independence and is highly unlikely today. The political opposition looked strong in the late 1980s and early 1990s, but it has never really succeeded in mobilizing popular dissatisfaction with the military government into sustained political action, and its leverage today is minimal. The decision by the National League for Democracy (NLD) in May 2004 to boycott the National Convention has further marginalized the party which looks increasingly unlikely to assume a future leadership role in government, at least in its current configuration.

Economic sanctions, by limiting the regime's access to foreign exchange, may have curtailed its arms purchases, but this curtailment has primarily affected Burma/Myanmar's conventional defence capabilities. It has had little effect on the regime's ability to suppress internal dissent, which relies largely on political and social controls backed by a proven commitment to use violence to suppress dissent, not on high-tech weapon systems or even on large numbers of troops. Instead, the military has responded to the resulting resource constraints by cutting back government expenditure on health and education, thus passing the burden of sanctions on to the poor. International attention may have helped protect Aung San Suu Kyi and her party from elimination, but the lack of economic reform and development, to which sanctions contribute, works against any processes of social change that over time could facilitate genuine political change.

The International Context

In theory, the lack of progress toward democracy and human rights could be due to the failure by the international community to agree on comprehensive sanctions that would raise the costs for the regime to a level high enough to force change. In reality, effective global sanctions are not — and never were — a realistic option, given the positions and interests of Burma/Myanmar's regional neighbours. Instead, by seeking to force regional countries to adopt a Western strategy that runs counter to their own interests, the US and the EU have undermined any chance of developing a common platform and influencing all-important regional dynamics in a positive direction. This has also significantly weakened the capacity of the United Nations to play an effective mediating role.

Transitional Challenges

The push for regime change not only disregards realistic scenarios for change, but also ignores the many inter-linked and highly complex challenges Burma/Myanmar must overcome in order to break its present, self-reinforcing pattern of conflict, repression and poverty. The installation of an elected government would be an important step forward, but such a government could not function properly in the absence of supportive socio-political structures, nor would it provide a panacea for the country's deep-seated development problems. The central state has neither the authority nor the institutional capacity nor the financial strength to implement policies across its realm effectively. The expansion of stable, modern governance structures and of the rule of law into areas currently under control of local army commanders or former insurgent groups will be a particularly difficult and extended process. Meanwhile, the low level of development and the deepening humanitarian crisis leave the general population disempowered and unable to play a meaningful political role, even if the political system were freer. Unless more is done to prepare the ground for political change, democracy is likely ultimately to disappoint, and could all too easily fail.

The Social Costs of Sanctions

Many proponents of sanctions, while admitting their limitations, nonetheless maintain that the benefits outweigh the costs, and that the harm done is insignificant. This is a serious misreading of the situation. While it is certainly true that the macro-economic effects of the sanctions are overshadowed by the regime's own economic mismanagement, the sanctions have increased the sense of threat within the government, and have thus directly contributed to the increased allocation of scarce resources for improved armaments and other security capabilities. By reinforcing the political deadlock and making the search for domestic compromises more difficult, sanctions also contribute to maintaining the current zero-sum struggle for power, which diverts attention away from vital governance and development issues. More direct negative social effects arise from the denial of foreign aid, investments and trade, which limits job opportunities, contributes to inflation, and reduces the provision of social services as well as broader community development activities, thus significantly diminishing opportunities for the general population to improve their livelihood.

Another Way Forward

Any effective international approach must recognize that the challenges of transition in Burma/Myanmar — one of the poorest, most heterogeneous and conflict-prone societies in Asia — are more difficult than in most of the countries that over the past few decades have made the transition to some form of democratic rule. The path to the creation of a government and society capable of realizing Burma/Myanmar's great potential will necessarily be long and tortuous — and those who genuinely wish to help the general population need to match commitment to principle with a more pragmatic search for solutions. For any policy to be effective, it must take into account the huge power imbalance between the military and the pro-democracy forces, as well as the broader structural obstacles to political and economic development, including armed conflict, deep-rooted poverty, and low levels of education. This requires a long-term perspective, measured over perhaps decades rather than years, and more humility regarding the prospects for reform and the influence of external interventions.

Policy Recommendation: Broaden the Aims

However laudable, the West's singular pursuit of democracy does not provide an effective strategy for promoting freedom, security, and welfare for the general population of Burma/Myanmar. First, the probability for a transition from military to genuine civilian rule in the foreseeable future is close to zero. The military will remain in power in the foreseeable future; any transition, including important governance and economic reforms, will have to be negotiated and implemented in cooperation with the military leadership. Second, democratization is a long and difficult process, not a one-off event. The establishment and maturation of genuinely democratic institutions in any country, not least one as poor and inexperienced with democratic practices as Burma/Myanmar, requires fundamental changes in attitudes and behaviour at all levels of society, which take decades, if not generations, to occur. Finally, the association between democratic governance and welfare is imperfect and not necessarily positive, at least in the short to medium term. To push for a revolutionary transformation of the formal political system without paying attention to important underlying or complementary development processes is short-sighted, unlikely to succeed, and could do more harm than good.

Instead of pushing for regime change at this stage, the international community should work to promote three longer-term processes of change — political liberalization, peace-building, and socio-economic development — which would not only produce immediate benefits for the general population, but could also begin to lay the ground for an internally-driven and thus more meaningful and sustainable reform process. This approach would also create wider space for working with domestic actors, who, with the exception of the NLD and a relatively small number of political activists, do not see democracy as the immediate, or even the primary, goal for society, but are working towards other goals — for example, to strengthen national unity, to promote local autonomy and ethnic rights, or simply to re-establish their fields or businesses after decades of armed conflict. The three processes of change, of course, are closely inter-related and mutually reinforcing, which is another reason why they need to be pursued in tandem.

Political liberalization

The overwhelming power imbalance between the military regime and the opposition, as noted, virtually rules out any democratic break-through at this time, whether through a power-sharing compromise with the political parties or a revolutionary social challenge from the grassroots. Since 1988, however, the military junta has allowed a number of political openings, including the formation of political parties and the convening of the National Convention, as well as a limited expansion in popular access to information and in space for public debate and civil society organizations. Although these steps are primarily aimed at shoring up the regime's power rather than facilitating increased popular participation in politics, they have begun to transform public life and may over time fuel a process of "creeping democratization".

We know from countries such as Singapore that limited political liberalization, even when reinforced by comprehensive economic liberalization measures, does not necessarily lead to liberal democracy, even in the longer term. It does, however, inevitably strengthen civilian institutions by giving them space to form and exercise at least certain basic political functions, thus improving the prospects for an effective challenge to authoritarian rule and the consolidation of a meaningful democracy. This is particularly the case if the expansion of political freedom and activity combines with peace-building and socio-economic development that spread the possibilities and resources for civilian political activity to a wider section of the population.

Peace-building

Burma/Myanmar's long-running, internal armed conflicts were a root cause of the military's rise to power in the 1950s, and continue to present a serious obstacle to any future military disengagement from politics. The spread of ceasefires since the late 1980s has brought within reach a nationwide stop to fighting. However, continued political tensions, serious human rights abuses by the army in newly-occupied areas, and the lack of development of former war zones means that peace is still far off. While the leaders of the ethnic armed groups, including those still fighting the government, appear to be committed to stopping the fighting, frustrations among the younger generation, who have little prospect for a meaningful future and do not remember the suffering caused by the war, are mounting. Resistance on the part of many army officers to cooperating with their former enemies means that even minor flare-ups could quickly escalate into renewed fighting on a significant scale. This, in turn, would reinforce the military's reasons for maintaining a stranglehold on government and would justify even larger budget allocations to the armed forces.

The absence of peace also presents a major threat to a future democracy. Although supporters of the NLD argue that democratic governance would resolve the ethnic conflicts, it is equally likely that its introduction would bring new tensions to Burma/Myanmar's pluralist society where ethnic and religious identities are extremely strong. To be successful, democratic government requires political activity to be moderate rather than extreme in nature, with a strong emphasis on mutual trust and accommodation among contending groups. It is vulnerable to extremist politicians who use ethnic and other cleavages as a basis for generating support for confrontational positions. While the democratic process might facilitate inclusion of excluded groups and interests and allow the healing process to begin, it could also open the way for demagoguery and agitation based on ethnic and religious identity that would fuel latent conflicts. The search for peace, therefore, is not subsidiary to the quest for democracy, but is central to any meaningful political reform process.

Socio-economic development

A truly inclusive and democratic political system that gives all groups a voice in the governance of their areas and protects both individual and group rights does not result simply from reform of the formal structures of government, but depends on the empowerment of ordinary people. Failing this, the "democratic" political system will remain elitist and will do little to overcome the root causes of conflict and inequality. Yet the large majority of the population in Burma/Myanmar is subsistence farmers, often semi-illiterate, who have little or no experience of the world beyond their village. Many people have had little contact with the central state and thus can hardly be expected to show commitment to its political arrangements, whether democratic or not. Moreover, local power structures in many areas are basically feudal, with little space for popular participation.

In these circumstances, even if democracy were introduced, the poor majority would remain voiceless and subject to the powers that be. Political and socio-economic development therefore cannot be separated. Before a future democracy can take root and be meaningful for many people and communities, those people and communities will have to transcend the barriers created by the daily struggle for survival on the one hand, and the cultural and structural legacy of militarization of society and repressive, autocratic rule on the other. This will require improved economic conditions, broader access to education and information, and stronger local organizations as the foundation for a vibrant (but moderate), pluralistic civil society.

Policy Recommendation: Revise the Strategic Objectives

The West also needs to reconsider its strategic objectives. Rather than helping Burma/Myanmar move forward, past efforts to weaken the military regime have simply deepened the siege mentality of the top leadership and caused the divisions in society to widen, provoking further reactionary measures by an institution whose knee-jerk response to any perceived threat has always been to strengthen its control over the state and society. Further isolation that undermines whatever limited government capacity and economic activity still exists, will simply reinforce current repressive, predatory, and corrupt practices, and make it more difficult for any future government to reform the existing system.

To avoid such a scenario and to support the three overarching processes of change outlined above, the international community should work instead to establish the conditions for a gradual transfer of power to a stable and competent civilian government. This requires less focus on weakening the military regime and more on encouraging new thinking within the officer corps, building capacity across the state and society to deal with the country's development needs, and strengthening the nascent democratic infrastructure.

Encouraging new thinking within the officer corps

Considering the immense power imbalance between the military and civilian forces and the proven commitment of the generals to quell any challenge to their rule, progress is all but inconceivable without the cooperation of reform-minded officers. The current leadership, however, is locked into traditional ways of thinking that are rooted in the country's troublesome past, and is so fearful of instability that any criticism or sign of popular mobilization is seen to threaten the survival of the state. One of the first steps in any strategy for promoting freedom, security, and welfare must therefore be to open the minds of the officer corps to more participatory and responsive governance. It is imperative that the next generation of military leaders comes to perceive alternative ways of governing that, while protecting vital "military" interests, including Burma's national sovereignty and territorial integrity, also support broader development objectives.

Strengthening capacity across the state and society to deal with the country's development needs

In order to ensure that the military regime derives minimal legitimacy and financial benefits from international assistance, most Western donors stipulate that contacts with the government should be minimized and that aid should be provided outside state structures either directly to the beneficiaries or through civil society organizations. Such limitations not only fly in the face of "best practice" and limit the impact and sustainability of aid programmes; they also ignore the requirements of gradual, evolutionary change throughout government structures, which provides certainly the most likely and, arguably, the preferable path towards transition. Realistically, state power will only gradually move from the military to civilian institutions, and only in response to successful development and growing confidence on part of the military that civilian government will not threaten national security. This will require cooperation between military officers and civilian politicians and bureaucrats within a governance framework that engenders the trust and cooperation of a skilled and well-educated population. Donors and aid agencies should therefore work to improve the capacity of the existing state to formulate and implement pro-poor policies, as well as the capacity to raise revenue legitimately for public investments in physical and social infrastructure that support these policies. Much more also needs to be done to develop the capacity of the general population through improved education, health and welfare to support and complement the state. Most importantly perhaps, bridges must be built between the state and society — connections that will extend beyond what is necessary for the development of a future electoral system to establish a widespread network of two-way communication structures through which the state may inform its citizenry and elicit information and ideas. Such efforts may reinforce the military regime in the short term, but over time will strengthen the basis for a successful transition to meaningful democracy by challenging current notions of military supremacy within the officer corps and building a credible civilian alternative to military rule that will be able to deliver on the population's high hopes for peace and prosperity.

Strengthening the democratic infrastructure

While conservative leadership and weak capacity for good governance present immediate barriers to progress, the biggest challenge for promoters of democracy may be to build the infrastructure necessary to make a future democratic system truly representative and participatory. Burma/Myanmar's experience with democracy in the early post-independence period was extremely short and ended more than forty years ago; in the country today no one under sixty years of age has any experience of participation in democratic politics. There are no long-standing political parties, no politically significant civil society, and no widespread commitment to democratic values and behaviour among the population at large. Indeed, the strong hierarchy, top-down approach to governance, and inability to deal with dissent associated with military rule are replicated within most civilian organizations, including the NLD and most exile groups. Although present conditions do not determine future outcomes, this democratic "deficit" is likely to persist long after the establishment of electoral democracy, and should be actively addressed, even if, at the present stage, this will have to be done indirectly within a broader capacity-building agenda.

Policy Recommendation: Get the Policy Mix Right

The framework set out here does not rule out the use of coercive or punitive measures *per se*, but the policy implications of taking a longer-term, evolutionary approach to reform are clear. In order to contribute to social change processes, international actors need to be engaged on the ground in close proximity with the people and institutions they are trying to influence. This requires a shift away from censure and sanctions toward "critical engagement'. There is a need to downplay public condemnation and overt pressure in favour of more constructive efforts to foster policy dialogue and capacity-building.

Diplomacy

Although coercive diplomacy may exert some pressure on the military rulers to improve their human rights record for purely instrumental reasons, it has the unfortunate effect of closing minds and freezing social developments, something which contradicts the overriding need to build a stronger grassroots support and capacity for participatory government and the rule of law. Essentially, coercive diplomacy encourages only defensive measures by the regime, not far-reaching genuine reforms, which depend on fundamental shifts in the perceptions of top military leaders, as well as empowerment of civilian institutions.

The aim of a "new" diplomacy should be to improve communication with the military regime in order to allay its fears and establish the basis for critical dialogue about core international concerns. It is crucially important to draw the generals out of their shell, lessen their suspicions about the ultimate intentions of Western governments, and help them embrace international cooperation and interaction. Although this will be a long-term process, it is the only way to make them see the value in, and the prudence of, complying with contemporary international norms of behaviour.

A "new" diplomacy should also encourage the establishment of institutions that over time can become independent agents of change, especially through reform of laws and official processes. The ongoing process of drawing up a new constitution, for example, however flawed, is preferable to the alternative, which would see the military continue to govern essentially unconstrained by legal institutions. The formation of a parliamentary system, even if initially constrained and largely *pro forma*, would establish a platform for policy discussions which so far have been ignored by all sides in the ongoing power struggle. It would also provide more space for political party activities and thus over time help to build a more credible alternative to military rule. Similarly, the government's establishment of a Human Rights Committee and the ratification of core human rights instruments such as the Geneva Conventions has provided new access points for dialogue and capacity-building. Even if such instruments are weak at first, the mere fact of their existence helps to build a constituency for change within the military state that is currently lacking. Conversely, rejecting them as irrelevant easily becomes a self-fulfilling prophecy as the new structures are left inactive and their domestic supporters abandoned and isolated.

Sanctions will, no doubt, remain part of Western policy for the foreseeable future, but there is a need for much clearer, more realistic benchmarks for progress towards agreed international objectives, together with a firm commitment by Western governments and international organizations to reciprocate with concrete, valuable gestures when positive steps are taken. In order to avoid disagreements in one area becoming an obstacle to progress in all other areas, there should be distinct "roadmaps" for progress towards political liberalization, basic human rights, and economic reform. The incentives associated with each of these roadmaps should be relevant to the particular issue in question, as this would facilitate dialogue also at the working level of the government, where officials may not always see the bigger picture. For example, since the worst human rights abuses are committed by local army units, reciprocal gestures for improvements should incorporate benefits for active army commanders and could, for example, focus on military exchanges and training. Similarly, concrete improvements in the access given to international aid agencies to remote or conflict-affected areas could be acknowledged by releasing assistance for road or other infrastructure-building, which may not take priority from a developmental point of view but would serve the national development agenda. Any such assistance should be additional to existing aid programmes, which should be provided according to technical criteria alone.

Foreign aid

Apart from refocusing their diplomacy, Western governments need to significantly strengthen their engagement with the state and society on more technical issues using foreign aid. The efficacy of international assistance depends on a comprehensive and coherent package of policy dialogue, selective capacity-building, and financial support. The current political limitations on assistance to Burma/Myanmar constrain efforts in each of these areas and are not conducive to promoting sustainable development. Although aid agencies are making a significant difference in the lives of many poor families through community development and livelihood activities, most of these activities leave the policy environment for development untouched and therefore are of questionable sustainability.

While opponents of development aid are correct in arguing that the security priorities and economic policies of the military regime currently limit the sustainability of aid, the true potential of assistance has never been tested. It is hardly surprising that the military government has flatly refused sweeping calls for structural adjustment reforms when they are denied support from the international financial institutions which usually provide the necessary technical and financial assistance and encouragement for such reforms in low income countries. It is no wonder, either, that the current leadership is generally suspicious of the activities of aid agencies when the rhetoric and conditionalities of major donors are so blatantly partisan and show little concern for the overall development needs of the country.

There is no doubt that the military is hostile to economic and administrative reforms that would directly weaken its hold on power, and less than enthusiastic about community development and other programmes that contravene its own notions of development which lag several decades behind current international development thinking. There is no doubt either that the state and society both lack the capacity to absorb and effectively apply large amounts of assistance, and that this capacity will have to be built up gradually, ahead of any major new financial commitments. However, the international aid community is hardly unfamiliar with such obstacles. On the contrary, it has a range of strategies and tools available that have proven effective in other countries with arguably less government commitment to development and certainly less potential for long-term progress.

Importantly, the future is not without prospects. The next generation of military leaders, which is likely to take over within the next few years, has quite different educational and military career backgrounds from the current leadership, and has experienced at close hand the economic progress made by their neighbours. Once in charge, like all new governments, they will want to make their mark and improve on the performance of their predecessors. Thus there will be an important window of opportunity for reviving the reform drive — at least, if the international community is prepared to offer the necessary technical and financial assistance.

Conclusion

While the international community should defer the goal of democracy for now, this does not mean giving in to authoritarianism or accepting the continuance of human rights abuses. Rather, it would be a rational reorientation of international efforts to facilitate political and economic reform in a country where little progress has been made during the past sixteen years, nor seems likely in the foreseeable future if the current international policies are maintained. A broader, more process-oriented approach is both necessary for overcoming military resistance to reform and prudent, given the difficulty of instituting a genuine democracy, particularly if it is born out of major political or socio-economic upheavals rather than through a incremental, negotiated transition. By supporting national reconciliation and development, the strategy outlined here would help pave the way for meaningful and sustainable political change.

Index

National Convention, xx–xxi, xxii,
    xxvi, 6, 34, 37, 60, 63, 64, 65–66,
    67, 282
  in 1993–1996, 54
  constitutional issues, xxii, 22, 23
  ethnic groups, xxvii, 31, 34–35, 45,
    63, 64, 65
  and NGOs, 158
  resumption of, xx, 39, 46, 50, 66
  and "road map", 30
  view of UN, 61
National Council Union of Burma
    (NCUB), 51
National Day of Action, 244
National Democratic Alliance Army, 64
National Democratic Front (NDF), 43,
    44, 51, 64
National Human Rights Committee,
    185
National Intelligence Bureau (NIB), 4,
    16
National League for Democracy
    (NLD), xx, 4, 7, 12, 23, 39, 50,
    168, 251, 236
  and 1990 election, 6, 237, 249
  ceasefires, 54
  Central Executive Committee
    (CEC), 10, 168
  insurgency, 51
  marginalization of, xxiii, 13
  military regime, 31, 160, 161
  and National Convention, xxi, xxvi,
    6, 10, 11, 30, 31, 46, 63, 66, 278
  and NGOs, 158
  policies, 11, 52, 281–82
  Premier Oil, 185
  re-opening of branch offices, 11
National Program for Development
    of Irrigation and Rural Water
    Supply, 114

National Program for Nine Districts
    Greening, 114
national reconciliation, xxxii, 39, 161,
    282
National United Liberation Front, 44
National Unity Front, 155
NCUB, *see* National Council Union of
    Burma
NDF, *see* National Democratic Front
Ne Win, 7, 155
  "Burmese Way to Socialism", 43
  and Khin Nyunt, 14
  and pluralism, 167
  army organization under, 14
  caretaker government in 1958, 169
  isolation of, 17
  opposition to federalism, 43
  purges of rivals, 33
  resignation of, xxiii, 17
  takeover of power in 1962, 43
Ne Win era, and popular dissent, 235
  authoritarianism, 159
  civil society organizations, 219
  damage to human capital, 251
  economic misrule, 43
  end of, 233
  repression of free speech, 268
Nehru, Pandit J.L., 105
nepotism, 251
Ner Dah, Colonel, 62
New Light of Myanmar, 18
New Mon State Party, 58, 64, 164
  and ceasefire movement, 53, 54
  and U Nu, 44
Newcastle disease project, 112, 140–44
Nixon in China, 24 n. 1
Nong Hkam, Farmer Field School, 58
non-government organizations
    (NGOs), xxv
  access to ceasefire areas, 55

www.ingramcontent.com/pod-product-compliance
Lightning Source LLC
Chambersburg PA
CBHW020752300326
41914CB00050B/149